Additional praise for *Winning Gifts*:

"Tom Wilson writes in an easy to understand and highly relevant style that guides the reader through some very concrete examples of how to succeed in the increasingly competitive world of philanthropy. In a word this book is <u>indispensable!</u>"
—Leo Arnoult, CFRE, President
Arnoult & Associates Inc., Consultants to Nonprofits Since 1987

"Tom's bundle of scar tissue gained through 30 years of fundraising is now yours without the pain and bleeding by transfusing the practical wisdom of *Winning Gifts*."
—Charles Bernard Maclean, PhD, Founder
PhilanthropyNow.com

"A very good book and a powerful tool that will benefit fundraising professionals from novice to seasoned veteran. This is more than expert advice; it reflects a career of distilled expertise. The step-by-step lists Tom Wilson includes to help people systematically put into practice his advice is very helpful. The summary at the end of each chapter invites readers to do things to retain their learning from the book."
—Jim Paglia, President/CEO
In's & Out's, Inc.

"This was enjoyable reading. There is so much distilled information in there that it can serve as a guide for newbies as well as reminders for those who have been doing it for awhile and are getting stale. In Chapter 2 you have brought together a variety of viewpoints and information that truly fill out what Donor Values are all about. You can tell in Part II with Make Your Case and The Win Win Ask you are in your element, you are hitting your stride and writing about things that you know so well."
—Chuck Howard, GrantsCrafter Consultancy

"How refreshing to read useful, pertinent information! I loved the chapter on listening. Once again you have proven how you have mastery over your field. I always learn from you."
—Evelyn C. Lamb, Director of Development
The Center for Women's Health Oregon Health & Science University

Winning Gifts

Make Your Donors Feel Like Winners

THOMAS D. WILSON

BICENTENNIAL
1807
WILEY
2007
BICENTENNIAL

John Wiley & Sons, Inc.

Published by John Wiley & Sons, Inc., Hoboken, New Jersey.

Wiley Bicentennial Logo: Richard J. Pacifico

Published simultaneously in Canada.

For general information on our other products and services, or technical support, please contact our Customer Care Department within the United States at 800-762-2974, outside the United States at 317-572-3993 or fax 317-572-4002.

Wiley also publishes its books in a variety of electronic formats. Some content that appears in print may not be available in electronic books.

For more information about Wiley products, visit our Web site at http://www.wiley.com.

Library of Congress Cataloging-in-Publication Data:

ISBN: 978-0-470-12834-3

Printed in the United States of America

10 9 8 7 6 5 4 3 2 1

The AFP Fund Development Series

The AFP Fund Development Series is intended to provide fund development professionals and volunteers, including board members (and others interested in the nonprofit sector), with top-quality publications that help advance philanthropy as voluntary action for the public good. Our goal is to provide practical, timely guidance and information on fundraising, charitable giving, and related subjects. The Association of Fundraising Professionals (AFP) and Wiley each bring to this innovative collaboration unique and important resources that result in a whole greater than the sum of its parts. For information on other books in the series, please visit: http://www.afpnet.org.

THE ASSOCIATION OF FUNDRAISING PROFESSIONALS

The Association of Fundraising Professionals (AFP) represents 28,000 members in more than 185 chapters throughout the United States, Canada,

Mexico, and China, working to advance philanthropy through advocacy, research, education, and certification programs.

The association fosters development and growth of fundraising professionals and promotes high ethical standards in the fundraising profession. For more information or to join the world's largest association of fundraising professionals, visit www.afpnet.org.

2006-2007 AFP Publishing Advisory Committee

Samuel N. Gough, CFRE, Chair
Principal, The AFRAM Group
Nina P. Berkheiser, CFRE
Principal Consultant, Your Nonprofit Advisor
Linda L. Chew, CFRE
Associate Director, Alta Bates Summit Foundation
D. C. Dreger, ACFRE
Senior Campaign Director, Custom Development Solutions, Inc. (CDS)
Audrey P. Kintzi, ACFRE
Chief Advancement Officer, Girl Scout Council St. Croix Valley
Robert J. Mueller, CFRE
Vice President, Hospice Foundation of Louisville
Maria Elena Noriega
Director, Noriega Malo & Associates
Leslie E. Weir, MA, ACFRE
Director of Family Philanthropy, The Winnipeg Foundation
Sharon R. Will, CFRE
Director of Development, South Wind Hospice

John Wiley & Sons:
Susan McDermott
Senior Editor (Professional/Trade Division), John Wiley & Sons

AFP Staff:
Jan Alfieri
Manager, New Product Development
Walter Sczudlo
Executive Vice President & General Counsel

To my loving wife, Sue, who has been patient with my crazy dreams and ideas all of these years; to my children, Christine Wilson Goodner, Richard Wilson, Charlie Wilson, and KT Wilson; my sister Cheri Wilson Hansen and to my late parents, Richard and Charlotte Wilson.

Contents

Preface

Everyone loves to win and to be a winner—the satisfaction, the glow of success, the admiration of your peers, your spouse, your parents, your children. Who doesn't want to win?

Those of us who have been fortunate enough to develop careers in philanthropic fundraising have learned that successful fundraising is developing winning gifts—gifts that the donor enjoys making.

I'm a musician by training who fell, by dumb luck, into what is now a more-than-a-quarter-century career in philanthropic fundraising. I love my work. There is nothing more fun than seeing a donor's excitement in making a transformation gift—for my institution, for our community, and most importantly, for the donor and his family.

As a longtime fundraising consultant, first with DMA, then with my own consulting firm in the Pacific Northwest for 10 years, and now with Campbell & Company nationally, I have had the pleasure of interviewing nearly 2,500 donors through the philanthropic market research study process (feasibility study). I have made close to 1,000 gift requests and closed hundreds of millions of dollars of gifts. In listening to donors I have heard their delighted stories about giving—and their horror stories of bad asks.

Consultants are nothing but bundles of scar tissue. This veteran of decades of fundraising and consulting hopes you will learn something from this book. Please note, at the end of each chapter you will find three tips that you can use from the information in that chapter.

This book belongs to my donors, my clients, and my colleagues in the field of philanthropic fundraising. We do the greatest work in the world—enabling donors to find fulfillment through their philanthropic investments.

Lifelong learning is critical to everyone's success. I welcome your feedback, your pushback on the ideas presented here—how can these ideas be improved? What have I missed?

What stories would you like to add for the next edition? What has worked for you? For your volunteers? What do you agree with? Think I'm off base about? Send in your ideas by checking this book's web site at www. WinningGifts.INFO or e-mail me at Tom.Wilson@WinningGifts.INFO. Thank you in advance.

Acknowledgment

I want to thank the Association of Fundraising Professionals Publishing Committee for their partnership with John Wiley & Sons. Their encouragement and book development process helped shepherd this project to completion.

Special thanks to my friends and colleagues who helped review the entire book and give me advice: Kathy Marty, my ace proofreader; Vic Atchison; Thayer Willis; Chuck Howard (for his insightful challenges to my thinking); Richard Wilson (my son and webmaster); John Castles of the M. J. Murdock Charitable Trust; Paul Hansen, my brother-in-law, for his actuarial advice; Dr. Chris King for the use of his personal story, Evie Lamb, Charles Maclean of *Philanthropy Now*, Jim Paglia of In's and Out's, Pat Scherer, and Tom Holce for his friendship and assistance in developing The Six I's of Philanthropy so many years ago. I want to thank additional assistance from Robert Cialdini, Ph.D., Bill McGinly of AHP, Val Vaden and Lilli Rey, Mark Neville, Linda Wright, and Leo Arnoult.

I also want to thank my inspirations—authors Marilyn Sewell of First Unitarian Church of Portland and Harvey McKinnon of British Columbia. They encouraged me to write a book too.

I want to particularly acknowledge the hero I never met . . . Thomas Broce, whose book helped launch my career so many years ago. From one Thomas to another . . . thanks.

About the Author

Tom Wilson started his philanthropic fundraising career more than a quarter-century ago as a campaign fundraising consultant for the Ravinia Festival,summer home of the Chicago Symphony (he read a book and survived his first year as a fundraiser).

Tom really is just a musician. He studied music education at the University of Nebraska–Lincoln, where he was drum major of the Cornhusker marching band, coprincipal clarinet of the college orchestra, and a member of numerous performance groups. Tom went to Northwestern University, where he received a master of music in clarinet performance, studying with Robert Marcellus and Larry Combs, principal clarinet of the Chicago Symphony. After teaching two years of high school orchestra and music, Tom returned to Northwestern, where he pursued a doctorate in music education (and is currently ABD—all but dissertation) and served as a teaching assistant and graduate fellow.

Tom served as general manager, chief fundraiser, and assistant conductor for the Lake Forest Symphony (in suburban Chicago, Illinois), corporate and foundation fundraiser for Field Museum of Natural History in Chicago, vice president for development with the Phoenix Symphony, resident campaign consultant for Del E. Webb Hospital's planned estate giving campaign in Sun City West, Arizona, resident campaign director for Oregon Public Broadcasting, vice president for development for Oregon Graduate Institute of Science & Technology (where he started with a blank desk, recruited a staff of eight, and raised $30 million in five years), owned his own fundraising consulting firm for 10 years, and now works for a prominent national consulting firm, Campbell & Company.

Tom Wilson leads fundraising training sessions throughout the country. The Winning Gifts concept came out of presentations to fundraisers and clients over the last two decades.

While he has worked with all types of clients, Tom now specializes in healthcare and higher education fundraising.

Tom's personal mission statement is—"transforming people through philanthropy to improve our community."

PART I

A Winning Gift For Your Donor

I've given millions of dollars away to many causes. I chaired our university's board and chaired its capital campaign. I created endowed scholarships. My best gift? The tennis courts at the university. Every time I drive by them and see the students and faculty playing it brings a great big smile to my face. What a fun gift.

—DONOR INTERVIEWEE

In listening to donors it's great to hear a winning-gifts story like this. Hearing stories like the one above is inspiring.

The true joy of philanthropic fundraising is creating your own stories as you work with your donors on behalf of your organization. Try to draw out these stories from your best donors. Their stories will help to illustrate the values they hold dear and will help to demonstrate where their passions lie and what excites them about making a philanthropic gift.

Too often in our field of philanthropic fundraising, the bottom line—the fundraising goal—becomes the only line. The need to fund institutional priorities to meet the plans of a president or a board of trustees becomes more important than presenting a winning gift concept to a donor. Ideally the philanthropic fundraising professional will be able to balance the urgent, immediate needs of the institution with the lifelong, personal values of the donor. If done correctly, fundraising is the job of presenting attractive opportunities to donors.

While most donors are individuals, foundations are governed by trustees who are people, too. At a university that needed a new computer science building, a major foundation was approached for support. One of their trustees indicated a grant would be highly likely. The foundation could do something in the neighborhood of $100,000 to $250,000 to meet this institutional need. However, if the university had a project that was library related this would be more exciting to the foundation's trustees, and the foundation should be approached for a $500,000 to $1,000,000 grant. It was up to us to decide.

Don't we wish all people were this clear in their thinking? Foundation grants are easier to discuss because it's not the individual's money. Yes, the foundation's trustees have to watch out for the best interests of the founder. But, foundation trustees become practiced in negotiating gift deals with nonprofits. In most cases, discussions with program officers and foundation trustees can be direct and open. Large foundations will review hundreds of proposals in a year and have staff members that analyze proposals and conduct site visits. While foundations can go through changes in their grant-making priorities, they tend not to be as shy as individuals about discussing gifts. After all, foundations by law must give money away each year—that is their business and only reason for existence.

Our job as philanthropic fundraisers and as volunteer fundraisers is to empower people to be as open in their giving intentions as corporations and foundations are in their philanthropic agendas.

As you think about donors as people first, remember that in almost all cases we need to define potential donor people as couples—not individuals—who make gift decisions. When you only see one name of a couple recognized for giving, don't assume the nonprofit organization got the listing correctly. Always assume gifts are a joint decision. This is especially true when you are talking to board members about giving. Yes, the board should give first and generously. But, don't assume their spouses are as knowledgeable. When it comes time for a major gift, sit down with both your board member and that individual's spouse or partner to see how both people respond to your case and your request for a significant gift.

WINNING VERSUS LOSING

Having served as a consultant for more than half of my career, I frequently interview key prospective donors for our clients. One of a consultant's key questions is: "Will you work on the campaign in some way?" If the person answers yes, then the follow-up question is: "Are you comfortable asking for gifts?" We always find a few people who enjoy making the ask. They are naturals, or that is a primary role in their professional life, or they have been through a fundraising campaign already and have learned how to ask for philanthropic gifts.

Interviewee responses to the "Will you work?" question can be revealing—from "I love to ask, no problem" to "I would rather you pull out my toenails with a pair of pliers than ask someone for money."

Why do so many people hate fundraising while others of us enjoy it? Many people are amazed that professional fundraisers love to ask for money. For people who dislike fundraising their impression of the process is "win/lose." Stephen Covey's enduring and popular book, *The Seven Habits of Highly Effective People* focuses one whole section on the key concept of everyone winning—Habit #4: Think Win/Win.[1] Reading Covey's book is a revelation. This concept of everyone winning or no deal is why some people are open to fundraising (see Exhibit I.1). The fundraiser enjoys watching donors experience the joy of philanthropy knowing the impact of gifts on the institution is profound. This is a winning gift—both sides win—the donor and the nonprofit organization.

For many volunteers, asking for a gift feels like taking money away from their friends. Unfortunately, some of these discomforting thoughts and bad feelings come from unpleasant ask experiences the volunteer has personally gone through. Her arm was twisted; he was forced to make a gift; she made a

---

EXHIBIT I.I   STEPHEN COVEY HABIT #4—THINK WIN/WIN

Win/Win is a frame of mind and heart that constantly seeks mutual benefit in all human interactions. Win/Win means that agreements or solutions are . . . mutually satisfying . . . all parties feel good about the decision and feel committed to the action plan. . . . an even higher expression of Win/Win—Win/Win or No Deal . . . . When you have No Deal as an option in your mind, you feel liberated because you have no need to manipulate people, to push your own agenda, to drive for what you want. You can be open. You can really try to understand the deeper issues underlying the positions. With No Deal as an option, you can honestly say, "I only want to go for Win/Win. I want to win, and I want you to win. I wouldn't want to get my way and have you not feel good about it, because downstream it would eventually surface and create a withdrawal."

gift because she was on the board and was required to. There was no joy in this philanthropy—only guilt, reciprocation, or obligation.

The role of volunteers and staff in the fundraising process is not to twist arms, but rather to help the donor understand the case for support (the organization's story of why funds are urgently needed), and the benefit to the community. If we can match the donor's philanthropic values with the organization's needs, then asking for a philanthropic investment isn't taking money away from the donor but rather doing the donor a favor. How can everyone feel like a winner?

Here's a true story from a consultant who ran into a philanthropist friend in town. Sam had been asked to make leadership gifts for two arts organizations at the same time: one for an art museum's big capital campaign, the other for a small contemporary art society's endowment effort.

> Sam: Our family foundation is supportive of many things in the community. What should I do? We're just too visible in town not to give to both. I really like the contemporary art society, while the major art museum in town is okay and I know it is good for the community.

It's each organization's job to tell its story to him; then it's up to Sam to decide where he wants to donate his money. What questions did he have for each organization? Where was his real interest? Where was his heart?

> Sam: I really love the contemporary art, the society's vision for its programming, its fiscal responsibility, and its stability of management. I think I'll give $25,000 to the art museum as a token of our appreciation for its role in our community and $100,000 to the contemporary art society because it does such a great job and I love its work.

Both organizations won. The contemporary art society had obviously built a good rapport and relationship with Sam so that he was moved to contribute more to them. This story provides hope for new, younger nonprofit organizations; sometimes you have the creativity to attract the attention of donors who might be taken for granted at more established institutions.

How Do You Know if It's a Winning Gift?

The first section of this book focuses on the donors—their values and motivations as found in literature and research about donors and written by donors.

Of course the best way to determine if a gift request is a winner—ask the donor. As the donor makes the gift, does he feel good about it? How about six months later? Three years later? To build long-term relationships between people and nonprofit organizations, seek winning gifts over time. Many of the $10 million and $100 million gifts we read about in the trade literature sound miraculous. And while they are, usually they are the result of years, sometimes decades, of relationship building and a series of gift investments by the donor.

You can also look in your own heart—does the gift request inspire you the volunteer or professional fundraiser? Do you feel passionately about the organization and its mission? The project for which you are seeking funding? The impact the donor's gift will make in the community and in your institution? Even as a consultant who works with many clients I want to be inspired by the case and by the impact of the nonprofit organization on the community. For a new staff member, they need inspiration, too (for the long-term staff fundraiser this sense of mission and purpose is even more important to constantly renew their passion for the organization).

If you get yeses to all of these questions, you will have a lot of fun raising money.

WHY PHILANTHROPIC FUNDRAISING?

A lot of people and organizations raise money: politicians, venture capital funds, hedge funds, and small companies seeking investors. Fundraising has broadened to mean many things. Those of us raising funds for nonprofit organizations should start describing ourselves as philanthropic fundraisers. We are seeking funds to benefit the community, to help nonprofits make a difference in society—transformational fundraising. Keeping a people-centered focus suggests a different perspective to fundraising. Just meeting the yearly annual fund goal is not enough; that's institutionally centered fundraising. Ideally, you want donors to delight in making their winning gifts, gifts that make a difference. This people centered, winning-gifts philosophy keeps everyone focused first on the customer, the donor, rather than the institution receiving money as the primary objective.

INSPIRE GIVING

If you aspire to be a people centered fundraiser, then winning gifts come through inspiring donors to the aspirations and vision of our organization. Through inspiration donors feel like they have made a winning investment to help their communities.

This sounds easy. But, as fundraisers we know the challenge is to take the mundane operating budgetary needs of our organization and repackage and repurpose those needs to inspire great philanthropic gifts. This needs to be authentic and honest repackaging.

For example, one ballet company did a wonderful job of creating an annual giving Pointe Society (people who donate $1,000 or more every year), emphasizing how much of the operating budget went to purchasing ballet shoes each year. Donors were amazed at the cost of one pair of ballet shoes and the number of pairs of shoes each ballet dancer went through each year. Before this initiative the cost of buying ballet shoes was buried in the operating budget. Through good fundraising work, a marketing campaign for the Pointe Society resonated with donors and raised a lot of money.

THE SIX I'S OF PHILANTHROPIC FUNDRAISING

The philanthropic fundraising process seems mysterious to many people. Or, worse yet, the process is clear . . . and unpleasant. Joe has money; let's go get it from him.

In the late 1980s, Buck Smith, a college fundraiser who became the president of Chapman College, began thinking about the process of fundraising and came up with the concept of *moves management*. He watched his own behavior in closing major gifts and decided the process could be written down and tracked and a management system followed to help teach others the process.

In capturing Smith's ideas and sharing them with major donors and fundraising volunteers, I found that more clarity was needed and some type of graphic required for displaying the process. Tom Holce, a high-tech serial entrepreneur, suggested adding a step to Smith's five-step process, using a number-6 graphic, and starting each step with the same letter of the alphabet so the process would be easier to visualize and remember. He challenged my thinking. After a few iterations, I created The "Six I's of Philanthropic Fundraising" (see Exhibit I.2) in the early 1990s and began teaching it at conferences and to my clients. It has been fun to see the field adopt some of the I's in other versions of this fundraising management model.

While the Six I's process may seem like a gift-solicitation tool, and it is, we introduce it now as an organizer for this book.

The Six I's of Philanthropic Fundraising

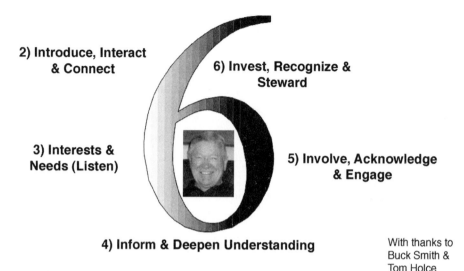

1) Identify, Qualify & Research

2) Introduce, Interact & Connect

6) Invest, Recognize & Steward

3) Interests & Needs (Listen)

5) Involve, Acknowledge & Engage

4) Inform & Deepen Understanding

With thanks to Buck Smith & Tom Holce

EXHIBIT I.2   THE SIX I'S OF PHILANTHROPIC FUNDRAISING

Think of the first three steps of The Six I's as donor oriented—Step #1, Identify, Qualify, and Research to find out who has the capacity to make a gift; Step #2, Introduce, Interact, and Connect to invite those qualified donors to learn about your organization and its impact on the community; and Step #3, Interests and Needs (Listen) to find out the values and motivations of these qualified donors who have started to become connected to your organization. All of these people-focused steps involve finding qualified donors and building an authentic relationship with them. Don't worry about asking for a gift. In fact, to get potential donors to relax, you need to promise them that no solicitations will take place during Steps #2 and #3.

The final three steps of the Six I's are more institution focused—Step #4, Inform and Deep Understanding uses traditional fundraising materials to make sure your story is told in depth; Step #5, Involve, Acknowledge, and Engage uses traditional volunteer techniques to ensure the potential donor feels a sense of ownership in the organization and its projects requiring funding; and Step #6, Invest, Recognize, and Steward is where the gift request is made and honored.

We will examine all six steps quickly now and then spend the balance of Part I of this book describing the first three steps in depth. In Part II, look for more information on the last three steps, particularly the last important one of asking for and closing the gift.

Six I's: Step #1—Identify, Qualify, and Research

One of the most obvious but important steps is to determine if the potential donor has any money to give away. You want to avoid getting someone interested in your organization, becoming good friends, and then destroying that relationship when it comes time for a gift request because the person has no money to give away (it's not good job security either).

In many ways, Step #1 of the Six I's—Identify, Qualify, and Research—is the most important. The rest of the process is donor-oriented relationship building, and usually culminates in a significant gift (not always, of course) as long as the person has disposable assets to give away. For the Six I's process to work, for any fundraising process to work, you must work with qualified donors.

Identify—ideally you want to start with your own organization's largest donors. Who are your best 25 donors for this fiscal year? For many organizations with a strong fundraising background, reviewing the list of the top 100 cumulative donors in the history of the organization will show people of significant wealth and affiliation who can be approached again in the future. Hospitals are particularly good at establishing their donor recognition systems on cumulative giving, where arts organizations tend to be wonderful annual fund list keepers. Do both formally—list your best annual fund donors by gift level in your annual report and your donor wall as well as maintain a separate listing of cumulative donors throughout the history of your organization.

With cumulative lists you must still do qualification work. You need to carefully review the names to make sure everyone is still alive, still in the area, and still in a position to give away money. Research is needed to update the capacity of the donor to give to your current effort. Receiving a $100,000 gift to your last campaign ten years ago is great, but what is the donor doing today? How is his company doing? Has the donor been in the news making large gifts to your friendly competitors? What is the donor's liquidity? Private business owners may have a tremendous net worth but until they sell the company or "go public" there may not be much cash to give; likewise real estate investors can have excellent net worth but be cash poor as they are always investing in the next deal. Ask board members to give you an update on that person. If in doubt, conduct a discovery call with the donor to ask about his current activities (see more information on discovery calls in Chapter 3, Listen).

For many organizations, the best indicator of future giving potential is not the size of donations but the duration of giving. If your organization has not been in a full-scale capital campaign or concerted annual fund, major-gifts effort, donor giving histories will be flat and not very helpful. Look for length of giving and length of affiliation (if you have a membership program or a subscriber program in addition to giving records).

Another good list to look at is largest-gift-ever listings. Go back 10 or 15 years and ask to see all gifts of $10,000 or more, $5,000 or more, $1,000 or more. Don't worry if a donor who made a large donation has not given to you in years or if last year's gift was $100. One special gift indicates gift capacity and donor interest. Most donor database systems have a "largest-gift-ever" field that is very helpful in qualifying donors in this way.

Look for odd gift amounts. Instead of $1,000 for your gift club, the donor record shows $1,003.26. Was does that mean? Usually, odd numbers like this indicate a stock transfer. For one client, a religious institution that we were helping to prepare for a capital campaign, we had a hard time building a qualified donors list. Because all church members were like "family" to each other, discussions of wealth capacity were avoided by our volunteers (usually they honestly didn't know and didn't care). We began looking for lump-sum pledge payments at year-end rather than weekly or monthly giving and for "odd" gift amounts. Both are indications of stock transfers to fulfill pledges. Stock gifts are a capacity indicator as the donors understand they can avoid some capital gains taxes by making gifts of stock.

Another technique is to take a relatively "flat" donor list and conduct qualifying screening with other donor lists in the community—get your local symphony and opera program book where they list all of their donors, look for donor plaques at nonprofit organizations, ask for copies of annual reports of your local university and hospital. Work top down. Look at the $10,000 level in all of these reports. Then go to $5,000, $2,500, and $1,000.

If a name is on their list and in your database, note the giving organization and gift level on your system. Keep going through lists until you have covered the major organizations in your city and then your state.

Qualify—soon you will begin to see a pattern of names emerging. Sure, some people will only give a substantial gift to one organization, but more often than not you will start to see the same names giving $5,000 or $10,000 to many organizations in town. If they are not in your database of donors, you have some work to do. But at least you have the name of a qualified donor. Start sending these people your newsletter. Invite them to cultivation events.

If, on the other hand, you find the donor has been giving you $50 for five years, you can move much more quickly. Maybe the only reason the donor has not given you a major gift is that nobody asked. You have a winner. Clearly this person is philanthropic, cares about the community, and is also connected with you.

Exhibit I.3 shows a wealth and interest chart (thanks, Vic Atchison). It helps to explain the early steps of identifying and qualifying donors so that when it comes time to ask for an investment in your organization you are more likely to be successful and the donor able to respond to your request. All of the dots on the chart represent a potential donor to your organization within your universe. This chart may be your town, your state, your country, or the world. It depends upon your mission and geographical scope.

The process of identifying donors is putting faces on each of the dots. Qualifying donors is putting them in the right quadrant for future work.

The upper-right quadrant shows your immediate prospects for gifts. They have wealth and interest. This group may be the best 25 of your top 100 cumulative donors and could include some long-term donors whom you have researched and determined could give away significant gifts.

The lower-right quadrant may represent the people you found on everybody else's lists but not yours or those who are at a low level of giving to you currently. These people might be wealthy business owners you are aware of but have not yet connected to your organization or the new board members that the chair recruited.

Your real task in fundraising is to get the wealthy, already-interested people even more interested and engaged with you. And, to get the wealthy uninterested people intrigued and enamored of your organization. Ideally, the entire right half of the chart is made up of asset donors rather than salary donors. To qualify donors at this level, look for second and third homes,

Universe of Interested and/or Wealthy people

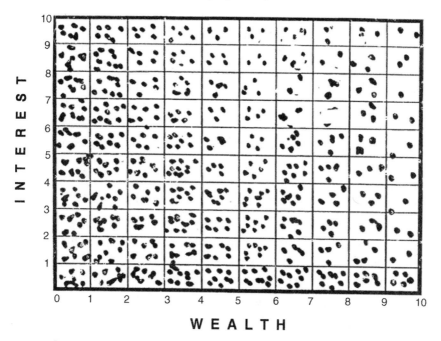

Rated on a scale of 1–10 with 10 denoting greatest interest/wealth.

EXHIBIT I.3   WEALTH AND INTEREST

frequent exotic travel, Securities & Exchange Commission (SEC) primary stock listings (people holding 5 percent or more of publicly traded company stock are listed in the SEC filings by these companies as are all officers and directors). Warren Buffett would be considered an asset giver even though it took him until age 75 to give away those assets. Of course, until that time he had been giving some small donations out of his yearly salary. Timing is everything.

The people in the upper left-hand corner of the chart, the highly interested but not wealthy people, are wonderful candidates for a planned estate gift. While of modest net worth, most people have several hundred thousand dollars of home value and usually more than that in retirement assets. Until death, these assets are not liquid and can only be committed in estate plans.

The lower left-hand people have no interest or money, so leave them alone.

The theme here is: **It is easier to make wealthy people interested than interested people wealthy**. Make sure to qualify donors to ensure they have the money to give away once they are highly interested.

This is the nondemocratic part of philanthropic fundraising. But, it does prevent you from over-asking donors without the capacity to respond. It is a winning-gifts technique.

Research—when I started in the field more than a quarter of a century ago, prospect research was unheard of. We did identification and qualification but there were few tools for in-depth prospect research as there are today. In fact, there is now a professional prospect research association of fundraising professionals who do nothing but this. There are also consulting firms that specialize in digging through data generated from electronic screenings, searches of national databases, and online searches of names.

For the small shop with one or two people, do as much in-depth research as you can on your top 25 donors. Look them up online, even pay for a research subscription where the vendor will provide in-depth profiles for a small fee. This information helps give you confidence on how much to ask for. For the large shop, consider cross-training one of your staff to become an expert in prospect research. Ideally, hire an experienced professional who comes to you with previous experience of how to do this well and ethically.

Six I's: Step #2—Introduce, Interact, and Connect

Now that we know whom we want to approach for a gift, how do we do it gracefully? Most people dislike fundraising because they figure out Joe has money and then they go ask for it. In a winning-gifts approach, Step #2 is never the ask but rather the introduction. For many board members who say they do not like fundraising and are not good at it, focusing their energy on introducing their friends with the capacity to give to the organization is a good role.

Introduction meetings can be a lunch with the university president, a breakfast with the hospital chief executive officer, joining a table of friends at the dinner auction, or going to campus for a tour and lunch with a faculty member. Be inventive; do everything you can to start connecting with your potential donors. Just follow one rule—no asks. These are education sessions, not solicitations.

Some capital campaigns will have an entire volunteer committee dedicated to introduction and interaction events. How can the organization tell its story through compelling activities at these events? How do we make these events special?

Six I's: Step #3—Interests and Needs (Listen)

Step #3 is the marketing approach to fundraising, the listening approach. This issue is so important that all of Chapter 3, Listen, is dedicated to techniques for collective and specific donor listening.

To build strong and lasting relationships with people, to find out their values and motivations around philanthropy, you need to be a deep listener. All of us can do it better. Chapter 3 will provide some insights from my experiences and from other sources to provide you with tools you can use.

Six I's: Step #4—Inform and Deepen Understanding

This step is all about traditional, ground-softening fundraising communications with some new twists for the Internet age. For many organizations that can say "we are the best-kept secret in town," Step #4 is critical. While a great deal of information can be transferred through face-to-face interviews and meetings, this is an inefficient way to inform the best 500 prospective donors for your organization. Some type of mass marketing and target marketing has to be used.

One marketing adage goes like this: 27 exposures for one understanding. That is why we see so many car ads, so many hamburger fast-food ads—repetition helps to burn in the brand and the message. Should nonprofits play that game? Can they play that game?

Unfortunately, the answer is no. The kind of television exposure that major, national brands can buy costs tens of millions dollars. Nonprofit organizations need to target markets for efficiency.

For some wonderful ideas on creative marketing on a limited budget, read the *Guerrilla Marketing* books produced by Jay Conrad Levinson and look at *Marketing for Dummies* by Alexander Haim.

While cold list direct-mail fundraising is expensive, direct-mail focused to a target list of your 500 best potential donors does work. Once people make philanthropic investments in your organization, they are willing to be informed more deeply about how the organization is using their money. We have found that communications to donors need to be short and frequent. Through testing during listening exercises (see Chapter 3, Listen) we found that donors, who are typically busy people and who are approached by many charities, tend to read "propaganda" from nonprofits sparingly.

E-mail will help, but the same admonition applies—keep it short. The best online newsletters have only a few graphics (so they load quickly), brief three-line outlines of an article, and a link to the full news article. Just remember to ask your donors if they are e-mail capable and if they like to receive information in that format. Short term, you should probably duplicate your communications online and through snail mail.

Continue cultivation events started in Step #2, Interact, Interest, and Connect, as most people will need to see your organization numerous times in a variety of settings to finally "get it." Use your socialites (*The Seven Faces of Philanthropy*, Chapter 2, Donor Values, found 11 percent of your donors fit this category) to help provide a continuous social presence to your donors.

Six I's: Step #5—Involve, Acknowledge, and Engage

If you want to speed up implementation of the Six I's system, find ways to involve your best potential donors with your organization in a meaningful way—utilize Step #5, Involve. Transfer the ownership of the organization from the staff to the community. In this way you are acknowledging donors as more than bank accounts—you are confirming they have good ideas and abilities to help your organization. Engage your donors in meaningful activities so they can grow into your organization.

Of course, the ideal way to involve potential donors is have them join your board of trustees. But, this path is usually reserved for donors who have already made substantial investments in your cause. What can you do for those who are still in the "potential" phase of your fundraising courtship? In Chapter 5, The Win-Win Ask, we'll spend the entire chapter on ways to use volunteers effectively in fundraising. We mentioned in Chapter 2, Donor Values, that the best way to keep people centered is to involve volunteers in all aspects of your fundraising program.

By using the power of your board members and volunteers, you can recruit new volunteers just because they are connected to your old ones. One recent interview with a potential donor and community leader was a classic:

> I didn't even know what this children's organization did but I was new to town and my friend George suggested I join his board. Over the first year I learned a lot and now I am one of their most active board members. I love what this organization does.

A recent survey found that high-net worth donors gave to organizations because 61% were on the board and 80% had volunteered. Those people volunteering 51 or more hours a year gave significantly more than people whose volunteerism was at a more "token" level.

Six I's: Step #6—Invest, Recognize, Steward

Process in fundraising is critical to a winning-gifts approach. But, at some point you need to ask for the order, close the gift, and seek the investment in your organization. In Chapter 5, The Win-Win Ask, we'll focus on making a successful gift request, and then, in Chapter 6, After Winning the Gift, we will examine ways of thanking donors, recognizing them, and stewarding their gifts over time.

A tracking and accountability chart tied to The Six I's of Philanthropy can be found at www.WinningGifts.INFO.

READ ON

Part I of this book focuses on these first three steps of the Six I's—qualifying donors, understanding their motivations for giving, and listening to them. Part II, Seek Winning Gifts for Your Organization, will describe the final three steps—how to seek winning investments from donors to benefit your organization's mission by making your case, involving donors, making the ask in terms that inspire the donor, and thanking them appropriately.

The Six I's looks like a linear, one-cycle process. But remember, people are complicated and organic—they start where they are, not where you want them to be. The real-life process is ongoing, ever spiraling upward in a growing concentration of good relationships, mutual respect, and trust. Think of the Six I's as a three-dimensional spiral moving upward from the platform of the six as the donor's life and the organization's growth mature over time. The spiral gets ever closer as the relationship tightens. This is where you would love the donor and organization to be—a philanthropic team for the good of the community—in 20 or 30 years, and through an estate gift, forever.

The time to take a qualified prospect through the Six I's ranges from 18 months to 4 years and 6 to 10 interactions. Of course, time spent by a donor participating on your board will increase the number of interactions and cut the time needed to secure a winning gift. Remember, once started, the process of a philanthropic partnership is lifelong. You need to establish systems to institutionalize the relationship. You must facilitate the ability of your successor to take over the donor relationship on behalf of your organization. The donor needs to have enough connections to the organization that transitions in fundraisers, presidents, and program staff will not sever ties and destroy the lifelong relationship between the donor and the organization.

NOTE

1. Stephen R. Covey, *The Seven Habits of Highly Effective People* (New York: A Fireside Book published by Simon & Schuster, 1990), 207, 213.

CHAPTER 1

People Centered Fundraising

*I have more fun and enjoy financial success when I stop trying to get
what I want and start helping other people get what they want.*

—Spencer Johnson and Larry Wilson,
The One Minute Sales Person[1]

In this chapter, we will cover three key ideas about people centered
fundraising:

1. Start with the peoples' needs and articulate how your organization
   benefits the community rather than focusing initially on institutional
   needs.
2. Use a marketing approach to fundraising.
3. Help your nonprofit become a people centered fundraising
   organization.

While some may think this chapter should be titled donor centered or
constituent centered or customer centered, think about people first. Your
family, your friends, your neighbors, your parents—they're all people first,
then constituents of various organizations, customers of a variety of
businesses, and donors to a few nonprofit organizations.

Great fundraising is all about relationships with people—people who have
their own interests, stories, motivations, and needs.

Start with Peoples' Needs

The winning gifts approach to philanthropic fundraising is a marketing approach. It is customer focused, and people centered. While we raise money for organizations, for the organization's board, or for the organization's executive director, ultimately nonprofit organizations are run to benefit the community. The board of directors sets policies for the organization as owners-in-trust for the community. Therefore, as contributed funds are sought it should be done in the long-term context of the organization benefiting its community.

So what do people need? What motivates them to give money away philanthropically? Chapter 2 will deal with these issues extensively in a historical and comprehensive way. Research studies have probed to find donor values around giving. In Chapter 3, listening skills to determine motivations for individual donors that you work with will be discussed. The best way to find out someone's philanthropic worldview is to ask them.

- "I just sold my company and am too young to retire. I want to join your board and observe Ed and John and the other community leaders who give of their time and wealth. I need role models."

- "My family is from Chicago where Granddad was on the museum board and Dad on the symphony board. We have a family tradition of philanthropy and board work. I need to learn how to do this in my newly adopted city."

- "Our company employs a lot of people in this county. We want to help make this a great place to live for our families and to be known as good corporate citizens."

- "I'm an entrepreneur. I'm willing to make a gift, but I want to see how the organization can leverage my money by raising additional funds. And, I want to see a multiplier effect of my gift in making a difference for poor children in our town."

- "Our founder is dead, so we as foundation trustees try to envision what he would have wanted us to fund. He was interested in economic development and children. We want to honor his generosity in setting up our foundation."

Every donor has his or her own unique set of needs, aspirations, family history, and understanding of philanthropy. And every donor is on the path from making his or her first gift, to having donated dozens of times, and to learning what an endowment is and how it differs from operating or building gifts.

In developing a winning gifts strategy for all of your donors, think through the benefits they receive through their gift investment. Most of these benefits will be intangible, psychic, and emotional. For many people of affluence, once they have bought a huge house, a second home, traveled everywhere they can imagine, and bought everything they want, they begin to see that things can only bring you so much pleasure. True happiness takes meaning and permanence. Becoming a philanthropist can provide people with more satisfaction than almost anything else. Finding peoples' passions and emotional values can be the winning-gifts secret to your fundraising success.

And, as you present gift opportunities remember that no matter how good the college president is, another job or retirement will mean change in the future. No matter how talented the fundraisers, they, too, will retire someday. What lasts is the mission and vision of the organization—and the generations of donors who invest their personal funds to help pay for that vision.

Fundraising for nonprofits started because there was a need for money. At private universities, students could not pay enough tuition to fully cover faculty salaries or fund the construction of new buildings; at hospitals, patient fees could pay for immediate services but not for all the new equipment needed in a given year; and at animal shelters, perhaps a treatment hospital is needed. These are all real concerns but they are focused on what the institution needs. For the board members of these organizations, many of these needs became evident through discussions at board meetings and with staff members.

How do we match up the needs of the organization with the values and motivations of donors? How do we do this for people who are loosely connected, if connected at all, with the organization in need? What's the 30-second elevator speech to capture the attention of people busy with their own lives and with the many other causes in the community?

The first step is converting these organizational needs to community benefit.

How Does Your Organization Benefit the Community?

When you first start thinking about how to convert organizational needs to community benefits, it can be numbing to your brain. What does this mean?

Try to look at your organization from the community perspective. What does it do that makes the community better? What's the added value? Sometimes it helps to think about what holes would be left in the community if your organization disappeared.

These ideas tap into the prominent donor motivation of communitarians—giving back to the communities that helped enrich their lives and lives of family members.

For example, colleges need money to pay for faculty, to keep their facilities clean, for administrators, to construct new buildings. But, what is the community benefit? Sure students go to classes. But how do I, the little old lady living three miles from campus, benefit? One of the great sayings is, "The only thing more expensive than a fine education is the lack of one." A study showed it costs more money to put a 20-year-old in prison for a year than to send that individual to Harvard for a year. Young people need a safe environment, one step away from home, to finish their emotional development and to gain knowledge and skills that will pay off for their lifetimes. College graduates work at local business and industry. They create companies, they work, they vote, they pay taxes, and they make good health-care decisions. They become a community asset rather than a community drain. A great college will bring students from far away to your town and your state. Many will stay to strengthen the local economy. A strong college creates an academic atmosphere by attracting faculty members and their families from across the country. College cultural events, plays and music performances, enable small towns to have the cultural life of a city many times larger. Sure, the college may need to raise money to pay for some projects, but one important reason people give is the community and societal benefit the college provides.

In people centered fundraising, you always need to ask the questions, How does the investment the donor makes in this organization benefit the community, society, or people in need? What difference will this gift make? What impact can we show the donor? What results is this organization producing in the world?

Here are two case histories that may be informative. These are true stories.

A Public Library   The local public library was able to operate on tax levies and modest revenues from library cards, overdue book fines, and a few government grants. Everything worked well for the past 50 years. Then the library building needed a major expansion. City budgets were tight and there was no money for capital improvements. The local citizens could not be asked to approve a bond measure for new library space. What to do? Undertake a capital campaign of course—raise the $2.3 million needed. But, that's a lot of money for a small, rural community of 7,000.

Why should people give money to the library, which is owned by the city, because the librarian wants more space? That's what we heard at our first consulting session with the client and some of its potential donors during a leadership briefing focus group session.

In asking what the problems were at the library, we learned that when the current library was built 20 years ago it was supposed to be 7,500 square feet, but the budget only allowed for 5,000 square feet. So what? Well, after two decades of successfully serving the public and after many changes in both the technology as well as the offerings of libraries—from card catalogs to Internet searches and from hardback books to the addition of paperbacks, audiobooks, VHS tapes, and DVDs—the stacks had expanded out to the walls of the library. All of the reading areas were now gone. As the town's demographics had changed, library patrons now came in using walkers, wheelchairs, and motorized chairs. The stacks were too narrow to accommodate these patrons. In fact, they were so narrow that when one person was browsing in an aisle there was no room for a second person to pass. One computer station had been added seven years ago and, through a grant from the Bill & Melinda Gates Foundation, three more computer stations were added a few years later. Computers were in such demand, users were limited to one hour. There was a sign-up list for Internet searches by senior citizens and by people who couldn't afford a computer or an Internet connection. The library needed more money for more computers and the space to put them in.

What other problems did the library have? Children's hour at the library had always been popular. It was a great activity for young moms to get out of the house and bring their children to hear some stories and browse the children's section for books they could check out. Everyone wants their children to learn how to read and become well educated. The problem? Too much success. As the children's section added more and more books there was less open space for the children's hour. The children's hour became more and more popular. Finally, critical mass was surpassed. The children's hour had to move out of the library into the nearby community center. It worked, but the opportunity for the children to move immediately from story time to looking for books was lost. Only half of the families took the time to walk one block to the library to look for books—especially in the winter in the pouring rain.

As we talked to potential donors who had the wealth to make gifts to help make the library expansion possible we found out they didn't know any of this story. They just yawned at the idea that the librarian wanted more space for her books. But, when they heard that their grandchildren couldn't look at books after the children's hour, that was a different story.

When we asked if they had checked out a book recently, they looked at us with puzzled eyes. If they wanted a book, they went to Barnes & Noble and bought it; they went online to Amazon.com and had the book sent to their home. They didn't need the library at all. And, you know what? They were right. A new library expansion had no value to them at all.

What we learned the hard way was the need to ask the value question in a different way. When did they use a library in their life? When was it of value? We heard some stories that were amazing to us—and even more amazing to the potential donors. One older gentleman remembered immigrating to America and coming to town not speaking or reading a word of English. He got a job with some cousins but spent every spare moment in the public library learning how to read English and understand the United States. He said that without the public library he never would have realized the American dream and come to own his own business and several buildings in the downtown area. Another person remembered going to the local library's book club as a seventh grader and reading 10 books a week during that summer, opening a whole new world through fiction and nonfiction. A lady learned how to turn her hobby of gardening into a nursery business. The stories were endless. All of a sudden, the needs of the library were aligned with the values of the donor and the benefits to the community. The donors' grandchildren would benefit. New people would move to the community because the library was so good. Poor families without computers and Internet connections would still be able to connect to the World Wide Web because the library was around.

The result? The campaign surpassed its building goal and started on its next fundraising phase, a permanent endowment fund for new book acquisitions.

A Graduate University   This private graduate institution granted doctoral degrees (primarily) and master's degrees (a few) in complicated high-technology, engineering, and science fields. The faculty members focused on their own research and supporting their graduate students' original research for their doctoral dissertations. A new president came to the school with a vision for the future and a fundraising team was created. Given the young history of the organization and the six to eight years needed to complete a doctoral degree, the alumni base was minuscule. How could funds be raised?

In developing a strategic plan, a new mission statement was forged: "ABC Institute of Science & Technology: educating leaders and creating knowledge through research." Sure, the organization still taught students, but the community benefit was educating leaders in science and technology for local and national high-tech companies. And instead of just doing research for its own sake (the common perception of donors), the faculty was actively engaged in creating knowledge to benefit humankind (this was always the goal; they just hadn't told their story well). The mission statement helped to articulate the community benefit. And, like most good mission statements, it started to serve as a guiding light to determine which new graduate programs the institution should offer in the community (e.g., the creation of a new master's degree program in technology management to educate engineers on business principles, thus meeting the needs of industry and its employees).

Take a Marketing Approach

A winning-gifts approach to fundraising takes a marketing approach rather than just a sales approach. In selling, you are going out to convince people to buy something. Using a marketing approach, you slow the process down to determine the interests and needs of your potential customers with the goal of coming back to them with a product they are already interested in buying.

Earlier in my career I was the corporate and foundation fundraiser for Field Museum of Natural History in Chicago, a wonderful institution. I loved wandering the halls learning about dinosaurs, exotic animals from around the world, the gem collection, and the primitive artwork of indigenous peoples. My young daughter used to tour with me occasionally and because of all of the stuffed animals at the time (the mid-1980s), Chrissy called it "the inside zoo."

One day, I got a call from volunteer services telling me they had assigned a new volunteer to help me. Volunteers always wanted to be tour guides in the museum or help with children's programs, not help with fundraising. I was amazed; this was going to be great.

Sally changed my whole perspective of fundraising. Her family had recently come to Chicago for her husband to take on a news anchor job. She was in her late 30s with a young child at home, but had a master of business administration in marketing and had worked at a big agency in New York City before starting their family and retiring. She wanted to volunteer somewhere her marketing expertise could be used.

At our initial meeting I described my responsibilities—raise $1 million a year from corporations to support Field Museum and write grants to foundations.

She tested me on what I knew about marketing; I flunked the oral exam. I was in my late 20s at the time, a kid. She was older than I and obviously had many more years of corporate experience. I was just a dumb musician who had recently finished managing a community orchestra. What did I know?

Being a good volunteer, she took control of the situation and laid out our mutual agenda. Her volunteer job was to teach me marketing. She brought in her MBA marketing books and lectured me, taught me, cajoled me into learning marketing concepts in her two volunteer afternoons a week.

I've never forgotten her main themes. Don't sell before you market, and listen to the marketplace. It's much easier to sell something people want to buy. Slow down and take the time to listen to your customers (donors) to learn about their interests and values. Then shape your sales proposal to meet their needs. Thanks, Sally.

Sales

What's the difference between marketing and sales? Selling is taking a product, or in our case a fundraising need, and convincing a person to make a decision to buy the product; making the pitch; making the sale. For example: Your college has a President's Club with a $1,000 yearly membership; they ask you to join them. That's a sales pitch.

Sales-focused fundraising emphasizes ways to make the ask, the amount of money raised this month and this year, how many prospects each fundraiser can handle, how many cold calls, and how many fundraising pitches have been made this month.

From Thomas J. Stanley, author of *Selling to the Affluent*:

> Are you an Apostle or Antagonist to the Affluent? An apostle to the affluent is a sales professional whose mission is to serve this target market. . . . They are also proficient at attracting, conditioning, and retaining the affluent as clients. Antagonists, more often than not, show more concern for their own needs . . . than for those of the affluent. . . . They often repel as opposed to attract the affluent as clients.
>
> First become an apostle to your affluent prospects before focusing on your own need—the need to sell your product.[2]

Stanley goes on to define an apostle as someone on a mission, someone who is there to serve.

Of course, you will always have an aspect of sales in fundraising; however, it should come after you have developed your marketing plan and tested your value proposition with your donors.

Many organizations rely on a sales approach through their emphasis on special events. Golf tournaments, auctions, and other types of special-event fundraising are transactional fundraising. The buyer is getting merchandise, usually at a discount, in exchange for her donation (her purchase). It's a sales approach to raising money. While nonprofit groups raise $5,000 to $500,000 using sales techniques in special events, donors may be only vaguely aware of the cause they are supporting. They are more interested in the great deal they got on the golf vacation they won at the auction.

Marketing

Marketing to understand your donors and potential donors means slowing down to find out the interests and needs of the potential buyers before making the sales pitch.

For example: What is your connection to our library? What do you know of our programs? Do you understand how we impact the community? Do you realize we need support from people like you to increase the size of our book acquisition fund so we always have the best research sources available? What would motivate you to consider making a $1,000 contribution to our organization?

A marketing approach can still involve metrics and measures of results productivity, but its emphasis is on relationships that lead to donors discovering they need to make a gift. Testing case statements through focus groups and face-to-face interviewing is a marketing approach (see Chapter 3, Listen). Relationship building is the heart of a winning-gifts strategy, a people centered approach to fundraising.

To create authentic relationships with your potential donors, you need to be convinced of your case for support (see Chapter 4, Make Your Case). Understanding the impact of gifts on your organization and society will help create your personal energy. It will motivate you to seek funding for your cause through charitable giving. In Part II, we will look at some ethical influence considerations as you put people ahead of money.

Good fundraisers know that the first gift is never the last gift. Your goal is to steward the first gift (see Chapter 6, After Winning the Gift) toward the objective of a lifetime relationship between the donor and the nonprofit organization. You may or may not be there the entire time of this institutionalized relationship, but hopefully you are the catalyst that starts and nurtures interactions as long as possible.

You can achieve the same results (for example, securing a $1,000 President's Club donation) through a marketing approach (taking the extra time to listen to the donor so you can begin to understand a long-term philanthropic path for this person with your organization). You may end up getting a much larger gift using this marketing approach rather than a quick-sell technique.

A fine example of this difference goes back to my days when I was on the Field Museum staff in Chicago. I was appointed by my supervisor to be on several museum committees, one of which was the "copier committee." We were in charge of helping departments get copy machines and duplicating services (this was back in the mid-1980s, when copying was a real chore). We asked Xerox to come in and make a sales presentation for a new machine for the fourth-floor curators. The Xerox representative came and politely listened to our request. She asked our permission to come back in a few days with a colleague to interview the curators and their secretaries to see what the ideal copier would be. They came back a week after the interviews and told us that while they could sell us the first machine we were interested in, they had a different model with more capabilities that Xerox felt met the museum's needs better and would be more efficient and cost effective over time. We listened to their defense of the proposal, bought the more capable copier, and thanked the sales team for their thoughtful work. This is a great approach—first-class marketing followed by the sales pitch.

In *The Portable MBA in Marketing,* authors Charles D. Schewe and Alexander Hiam note:

> It is not an easy thing to please customers. They already have so many choices. If you wish to sway even one purchase decision [think donor gift decision] in a new direction, you must discover and communicate something of unique value to customers.
>
> It all comes down to customers . . . you must, first and foremost, focus on *what you will do for your customer?*[3]

The essence of good marketing is customer satisfaction. As consumers of retail products in the United States, we know that. Toyota wants us to feel good about being environmentally conscious so the company offers us the Prius hybrid. As philanthropic fundraisers, we need to remind ourselves that while donors can be altruistic (one of the seven profiles identified in *The Seven Faces of Philanthropy* by Russ Alan Prince and Karen Maru; see Chapter 2, Donor Values), the donors are being bombarded by philanthropic requests almost as often as they are by car advertisements. Nonprofits compete for contributed funds—for the known donors who have publicly displayed the capacity to make million-dollar gifts, this competition is fierce. What will you do for these donors (these customers)? How will they be delighted by making a major donation to your organization? How can they be sure they have made a winning gift for themselves?

One way to satisfy customers is to provide direct feedback from the people they have helped or will help through their gift. For one college, we needed to get the scholarship message across to our donors. The staff found a young mom with two young children who was only able to go back to college because of a scholarship. We captured her and her children on video as the narrator read her heartfelt letter of thanks. The emotion of what this scholarship meant to her children and to her was clear to the donors and helped inspire many to give to the scholarship fund.

In their book, *Principles of Marketing,* Philip Kotler and Gary Armstrong comment on the importance of personal selling:

> People hold many stereotypes of salespeople . . . modern salespeople are a far cry from these unfortunate stereotypes. Today, most salespeople are well-educated, well-trained professionals who work to build and maintain

long-term customer relationships by listening to their customers, assessing customer needs, and organizing the company's efforts to solve customer problems.[4]

Many fundraising consulting firms have moved the concept of the feasibility study to that of a philanthropic market research study. Yes, they can still tell client nonprofits whether the campaign goal is feasible, but the higher purpose is to test the sales proposition (the case statement) with prospective donors to determine their reaction. Is the nonprofit helping to build a better community and society through this campaign project? Does the donor realize that a problem needs solving? Feasibility studies are fine, but you may want to consider expanding the scope of the study to include market research so you can understand your donors better.

In a recent interview, Kenneth Blanchard, co-author of *The One Minute Manager,* commented on college students and learning:

> I think the way you make anybody a raving fan is when you go out of the way to serve them . . . Satisfying customers is not enough, what you need is to create raving fans . . . by treating . . . the customers as if they really had brains and they were important to you and you want to listen to them and you're open to their ideas.[5]

In Chapter 3, Listen, we will examine specific techniques you can use to discover and uncover donor interests.

Importance of Strategic Planning

Strategic planning (scenario planning, long-range planning) should be important to every nonprofit organization. Planning helps set directions for the staff and the future of the organization. Visions of future successes for the organization are mapped during the strategic planning process.

Beyond organizational effectiveness, strategic planning creates a winning-gifts atmosphere. Why? First, the plan helps to confirm to the staff and donors the future vision and vibrancy of the organization. The time invested in planning by the staff and board also serves to create a common vision for the organization, and common words to describe the vision and the path to move toward that vision over the next several years. Second, to take a marketing approach implies flexibility. Because you have a multifaceted prioritized plan, you can react to peoples' interests and needs by shopping the plan. Of course, we always want to sell the first priority, but if the donor isn't interested, the strategic plan gives us a roadmap to other options.

We speak here about *vision* rather than just the three- to five-year strategic plan. While this type of plan is fine for operational purposes, philanthropic fundraisers need a longer-term view, a quarter-century vision. If we are to encourage our 60- and 70-year-old donors to include our organization in their estate plans, then we need to be selling the 25-year vision, not just the five-year strategic plan.

Planning helps your organization to define the ideal situation in 5 years, 10 years, and a quarter-century from now. It then looks at current resources to achieve that ideal. The gap between what is possible now and what is possible to reach the vision—the gap analysis—can be presented to donors for funding. For example: One organization had $500,000 set aside for an endowed scholarship. After strategic planning, the group found that to have an impact on the students it wanted to help through this scholarship program, it would need a $1 million endowment (the organization wanted to give two $25,000 scholarships to encourage minority students to enter the medical profession). Rather than lower its vision to one scholarship, the organization established a fundraising objective of securing an additional $500,000 in the next three years and a long-term vision of a $10 million endowment through planned estate-gift commitments (the organization knew tuitions would keep increasing over time and the number of students that needed scholarships was estimated at 10 to 15 students each year). You can see that without a strategic plan the fundraiser does not have a roadmap for future projects to share with donors.

Here is one donor's comment: "I was raised as a preacher's son and was told to give to those who asked, but as an adult, now, I want to know how my money will be used and need to see a vision and goal." The best way to respond to a donor like this is to share elements of your organization's strategic plan. Some donors will want to see, and deserve to see, the entire strategic plan. (Note: A person requesting such information may be an excellent board of trustees candidate).

Drucker Self-Assessment Tool   Peter Drucker (1909–2005) was an academic, a writer, and a consultant in strategy and policy for corporations and nonprofit organizations. He authored 31 books that have been translated into more than 20 languages. He was an editorial columnist for the *Wall Street*

Journal and frequent contributor to the *Harvard Business Review* and taught at the Peter F. Drucker and Masatoshi Ito Graduate School of Management at Claremont Graduate University (the business school was named in his honor in 1984). In 1997, he was featured on the cover of *Forbes. Business Week* described him as "the most enduring management thinker of our time."

In the early 1990s, Drucker turned his writing attention to nonprofit organizations. He created The Peter Drucker Foundation, which published the Drucker Self-Assessment Tool through Jossey-Bass Publishers (a division of John Wiley & Sons, Inc.), to aid nonprofit organizations with their strategic planning. More information can be found about the tool on the Leader to Leader web site—www.LeaderToLeader.org. The Drucker Self-Assessment Tool is an excellent way to structure a strategic planning process. We mention it here as it helps provide a context for planning. In the tool, Drucker asks five simple, yet deep and profound questions (see Exhibit 1.1).

The "customer" notion may seem foreign or awkward to your nonprofit organization. Drucker defines the customer as the person whose life your organization is trying to change. He asks that your organization consider the myriad sets of supporting customers who help the organization serve the primary customer. Of course, one always-important supporting customer is the donor. In addition to asking nonprofits to focus on their primary customer, another aspect of Question #2, Who is our customer?, Drucker asks that you consider sets of supporting customers. In Question #3, he asks nonprofits to think through the values of their primary customer and each set of supporting customers. By supporting customers, Drucker means all of the other people who assist the nonprofit in serving the primary customer. For a hospital, the primary customer is the patient; supporting customers would include physicians, nurses, lab technicians, cleaning personnel, family

---

EXHIBIT I.I   FIVE STRATEGIC PLANNING QUESTIONS

Question #1	What is our mission?
Question #2	Who is our customer?
Question #3	What does the customer value?
Question #4	What are our results?
Question #5	What is our plan?

members, administrators, health insurance companies, employers, the community, and so forth. Each of these supporting customers will have their own set of values.

> **What will encourage contributors** . . . to convert individuals who give money into "contributors," that is, citizens who take responsibility, neighbors who care. . . . What are that individual's personal reasons for giving money? To whom does he or she give? What results prompt the contributor to say, "Yes, that's what should be done. That's what deserves more of my support." What does this customer value enough to do more, to really become a partner in furthering the mission?

> **Listen to your customers**. . . . To formulate a successful plan you will need to understand each of your constituencies' concerns, especially what they consider results in the long term. Integrating what customers' value into the institution's plan is almost an architectural process, a structural process. It's not too difficult to do once it's understood, but it's hard work. First, think through what knowledge you need to gain. Then listen to customers, accept what they value as objective fact, and make sure the customer's voice is part of your discussions and decisions.[6]

Chapter 3, Listen, will cover ways of listening to the donor customers of your organization. Being sensitive to their values will keep you people centered in all of your fundraising work.

How to Be People Centered

Now that you understand the need to be marketing oriented, customer focused, and people centered, what does that mean for the different sectors of philanthropy? The first task is not to assume or to base our fundraising techniques on *our* values and *our* needs but to listen to people—therefore, there is a whole chapter on listening in this book. Don't guess at donor values and motivations—don't assume you are people centered until you meet with a donor or person in the community who might become a donor every working day of the year.

You can keep people centered by remembering to engage the other people in your organization, not just your fundraising team. Explaining your fundraising story to the academic vice president as well as everyone's favorite maintenance engineer forces you to remember that the people within your organization can be a marketing force for you, too. Alexander Haim, who wrote *Marketing for Dummies* as well as co-authored *The Portable MBA for Marketing,* notes the five P's of marketing:

1. Product—what aspects of the product itself are important?
2. Price—what does it cost for your customer to obtain and use your product?
3. Placement—when and where is your product available to customers?
4. Promotion—any and all ways you will be communicating to customers about your product.
5. People—all points of human contact with customers are important parts of your marketing program.[7]

In Chapter 4, Make Your Case, we'll look at product, placement, and promotion. Pricing will be discussed in Chapter 5, The Win-Win Ask. For this chapter, keep focused on item #5—people. Don't forget that the people who work with you and for your organization can be a wonderful aid to your fundraising program.

Individuals

With 80 percent of the charitable funding coming from individuals (see Giving U.S.A.—Sources and Trends in Giving in Chapter 2, Donor Values), we will spend most of the time in this book looking at this sector. In Chapter 3, Listen, we will go through a list of questions you can ask your best donors and best prospective donors regarding what they value.

One of the mantras throughout this book is to get out of your office at least 50 percent of the time to call on people. Interact with them, build relationships, ask them questions, and get to know their values. Philanthropic fundraising is a people business, so follow the one-a-day plan and visit with one qualified donor or prospective donor every day.

All good fundraising is a combination of marketing and sales. Once we understand a donor's value system and once we have created a case for support (see Chapter 4, Make Your Case) then we do have to go into a presentation and sales mode. To keep people centered, remember each individual is going through a learning curve and your donor community is

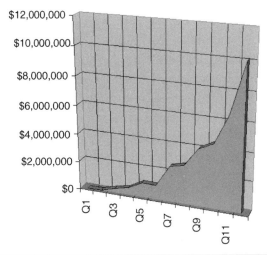

	Q1	Q2	Q3	Q4	Q5	Q6	Q7	Q8	Q9	Q10	Q11	Q12
Series1	$0	$0	$250,000	$500,000	$1,000,000	$1,000,000	$2,500,000	$2,750,000	$4,000,000	$4,500,000	$6,500,000	$10,050,022

EXHIBIT 1.2   LEARNING CURVE

going through a *mass learning curve* (a cumulative effect of all of the individual curves put together).

You can see in the fairly traditional learning curve in Exhibit 1.2 that education starts off slowly, some progress is made, and then a plateau is reached. Then, as time goes by, rapid learning takes place and finally mastery is achieved. Being a former high school teacher, this concept was presented to us in senior-level and graduate education courses so we as teachers could better appreciate why the students were so slow to catch on. It taught us to be patient, to be prepared for the plateaus in learning, and yet to keep our expectations high as rapid progress would occur over time. We were also taught that everyone in the class would have their own individual learning curve and that people would, on average, learn at about the same rate. But, to again teach us patience, our professor emphasized that a few people would catch on very quickly, thus getting bored with the slow progress of their classmates. And, a few others would be slow in the learning curve, take more of our attention, and probably need extra help outside of the regular classroom teaching setting.

As I got involved in fundraising, it became apparent that presenting an organization's vision and funding needs to potential donors required that they go up a learning curve. They do not get it right away. You have one meeting and they are nodding their heads, indicating that they understand. You go back one month later to see them again, and they have regressed back down the learning curve and have forgotten almost everything. They need to be retaught. One test of learning retention that works with students in the classroom as well as in fundraising is to ask the student (donor) to tell you the lesson (the case for support); tell it to others at a board meeting or leadership briefing focus group session. If they pass the test, you know they have mastered the material. And, in getting ready for the test, the public testimonial, the person needs to master the material and be able to articulate the case for support.

Look again at Exhibit 1.2. This indeed is a typical learning curve that would fit any individual student quite well. But, this is actually a campaign- dollars-over-time graph that tracked a $4.25 million campaign. Three years of time are captured here. You can see the plateaus where learning (fundraising) seems to have stopped. And you can see where mastery was reached and the campaign goal achieved (in fact, this campaign hit $10 million).

Patience is critical. It is not about us telling the story; it is about the potential donors understanding, internalizing, and being able to repeat the story of our organization in their own terms with their own passion and values integrated. We looked at The Six I's of Philanthropic Fundraising in Part I, A Winning Gift for Your Donor. The time it takes for a donor to go through this six-step process is somewhere between 18 months and four years, depending on his prior knowledge and experiences with an organization. Collectively, capital or comprehensive capital campaigns can take three to five years, with seven years the standard in large, complex campaigns for universities and medical centers.

Having worked in one community for 20 years now, it is fascinating to see how patient and persistent organizations need to be. The $50,000 donor of a decade ago is now making million-dollar gifts. The family who was new to town and cautious with their giving is now a recognized role model. Even though your organization needs the money now, each person is on his or her own philanthropic path. Give them time to mature and grow.

To be people centered, act like a teacher exhibiting high expectations but infinite patience with your students, the donors.

For those involved in teaching adults, it is important to remember that—because of the ever-growing body of knowledge about the brain—we now realize the older the person, the more experienced the person, the harder it is to introduce new concepts and new nonprofit organizations to support. Not impossible, but harder, as we are trying to position our organization into the already-established charitable giving patterns each donor has.

The old real estate mantra is "location, location, location." The philanthropic fundraising mantra should be "patience, patience, patience." But don't mistake patience for doing nothing. Children go to school five days a week because learning is enhanced through repetition. Frequency of interaction with concepts to be learned is critical. Another common way to look at fundraising is to assume through the Six I's process of up to four years that you will have 6 to 10 contacts with the donor over that time period. This time frame can be shortened through bimonthly written communications (through printed and/or e-mail newsletters). You want to get to a top-of-mind status with your potential donors. You want them to say that your charity is one of their top three philanthropic priorities. If you are number 10 on their list right now, you can see where a couple of years of hard work will be needed to bring your organization up to the top three. If you are not even on the donor's radar screen of charitable causes, you could be looking at the four years (or longer) to capture the donor's interest, heart, and pocketbook.

In *The Art of Selling to the Affluent*, Matt Oechsli notes:

> Your critical path to affluent sales success requires the mastery of *face-to-face* interaction . . . you don't simply manage the sale; you manage the relationship. . . . They do not want to be sold; they want to be served and assisted as they move through the decision-making process. . . . Face-to-face communication . . . is the richest medium of communication possible. It engages all five senses.[8]

In Planned Estate-Gift Fundraising   Many organizations seeking planned estate gifts want the money to help build their endowment funds. Just like people can never be too rich or too thin, nonprofits can never have too much endowment. But both statements are vain and self-centered. How do you become other centered? People centered? Why do you need an endowment? What impact does it have on the people you serve?

Basic, planned estate-giving fundraising techniques include: think family first; include all of the donor's major charities in your discussions; find out the person's values around giving money to children and grand-children; and what legacy the donor would like to leave the community or society. And, ask about the donor's views on endowment (some like it, some like it not).

To build a successful planned estate-giving program, you have to be 90 percent people centered or you will not be successful (more to come on this later in this book). Estate giving is so family-centric that to break into the inner circle of giving takes great persistence and intelligence. As one gentleman told me: "I have four children and twelve grandchildren, that's my estate plan." Unless we can show a person like this a legacy vision plus a way to reduce tax obligations, an estate planning proposition is impossible.

One classic people-centered story has to do with a fundraising-industry-jargon use of the words, *planned giving.* In this book, you will find the consistent use of *planned estate gifts.* Why? Here's the story: I was invited by a board member of one of my clients to present to one of his other nonprofit boards. The organization we were working together on was in the midst of a major capital campaign for endowment that was using both five-year pledges and planned gifts to reach the campaign goal. My board friend, Joe, was the president of one of the largest banks in the region and wanted his other board to get on the planned-giving bandwagon. Therefore, he invited me to do a training session. I started the session with a discussion about basic planned giving, noting that 87 percent of all planned gifts are made by simple bequest. He stopped me right there and asked me to repeat what I had just said. I repeated it. He interrupted again to ask, "Does that mean if I have ten charities listed in my estate plan that I am a planned gift donor?" I told him yes and realized that, to him, even as a long-term leader in banking and financial services, the term *planned gift* was meaningless. I immediately started using the more people-friendly *estate gift,* and, to help bridge this apparent gulf between people and professional fundraisers, started using *planned estate gift.*

Foundations

In many ways, foundations are the hardest area in which to be people centered as you are dealing with an organizational entity rather than an individual (this applies to large-staffed foundations, not family foundations). They may seem remote, bureaucratic, rule-bound, and somewhat adversarial. I had the luxury of being a rookie grant writer at a major Chicago cultural organization, which allowed me to ask dumb, rookie questions of grant officers at the major foundations in town.

In talking with these program officers, it was interesting to learn that they felt as restricted by their trustees' guidelines as did the grant requestors. But they had to follow the rules. Their real professional goal was to find exciting, solid grant proposals from nonprofit organizations to present to their trustees. If they did so and the trustees made a full or significant award, the program officer was successful; they felt like winners—they were delighted.

Understanding my customer, the foundation grant officer (and the grant officer's customer, the foundation's trustees), it was now clear that the nonprofit organization's grant writer's job was to follow the published guidelines, write a first-rate proposal, form a partnership with the grant officer (if at all possible), and revise and redraft the proposal to meet the values and expectations of the foundation's trustees. It didn't have to be an adversarial relationship, and, in fact, if you worked hard and did the process right, a partnership usually did develop with your program officer. The program officer became your internal advocate and champion in his written report and personal explanation of the proposal at the trustee meeting.

Through a relationship with your grant officer you can understand firsthand the values of the foundation instead of trying to tease them out of the written guidelines. Over time, your relationship becomes more important as the grant officers begin to share ideas the trustees are discussing for changes in the written guidelines that may not appear for some time in writing (you get on the inside track).

Of course, trying to build relationships with the trustees is also important but not as easily done as with the grant officer. Ideally, to understand the foundation's values you want to do both. Top-level foundation fundraising is not just about good writing—grant writing. But, rather, grantsmanship is the value matching of the foundation's vision of how they want to benefit society with your organization's strategic plans and projects. As the song in *Fiddler on the Roof* goes, "Matchmaker, matchmaker make me a match . . . find me a find."

Corporations

Many nonprofit organizations relate poorly to corporations when it comes to fundraising. The whole culture of most nonprofit organizations is academic, or social services oriented, or otherwise focused on service rather than profits. In fact, if the nonprofit does its job right, you create more losses through more services to people in need in the community. The difference in culture between nonprofits and for-profit corporations, which monitor quarterly earnings and profits like hawks, is gigantic.

To aid in your corporate fundraising work, elect some leading corporate officers to your board. Start reading your local newspaper's business section as well as the local business journal. Attend meetings of your local chamber of commerce; become a Rotarian.

If corporate fundraising is going to be important to you, reach out to understand their world. As you become more acquainted with corporate life, you will begin to understand the vast differences within the business sector— how banks operate so differently from high-tech firms, how publicly held companies differ from privately held ones.

Unlike foundations, which are formed to give money away, companies are formed to make a profit for their owners and shareholders. Their first job is profit. If you, as a nonprofit, can help the business be seen as a good corporate citizen, it may perceive that this is indirectly helping boost its profits. If so, the corporation will be more cooperative in helping you.

For example, when I was head of fundraising for the Phoenix Symphony, we had a great corporate sponsorship program in the community. We recruited a volunteer committee of public relations company executives. Their job was to understand what the symphony had to offer and to see how best to match that with client needs for corporate visibility. There were no promises, just a marketing opportunity if the right match came along. We did a few small projects and then we hit the big one. One of our PR volunteers called up to say that a major bank merger was in the works. It would take place in four months and the new bank name needed to be promoted in the community to build brand identity. The bank was looking at any and all creative ideas on how to do this. Did we have any projects coming up at that time period with a budget in the $50,000 to $75,000 range? In fact, we did. We put a presentation together for our volunteer who went to his client and sealed the deal. Ah, fundraising is fun when everyone wins.

We had visited Dr. Howard. He had formed several privately held corporations 30 years ago to develop products for his patients. He no longer practiced clinically except to perfect his products. He was passionate about their impact on patients. We hoped for a six- or seven-figure gift to jump-start our comprehensive campaign. In interviewing him we learned that he had a new product that he was bringing to market that required huge investments of capital. All of his thought, energy, and resources were going into this product. In talking to one of his senior managers, we learned that Dr. Howard had never taken on any debt, his companies were privately held, and that positive monthly cash flow was a high value to him. In conversations with Dr. Howard about a potential gift, he reaffirmed his monthly, positive-cash-flow philosophy and his commitment to eventually giving big gifts away to others and maybe us, but he said that the timing wasn't right. Anything we could do to partner with him to take in-kind gifts of the new product and help poor people would be just terrific. The organization was disappointed that no money was forthcoming. However, it was smart enough to start looking at several clinics where the in-kind donation of products could be used to help poor children without access to medical care. We approached a local community foundation to partner with us to support the pilot project. The end of the story? We'll see.

Remember that corporate philanthropy is enlightened self interest. Businesspeople want a stronger community that provides jobs for their customers so that people have the purchasing power to buy products and services. They also want to hire good employees and keep them healthy. As you discuss your organization's impact on any of these issues, figure out partnership opportunities between your nonprofit and the company to develop a winning-gifts strategy. This partnership may be in the form of a financial grant to your organization. Ideally, it can be much more. For example, in working for an art museum we approached a corporate donor. They said they would support the museum with a modest capital gift for the capital campaign. When we asked about their interests, we found the local manager had been on the school board for three years and the national company had a major emphasis on education. We talked about the possibility of endowing our arts-in-the-schools program for two inner-city elementary schools. All of a sudden, our $5,000 to $10,000 "okay" project went to a $50,000 discussion with high energy from the local manager. Meet their needs halfway as you seek funding for your projects.

Communications and Learning Styles Some people are readers and some are listeners. It is like being right handed or left handed; you are born with a learning style, a communications mode that works for you. People can try to improve their reading skills and their listening skills, but they have a natural tendency of knowledge acquisition to which you need to attend.

Do not expect people to read everything you mail to them or to listen to all of the speechifying at your cultivation events. Learning theory indicates that some people take in information aurally, some visually, and some in both forms. Use both communications forms (oral and written) for maximum effectiveness in your communications.

For example, at a donor dinner, as the president is telling the audience of donors about the mission of the university and the three key strategic issues that require investment during this capital campaign, have the president refer to the small three-inch by five-inch tent cards in front of each plate on which the university's name, mission statement, and a list of strategic initiatives are emblazoned. Some people will hear the message; others will read it. The card is a great take-home reminder for people, explaining why your organization exists.

While this information applies to every person, every type of donor, the corporate sector can comprise some of the toughest people to communicate with as they are busy and overwhelmed with communication opportunities. Once you master the concepts here, you can apply them in many other settings and with various types of donors.

Remember back in your school days when the teachers wanted quiet, stillness, and silence in order for learning to take place? Then think back to your most favorite classes—like chemistry lab, where you were able to set things on fire and mix chemicals to produce strange, new concoctions. Which was more memorable? Burning stuff up and watching beakers foam up or change colors, of course—*experiential learning.* Great schoolteachers are smart. They realize that concrete, real experiences in any subject are longer-lasting lessons than passive listening. Some great teachers tell memorable stories, while others assign challenging, if not impossible, homework assignments that burn concepts into your brain (like the high school journalism teacher who forced everyone to document 1,000 synonyms for "said").

To be people centered, remember to let your donors experience your organization, the challenges your constituents are trying to overcome, and how your organization makes a difference.

Fundraising is not about you or your organization's needs but about *providing donors with an opportunity to invest their money in the community to help people and society.* You want to be people centered so that donors can understand your organization's mission in the world, your vision for solving societal problems, and the role they can play in helping your plans come to fruition through a philanthropic investment. You're not so much telling and selling as allowing the donors to discover how your organization fits into their values, their aspirations for society, and the future.

How do you test to see if your communications are people centered? Ask people, of course. An example: At our university we were trying to get local business leaders to adopt our institution not only to help fundraising but more importantly to acquaint our faculty with industry needs for joint research collaborations and to place our graduates. In interviewing corporate CEOs on our board to probe for communication techniques, I asked them to review our standard six-page newsletter. Several of them chuckled and asked if we were kidding. I didn't get the joke. They said that they had so little time to read outside of their job duties that they would never get to my newsletter. After recovering from my hurt, I asked what recommendations they had. How could we fix it? They told me that every day they skimmed through their outside mail as fast as they could. The quick, short letters and information they read immediately and threw away or put in the outbox for action. The longer magazines, our newsletter, and other things they received went onto the to-be-read-later pile. After that pile got a couple of feet thick, they would spend five minutes and skim through the whole stack of materials with the aim of disposing of paper with lightning efficiency (you probably do this, too). They said we were always in the to-be-read-later pile, and, in spite of good intentions, they just did not have time. If we could get into their quick-read-and-toss pile, they would look at us.

We listened; we changed. We moved forward with an oversize, one-page, trifold, self-mailing newsletter on glossy stock with lots of pictures and captions, headlines, very brief articles on our faculty members' research, and highlights of past cultivation events on campus. We decided to mail on a bimonthly schedule rather than quarterly as the frequency kept us more visible and enabled us to shorten the articles. It was hard to write such brief stories and devote so much of the newsletter's space to pictures. But that's what it meant to be people centered, so we did it. By the way, they loved it. They appreciated the fact we had listened, and they really did read and toss versus putting us in the pile for later.

Another example: While waiting for a meeting with a venture capital investor who was one of our donors, I got to talking to his administrative assistant, Joan. I had been to the office many times and had gotten to know her over time. I happened to glance down at her desk and noticed one of our letters to her boss. She had highlighted several sentences on the page with a marking pen. That puzzled me. Our conversation went something like this:

Tom: Joan, if you don't mind my asking, why are you highlighting parts of that letter?

Joan: I always do that with all of John's correspondence. He is so busy that I pre-read the letters looking for the essential elements. If he just reads the highlighted sections, he'll know the key points and what action is being requested of him. If he's really interested, then he'll go back and read the whole letter. It saves him time.

Tom: Would it save you time if I did that to the letters I send here? That would help you, wouldn't it?

Joan: That's a great idea. Thanks.

We asked around and sure enough a lot of the high-level administrative assistants were doing the same pre-reading. It seemed strange at first to be taking a nice-looking letter and highlighting it by hand (now you can do it on your computer, thank goodness). Every time we went in for meetings, the secretaries would wink at us as we had saved them time. I don't think the bosses ever knew what was going on, but we had won over another customer—the gatekeeper to the donor.

INVOLVE VOLUNTEERS IN YOUR FUNDRAISING

To keep people centered, keep donors close to you. By forming an annual-fund, volunteer, fundraising committee, you have created an ongoing focus group of people who are just like the people you are trying to secure as donors. If your volunteers can get excited by raising operational money in the annual fund drive, then most likely so will your target audience of donors.

As you read this book, you will pick up many useful ideas; too many, perhaps. One of the ways to stretch the capacity of you, your staff, and your organization is to seek dedicated volunteers. I grew up in arts fundraising where fundraising budgets are tight and expectations high. The only way to survive was to use volunteers. As chief philanthropy officer, you have many jobs that will need to be done by your staff, your organization's staff, and your fundraising volunteers.

One caution though—make sure your volunteers model the characteristics of the target audience you are trying to reach. For example, if you want to secure the top 25 largest corporations in your community as donors, who on the volunteer committee you have formed leads, works with, or provides services for the largest 25 companies? Hopefully you have someone on your board and donor list who fits that description. Sometimes you won't have a company at that level yet. What about the top 50 companies? Do you have board members or volunteers who work with these top companies in some way, as a corporate attorney, accountant, banker, or so forth? Many times these volunteers understand their customers (the big companies) and can advise you on how to approach them. In seeking to answer the value-to-the-donor question, just ask your fundraising volunteers at your meetings.

In Part I, A Winning Gift for Your Donor, we discussed The Six I's of Philanthropic Fundraising, noting that not every volunteer will be comfortable with Step #6—asking for the investment (closing the gift). Some organizations make the mistaken assumption that all fundraising volunteers will be askers. If you understand that the most comfortable role for some volunteers in the fundraising process is everything *but* the ask, you can relax and be more understanding of your fundraising volunteers. In fact, a recent study on high-net-worth individuals found that peers were the second strongest influencers of giving (36%), second only to staff fundraisers (41%). Yes, you need a few volunteers to be your askers, but the volunteers' primary role is to help you with Step #1, Identify, Qualify, and Research—who should your organization be approaching for the $1,000 gift club or the $100,000 campaign gift society?; and with Step #2, Introduce, Interact, and Connect—what cultivation events can you offer potential donors so that you can start meeting with them and educating them about your organization?

Many potential volunteers, when asked about their willingness to fundraise, will say no. However, if you ask them if they can tell you whom to call on for a significant gift or to help to open the door for your organization, they are very willing to help. In *The Seven Faces of Philanthropy* (Chapter 2, Donor Values), authors Prince and File note that they found that about 11 percent of donors are socialites who love to help with Step #2.

They are the party and event people and Step #2 calls for social events to help connect potential donors with the organization (see Part II, Seek Winning Gifts for Your Organization, for the importance of "connectors" in the Law of the Few, *The Tipping Point*).

We cannot emphasize too highly, though, that you want to go through Step #1—Identify, Qualify, and Research—to identify your target audience and then select your volunteers from target audience members who are already affiliated with you. Sometimes this is easy; other times very difficult.

For example: In working with one alcohol and drug treatment center that wanted to build a new youth treatment center, we found only a very small number of donors. The center's operational funding came from governmental sources, so, except for a few foundation grants and a once-a-year direct mailing, the group did not do any fundraising. The board was small and not philanthropically savvy because, in the past, it had not needed to be. How to proceed was a puzzle. We always ask for a wide range of background materials when we work with new clients as you never know what you will need to know in the future. Digging through this information we found a list of board members that dated from the organization's launch 30 years earlier. One name leaped out—Albert. He was a major contributor in town and had a small family foundation. We had worked together on other projects, so after asking permission from the treatment center we interviewed Albert. He admitted he was a recovered alcoholic and that to pay back the treatment center for saving his life he had joined the board, served his terms, and drifted away. Would he come back to help the treatment center build the new youth center? Sure, he would help in any way he could. We asked that he recruit five people like himself to form the core of the campaign committee. Would he also agree to accept the first Freedom Award from the organization at a breakfast cultivation event to help make the treatment center visible in the donor community? He was brave and agreed to tell his sobriety story in accepting the award. He knew many friends who had gone through treatment and who would respond to an invitation to the event. This was the start of what would eventually be a successful campaign many years later. Did Albert raise money? Sure, indirectly. Was that his first and most important job? No.

Another important reason to involve volunteers is to deepen a potential major donor's relationship with an organization. Tanise L. Chung-Hoon's doctoral dissertation looked at higher education's donor relations and the role of organizational integration in creating long-term donor support for the nonprofit. While focusing on higher education because of her staff work at Brigham Young University and Utah Valley University, Chung-Hoon's research and an article co-authored by Julie Hite and Steven Hite applies to all nonprofit organizations. The authors noted that meaningful interactions lead to long-term relationships and donor investments.

> Enduring donor relationships are evidenced by high levels of personal relationships, economic interactions, social capital, and personal commitment; by significant personal integration into the formal structure and activities of the institution; and by high levels of trust. . . . Institutions must make strategic organizational efforts that go beyond transactional give-and-take exchanges. . . .[9]

Staff-Driven Fundraising?

Some professional fundraisers express frustration with volunteers in fundraising. Yes, it takes time to get someone up to speed on the project, have them help you review prospective donors names, find out how best to use them for cultivation events, and find out the hard way how good they are at asking for money. But, if you realize their first job is to keep you people centered and to remind you of donor values at all times, then the volunteers' role comes into context.

For universities with far-flung alumni, using volunteers is difficult. But seeking a fundraising volunteer in each major city where you have alumni to serve on a regional or national fundraising council will pay dividends in the future. Always remember Six I's Step #5 Involve, Acknowledge, and Engage. If you want to speed up the fundraising process, look for highly qualified donors in Step #1 and recruit them to your board and/or volunteer fundraising team (Step #5). As they become involved as volunteers you end up going backward in the Six I's to fill in the missing gaps in their knowledge and commitment to your organization. Through fundraising task force meetings you cultivate them for a bigger gift. Self-discovery is a critical part of the process.

Make no mistake: Volunteer-led fundraising will make you more successful only when it is staff driven. It takes a quick-working, smart, and dedicated staff member to keep up with highly successful, brilliant volunteers. When both teammates are working in tandem, your fundraising will be highly successful; the presence of volunteers will keep you people centered.

How to Help Your Organization Become People Centered

What do you as a professional fundraiser and/or sensitive fundraising volunteer do when you are people centered but your organization is not? The organization is not intentionally being selfish or malicious; it is focused on its own needs and simply wants money from donors. How can you start to effect a culture shift? How do you get your institution to see the light? How do you build a *culture of philanthropy?*

The first step, of course, is to have everyone in the organization read this book (*smile*). But what's next? First, appreciate the fact that you may have been personally involved with fundraising for 5 years, 10 years, or, like me, a very long time. You didn't learn everything in the first week. It took time. Your job is to help the organization begin to develop a winning-gifts approach to donors—a people centered approach to fundraising. The organizational leadership—the faculty, the staff, the physicians—may not understand right away why they need to be people centered; they just need to appreciate that you can raise more money short and longterm by taking this approach.

First step—be grounded yourself in the principles of people centered fundraising. You need to promote it every time fundraising comes up at board meetings, at senior administrative councils, at volunteer fundraising meetings.

Second step—we'll deal extensively with the case statement in Chapter 4, Make Your Case, but a very important step in transforming your organization to a people-centered institution is to take the case statement and make it community-benefit oriented. Take the needs of the organization and translate them into future benefits for the community.

Here are a few examples. The university wants to have more endowment funds because great universities are measured on their endowment per student and endowment per faculty member. It's basically an endowment arms race to catch up to Harvard University's $26 billion endowment. But that's institution centered. How do we take this institutional need and make it people centered? There can be several storylines—great institutions have endowed professorships as this helps to retain the best, most senior, star professors so they are not stolen away by other universities. Within the academic community, being named to an endowed chair is a prestigious honor that goes on resumes that get shared with spouses, family members, and colleagues across the country.

Tom Sanders, Ph.D., has been a star faculty member for 20 years. He does groundbreaking original research that benefits our local high-tech companies and his students love him—both his graduate research students and the freshmen who sign up for his standing-room-only lectures. We're worried that Dr. Sanders could be lured away from our campus by one of our less-than-friendly competitors. We want to honor his achievements and ensure his presence on campus until it comes time for his retirement. A $2.5 million endowed chair, in your name, would provide $125,000 of income a year for Dr. Sanders, his department, and our university. Dr. Sanders would get a significant portion of these funds each year to work on new ideas that are not yet fundable by the National Science Foundation and to support undergraduate and graduate research students in his lab. He'll also use these funds to help his students go to national conferences to present their team's research as well as to buy equipment and supplies for his lab.

The city's symphony orchestra is seeking funds for a capital campaign to provide bridge funding to balance its operating budget, record a CD of performances, and increase the size of the orchestra from 85 to 90 full-time musicians. That is what it wants and needs. How do we convert this to people centered fundraising? If we want our community to be seen as a viable metropolitan area that companies and their employees will want to come to, stay and grow in, we need a vital, active arts community. Otherwise, everyone will move to New York City, Boston, and San Francisco, where great symphony orchestras and other prominent cultural organizations thrive. The symphony is instrumental (so to speak) to our city's economic vitality. Did you ever play an instrument in high school or college? If so, you know what it means to have quality musicians in our city that we audition and recruit from around the world. Yes, they perform in the orchestra at evening concerts, but these same musicians teach private lessons to school children, perform in small ensembles, and enrich the cultural life of our community.

A public radio station needs a new building for its staff because the old building is 40 years old and terribly overcrowded. Consider a gift to our state-of-the-art digital broadcast center where we will expand our on-air offerings to include more international webcasts, move toward providing podcasts of our jazz programming, and protect our collection of 10,000 jazz records (one of the top three collections in the world; we must provide temperature and humidity control to protect this priceless archive). As you know, we ask for volunteers to help us in many ways. But, our current space is so overcrowded with staff that we can use only five volunteers at a time. We have people clamoring to help us. We can meet their needs only through this new broadcast center.

A hospital needs better communications systems for the staff, a new parking garage, and improved nurses stations. But, what is the hospital doing for the community? Well, we do hire certain specialists right out of their residencies to bring them to our community where they would not otherwise come. We let them work three-quarter-time so they can study for their national boards so they can be fully certified in their specialties. We help advise them on office management systems so they can learn how to start their practices. And for some specialties, we find them physician business managers to run their offices so they can be profitable and stay in our community. This result came after the fundraiser and consultant asked for more community benefit projects and didn't agree that the internal needs of the hospital were fundable by the community.

Apply What You Have Learned

In each chapter, we will give you three exercises to help strengthen your winning-gift muscles. Try each one as described or create your own variation. Keep a journal of what you learn from each of these exercises. Let me know how you do by e-mailing me at Tom.Wilson@WinningGifts .INFO.

1. *Volunteers to keep you people centered.* Go through each of your fundraising programs (major gifts, foundations, corporations, special events, planned estate gifts, direct mail, etc.) to see how many volunteers you have actively engaged in each program. How often do you meet with them? Have you empowered them to give you honest feedback on your plans? Are they really role models for the type of

donor you want to attract in each program? What could you do to improve your current situation?

2. *People centered audit of your fundraising materials.* Start this fundraising review with your staff. You may want to end it there, but this is a great 30-minute exercise for a volunteer fundraising committee meeting. Pull out all donor communications from the last year to see good examples of people centered communications (versus institution communications). Look through newsletters, annual reports, direct mail, and anything else sent out to donors in the past year. How often do these materials stress community benefit and impact? How many donor stories are there compared with institutional stories (e.g., "Faculty member gets research grant from NSF and we're proud of her" as opposed to "Joe and Mary made a bequest commitment to us because they were so excited about . . . ").

What did you learn from this exercise? How can you be more people centered in the next year? How can you monitor the process in the future?

3. *Your strategic plan.* Find your strategic plan. How recent is it? How does it share the vision of your organization? What visionary goals does it articulate that require the raising of funds? Does the plan need updating? How are you sharing the plan with your board members? With donors?

NOTES

1. Spencer Johnson and Larry Wilson, *The One Minute Sales Person* (New York: William Morrow, HarperCollins Publishers, 1984), 21.
2. Dr. Thomas J. Stanley, *Selling to the Affluent* (New York: McGraw-Hill, 1991), 20, 409.
3. Charles D. Schewe and Alexander Hiam, *The Portable MBA in Marketing,* 2nd edition (New York: John Wiley & Sons, Inc., 1998), 3.
4. Philip Kotler and Gary Armstrong, *Principles of Marketing*, 10th Edition (Upper Saddle River, NJ: Pearson Prentice Hall, 2004, 2001, 1999, 1996), 526.
5. Elliott Masie, "Interview with Ken Blanchard," October 2006, *Learning University 2006,* www.learning2006.com.
6. Peter F. Drucker, *The Drucker Foundation Self-Assessment Tool Participant Workbook,* Revised Edition (San Francisco: Jossey-Bass, 1999), 34.
7. Alexander Hiam, *Marketing for Dummies*, 2nd Edition (Hoboken: John Wiley & Sons, 2004), 14–17.

8. Matt Oechsli, *The Art of Selling to the Affluent* (Hoboken: John Wiley & Sons, 2005), 10, 29, 40, 93.

9. Tanise L. Chung-Hoon, Julie M. Hite, and Steven J. Hite, "Searching for Enduring Donor Relationships: Evidence for Factors and Strategies in a Donor/ Organization Integration Model for Fund Raising," *International Journal of Educational Advancement,* vol. 6, no. 1, 36.

CHAPTER 2

Donor Values

The question, "What do customers value?" "What satisfies their needs, wants, and aspirations?"—is so complicated that it can only be answered by customers themselves. And the first rule is that there are no irrational customers. Almost without exception, customers behave rationally in terms of their own realities and their own situation.

—PETER F. DRUCKER, SELF-ASSESSMENT TOOL[1]

In a winning-gifts fundraising model, the donor will be as delighted in making the gift as the institution is in accepting the money. To use a marketing approach to philanthropic fundraising, you need to understand the general interests and needs of all donors. This chapter on donor values and motivations is critically important.

In this chapter we will cover:

1. Sources of giving—where can you go to get funding for your organization?

2. Corporate motivations for giving,

3. Foundation values.

4. Knowing that individuals give 80 percent of the money, what stimulates their charitable giving?

Many of the sources noted here are familiar and are reviewed to help refresh your memory and to stimulate you, the reader, to go to these sources for additional information. This is not an exhaustive overall list of all resources of donor motivations and values (which would be its own book). Rather this chapter should help sensitize you to various donor motivations so you will begin hearing the "noises" of donor values in many of the conversations that you have when you are out raising money for your organization.

To create a winning-gifts attitude it is critical to review the history of giving in the United States through a few of the critical early voices for philanthropic contributions.

Common fundraising lore has it that Benjamin Franklin started the first capital campaign for a hospital in Boston. The recently ended eight-year Revolutionary War had depleted government resources and Franklin told his fellow citizens that if they raised a certain amount of money he would match it and then there would be enough funds to build the new hospital. He issued the first successful challenge grant in U.S. history (even if apocryphal, it's a great story).

Challenge grants remain to this day a wonderful winning-gifts strategy. Donors issuing the challenge feel good because they are doubling their money by stimulating others to give. The matching donors feel good because they are helping secure the challenge gift from a wealthy donor and doubling their gift as they do so. Nobody wants to leave the challenge money on the table so the campaign and the organization are big winners. It also provides fundraising volunteers with a wonderful excuse to ask for gifts—the challenge is making me do it. Challenge gift tactics will be discussed in Chapter 5, The Win-Win Ask.

Alexis de Tocqueville's *Democracy in America,*[2] which was published in two volumes (1835 and 1840), commented upon Americans' unique way of forming groups to help each other. De Tocqueville was born in 1805 to an aristocratic family that survived the French revolution. He and a fellow magistrate came to America in 1831 to study the judicial and prison systems. They toured for nine months before returning to France. De Tocqueville shared his insights on democracy and the differences between the aristocracy of Europe and the egalitarian nature of the United States.

> Americans of all ages, all conditions, and all dispositions, constantly form associations . . . religious, moral, serious, futile, general or restricted, enormous or diminutive. The Americans make associations to give

entertainments, to found seminaries, to build inns, to construct churches, to diffuse books, to send missionaries to the Antipodes; they found in this manner hospitals, prisons, or schools. . . . I met with several kinds of associations in America of which I confess I had no previous notion; and I have often admired the extreme skill with which the inhabitants of the United States succeed in proposing a common object to the exertions of a great many men, and in inducing them voluntarily to pursue it.[3]

De Tocqueville reflected on why the dictatorial aristocracy of Europe behaved differently from the democratic people of the United States:

Aristocratic communities always contain, amongst a multitude of persons who by themselves are powerless, a small number of powerful and wealthy citizens, each of whom can achieve great undertaking single-handed. . . . Among democratic nations, on the contrary, all the citizens are independent and feeble; they can do hardly anything by themselves, and none of them can oblige his fellow-men to lend him their assistance. They all, therefore, become powerless, if they do not learn voluntarily to help each other. . . . A people amongst whom individuals should lose the power of achieving great things single-handed, without acquiring the means of producing them by united exertions, would soon relapse into barbarism.[4]

Feelings and opinions are recruited, the heart is enlarged, and the human mind is developed, only by the reciprocal influence of men upon each other. . . . Nothing, in my opinion, is more deserving of our attention than the intellectual and moral associations of America.[5]

In 1984, the national United Way office recommended to local chapters that they establish a common major gifts club to thank their $10,000 yearly donors—"The Tocqueville Society."

Now, more than 170 years after de Tocqueville shared his insights, many other countries in the world are looking at U.S. philanthropic traditions. They are trying to emulate the successes of the United States and build their own philanthropic associations. Canada now has many local and regional chapters of the Association of Fundraising Professionals (AFP). Professional fundraising-consulting firms have active practices in both Canada and England. In 2006, the *Wall Street Journal (WSJ)* noted that Hong Kong, Singapore, and France have all established government matching funds and tax incentives to encourage philanthropy. The *WSJ* noted:

By most measures, Americans remain the most charitable people worldwide. In 2005, giving in the U.S. averaged 1.75% of gross domestic
product . . . compared to 0.75% in Great Britain, and 0.25% in
Germany, France, and Singapore.[6]

In the early 1990s, I was asked to help host a Japanese trade delegation that
was visiting our Pacific Northwest city. We spent the day with American and
Japanese business leaders touring major corporate and civic sites. Most of
sites the Japanese spoke excellent English. That gave us the chance to get to
know each other well during the day. I responded to many questions about
American culture and values. One executive, when finding out I raised
money for charitable causes (my university at that time), asked why
American companies were expected to give money voluntarily to such
causes. Why wasn't the government taking care of these issues? Several hours
later he came up to me and attempted to answer his own question. He
decided that the people who live in America left their home countries at one
time or another over the past 200 years. They fled from their native
governments to find a better life in the United States. Americans don't trust
the government. This distrust of formal authority means Americans depend
on each other for help, for assistance in times of trouble, and to improve their
local community. He said that in Japan, on the other hand, the government
had helped create industry and was trusted to take care of social needs.
Therefore in Japan there didn't need to be a culture of philanthropy for
companies or individuals. The role of Japanese companies was to create and
maintain jobs while the government took care of educational and social
needs. He and his colleagues did understand that when their companies did
business in the United States, they needed to be philanthropic to play the
game. But because they really didn't understand the culture of philanthropy
they needed guidance from U.S. companies and from their American
employees on how to be good corporate citizens. They sought out clues and
cues on how to play the American philanthropy game.

GIVING U.S.A.—SOURCES AND TRENDS IN GIVING

The Giving U.S.A. Foundation gathers yearly research data on philanthropy
in the United States. The research for *Giving U.S.A.* is gathered and analyzed
by The Center on Philanthropy at Indiana University. Its 2006 report

2006 Sources of Giving
Giving U.S.A

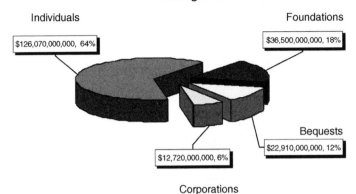

Individuals
$126,070,000,000, 64%

Foundations
$36,500,000,000, 18%

Bequests
$22,910,000,000, 12%

$12,720,000,000, 6%

Corporations

Sources of Giving not including giving to religion
by individuals of $96.8 billion

EXHIBIT 2.1	GIVING U.S.A. 2006 SOURCES OF GIVING WITHOUT RELIGION

shows $295 billion donated with 75.6 percent coming from individuals, 7.8 percent by bequest, 12.4 percent from foundations, and 4.3 percent from corporations. Of the $223 billion donated by individuals, nearly 43% ($97 billion) was given to religious causes.[7]

Exhibit 2.1 shows the relative amounts of philanthropic support in the United States when religious giving is taken out. Please note that religious organizations delivering social services (e.g., Catholic Charities) are not counted as religious organizations but rather in the sector where their work is delivered.

Even with religious giving removed, individuals account for the vast majority of philanthropy in the United States. It is amazing to think corporations only give 6 percent of the total. Of course, it is a very noisy 6 percent, while individuals tend to be quiet, and many anonymous, in their giving. Corporate giving is enhanced by marketing sponsorships to charities that are not counted in *Giving U.S.A.* as they are not technically gifts. Your organization may have a stronger corporate giving mix than the statistics indicated here. You should feel proud of this. But, this strength may also suggest you have far greater capacity for individual giving and that your fundraising program could use a re-engineering to diversify your sources of giving.

As you form fundraising teams of volunteers and staff with the goal of raising funds for your organization, review Exhibit 2.1 so everyone understands where the money comes from. It is often easy for volunteers to envision asking foundations for money as they are built to give money away. The group they are next most comfortable asking is corporations. They are visible and seem to have a lot of money to give away. A difficult concept for many volunteers is asking individuals for money, especially their friends. It is important that they understand the *Giving U.S.A.* statistics that individuals are the most likely source of money. And, if you can train them to stop thinking win/lose (the organization gets the money and their friends lose their money) and start thinking using a winning-gifts strategy, then individuals seem easier to approach.

An excellent example of the importance of individual giving comes from one of our clients who was raising $5 million for a new headquarters building. The client approached a major corporation, and received a warm welcome and a check for $75,000 toward the campaign. The organization could apply again the next year, but the company does not make multiyear pledges (most individuals will make multiyear pledges, increasing the return on your investment of time in closing the gift). At the same time, the organization was talking about the project to one of the company's officers who was a longtime donor to the organization. This donor and his wife committed $500,000 and hosted a large, catered dinner cultivation event in their home to recommend the campaign to their friends.

INDIVIDUALS

Giving U.S.A. research finds that individuals are responsible for the vast majority of philanthropic giving in the United States—more than 80 percent when you include bequests. While all of the principles of winning gifts can be applied in various ways to corporate and foundation donors, we will continuously focus strategies and tactics on individual donors.

Always remember that people, no matter how wealthy, like to be treated as people first, not just bank accounts, not just a source of funding for your organization. The relationship with the person should always come first— keep people centered in your fundraising.

The following sections provide depth of information concerning a variety of individual donor issues. We will look at the impact of the aging of America on philanthropy (especially planned estate gifts); then at Andrew Carnegie's *Gospel of Wealth* and its impact on recent philanthropic giving by individuals including Bill Gates, Warren Buffett, and Sandy Weill; and then we will conclude the chapter with a quick review of some in-depth research on donor values as published in *The Seven Faces of Philanthropy* and *The Millionaire Next Door.*

Sheehy's *New Passages*

Throughout this chapter are suggestions of books for further reading to help enlarge your understanding of donor motivations and values. One book I highly recommend is Gail Sheehy's *New Passages.*[8] Sheehy wrote the original *Passages* about 30 years ago. She described the generation gap and the various age ranges of generations that she found in the United States in the 1970s. She articulated Americans' acceptance of middle age at 40 and old age at 65 (whose roots date back to the establishment of Social Security's retirement threshold for full benefits—by the way, most people were dead by age 65 when Social Security was created in the 1930s).

Sheehy's publisher requested that she write *New Passages* to explore changes in American attitudes toward aging in the quarter century since her thought-provoking *Passages* was published. The highlight of *New Passages* was Sheehy's discovery that the stages of adulthood had shifted forward by up to 10 years. Because Americans are living so much longer and with more energy and health, middle age is perceived to be starting at age 50 instead of 40. This new definition of middle age is reinforced by the fact that more women are holding off on having children until they are older. The number of women having children in their mid-to-late 30s and early 40s may keep pushing this middle-age concept to 55.

Old age is now widely perceived as starting at 75. And, adolescence has been extended from 18 to 28—Sheehy references the many college graduates who come back home to live with their parents as they start their careers.

For fundraising, we used to say the golden age of philanthropy for donors was age 50, when they became empty nesters. All of the children are through college, careers are well established, and discretionary money is now available for philanthropy. In the quarter-century of this author's career (the same time scale as *Passages* to *New Passages*), this assumption has been turned on its head. Affluent professionals are having children later in life, with increasing burdens of college tuition and the perception that the best gift you can give your children is a great education (usually, a private, expensive education with costs going beyond the graduate years into doctoral programs, law degrees, medical degrees, and MBAs). In fact, a survey recently noted that the highest-spending age range in the country today is age 40 to 54. At first this didn't seem to make sense until you factor college costs in.

People in this age range of 40 to 54 are also known as the "sandwich" generation. They are taking care of children, paying for college tuition, and also taking care of aging parents. While these aging parents frequently have the resources to stay in their homes or assisted-living centers, there are emotional and time burdens in caring for parents that keep the sandwich generation from becoming as active on nonprofit boards and organizations as they used to be in the past.

This means many donors may not be entering their philanthropic years until age 60, maybe even later. (In fact, a 2007 Bank of America study conducted by the Center of Philanthropy found that the prime giving age starting at age 61.) These realities have powerful ramifications for the composition of nonprofit boards, timing of cultivation events, and when to consider people candidates for planned estate gifts.

I'm a great example. My wife, Sue, and I have been married 34 years and have four children. Our youngest daughter, KT, starts college in the fall of 2007 at a private university in New York City. By the time she graduates, I will be 60 years old. (As we edited this book, our story changed; KT, who is a wonderful dancer, got accepted to be a Radio City Rockette, so college will start even later now.) Only then can we start saving hard for retirement. And, while both of my parents have passed away, both of Sue's parents are still living and may need care.

> Sure we've been sponsors of the art museum's exhibits for many years and we have a small family foundation. But we can't make capital gifts right now. I'm 62 and we have three daughters all in graduate school—one getting a Ph.D. in Texas, another getting her dental degree at Tufts, and the other in medical school. I'm proud of them, but we're paying out over a $100,000 a year in tuition right now. When they're all finished, maybe we can be real philanthropists.

—MARKET RESEARCH STUDY INTERVIEWEE

I hear many clients asking for new, young blood for their boards. Getting new blood and new energy is always a great idea. After considering the societal factors listed above, you may want to engage "old" new blood for your board. You may want to seek out people who are in their late 50s and early 60s who have the energy, wisdom, and time to make a difference to your organization. Many hard-charging corporate executives do not have the time to devote to nonprofit boards during their corporate careers like their predecessors did, but you may have a wonderful opportunity to capture their attention the year right before or after retirement. Most want to decompress for a year after retirement to travel, play golf, and generally goof around. Many are worried about what they will do in retirement. And many discover that with their batteries recharged they are looking for ways to find meaning in their lives. How many rounds of golf a week can a person play? And, with their decades of work experience and wisdom, they find they can really make a difference by connecting with a nonprofit organization.

Cultivation events with teenagers at home can be a scheduling challenge. Yet, when the nest is empty (when couples are in their mid-50s to early 60s) they do experience a void that can be filled with community-building cultivation events for your nonprofit.

In Chapter 3, Listen, we'll review techniques to improve your listening skills. One of the things to listen for is this need for meaningful engagement during retirement (or after the children permanently leave the nest).

Implications of Americans Living Longer on Estate-Gift Fundraising

The demographic shift of people living longer is a fact. A male, nonsmoker, age 65, can be expected to live to his mid-80s, a female, nonsmoker, age 65, may live close to age 90. We should no longer automatically accept the assumption that people will leave their entire estates to their children. As we interview donors for philanthropic market research studies (feasibility studies), we ask them about their planned, estate-gift intentions. Since people are living longer, their children are now mature and are less in need of inherited wealth. Many people tell us that their children are making more money in their careers than the parents ever did so the motivation to help a child is reduced. Clear exceptions exist for special-needs children who will need protective trusts to care for them throughout their lives.

With children more established in their own careers and many not needing an inheritance, new family needs have surfaced. One of these is providing funds for high-quality education for grandchildren. With private-school tuition, books, and room and board approaching $50,000 a year, many parents can use the assistance of grandparents in helping college students graduate debt free. With housing costs going up, grandparents are also increasingly willing to help with a house down payment. After that, the need to pass down immense wealth to future generations weakens.

One donor told this story to me:

> I set up trust funds for each of my grandchildren, $1 million each. They could have access to the trust when they turned age 18. I assumed by then they would have the sense to use the money well. I certainly would have at that age [for him, that would have been in 1938 or so]. I assumed they would use it for college. Some did, but one granddaughter got access to this money and six months later it was all gone, blown. It almost destroyed her. I tell all of my rich friends this story. Don't leave a lot of money to your grandkids. You could destroy them.

I overhead the following conversation while waiting for a volunteer to finish a golf game in Sun City West, Arizona. Both he and his golf partner were in their mid-80s and were putting on the eighteenth hole. I was sitting on a bench not too far away, so I could hear the following:

> "How's your son doing?"
>
> "Oh, that ne'er-do-well. He's just a knucklehead. He can't figure out his life and is out of a job again. He's never going to amount to anything. It's so frustrating for my wife and me to watch."
>
> "How old is he?"
>
> "Oh, about 63."

I asked my friend about his reactions to his golf partner's family woes. He told me that with everyone living so much longer he heard this type of story a lot. It was making it hard to figure out where your money should go when you die. Either your kids have done really well so they don't need it, or, like his friend's son, they have never amounted to anything and so why give them a bunch of money to waste when you are gone? You made it the hard way and so should they. Of course, you should leave them *something* (you don't want them hating you forever), but giving them millions or tens of millions of dollars just does not make sense.

Another donor dilemma is created by the federal government. One would think that with the federal deficit, the government could use some extra money. One newspaper article a few years ago noted that a man had passed away and left the federal government as the sole beneficiary of his estate. He had been an immigrant and had done well in the United States and wanted to show his appreciation to his adopted country. The newspaper wryly noted that it took the U.S. government approximately two seconds to spend the $8 million this gentleman left to it. Nobody could ever track down what difference this gift made.

Andrew Carnegie—*The Gospel of Wealth*

The industrial revolution in America in the late nineteenth century allowed a select group of people to build fortunes of immense wealth. A real milestone in American philanthropic thinking came from Andrew Carnegie in 1889, with the publication of his *Gospel of Wealth*.[9]

Carnegie stated the following concepts:

Rich men can dignify their lives by organizing benefactions.

The rich are but trustees of the poor entrusted for a season with the wealth of the community administering it for the community.

Help those who will help themselves—provide part of the means to those who desire to improve to do so.

To assist, but rarely or never to do all.

The man who dies rich dies disgraced.

Carnegie tried to make the distinction between the everyday wealth of workers and professionals and the spectacular fortunes of a few individuals like himself. He felt that the rich had three options for their money: (1) leave it to their heirs (remember, this was in the days before estate taxes); (2) leave it to public purposes upon their death; or (3) give it away to charity during their lifetime.

Andrew Carnegie came to the United States from Scotland before the Civil War and started working as an uneducated bobbin boy at a cotton factory. He believed that education, particularly self-education, was the way that workers could improve their lives and the lives of their children. Consistent with his philosophy to help but not to do all, he challenged communities small and large throughout the United States to join with him in creating public libraries. He offered the capital to construct the library building if the local community agreed to raise the operating costs through taxes. More than 2,500 libraries were funded and Carnegie's legacy of public support of libraries continues to this day. In 1911, Carnegie created the Carnegie Corporation as the foundation to hold his assets after his death. He donated $135 million (which would be $2.8 billion in 2006 dollars).[10]

He felt strongly about *not* leaving vast sums of money to children and family members.

> Why should men leave great fortunes to their children? If this is done from affection, is it not misguided affection? Observation teaches that, generally speaking, it is not well for children that they should be so burdened. . . . Great sums bequeathed oftener work more for the injury than for the good of the recipients. Wise men will soon conclude that, for the best interests of the members of their families . . . such bequests are an improper use of their means. . . . The thoughtful man must shortly say, "I would as soon leave to my son a curse as the almighty dollar," and admit to himself that it is not the welfare of the children, but family pride, which inspires these enormous legacies.

He was not sure who would be as competent in the future after the person died to make these decisions to help humankind. Today, he would likely be in favor of the estate tax because it motivates people to give vast sums of money away during their life. He felt that the same competence and expertise that a person used to build a fortune should be directed at giving this money away to benefit society (we see this philosophy being implemented today through the Bill & Melinda Gates Foundation).

As you can see from this newspaper article, Carnegie's philosophy is alive and well in America today. Jules Knapp, speaking about his $25,000,000 gift to University of Chicago Hospitals, in the *Wall Street Journal*, February. 11, 2006, said:

> Research is very important to us. We tried to find a cure for my daughter. The philosophy I have is that when I die, I die broke.[11]

Bill Gates As Microsoft founder Bill Gates began to consider what to do with his vast fortune, his good friend and bridge partner Warren Buffett gave him a copy of Carnegie's *The Gospel of Wealth* to read. Inspired, one of the Gates Foundation's first rounds of significant funding was directed at providing 11,000 libraries with free computers and technology. Today 99 percent of libraries are connected to the Internet.

Bill and Melinda Gates crafted the following mission statement for their Seattle, Washington–based foundation: "Guided by the belief that every life has equal value, the Bill & Melinda Gates Foundation works to reduce inequities and improve lives around the world."

Writing on their foundation's web site, the Gateses explain: "We also believe that from those to whom much is given, much is expected. We benefited from great schools, great health care, and a vibrant economic system. That is why we feel a tremendous responsibility to give back to society."

As of this writing in 2007, the Gates Foundation states assets of $32 billion with grants totaling $10 billion to all 50 states and more than 100 countries since its founding in 2000.

In an article appearing in the *New York Times,* journalist Daniel Gross compares Gates's approach to philanthropy with that of Carnegie:

> Mr. Gates is approaching philanthropy in a fundamentally different way—call it Philanthropy 2.0. Just as Carnegie and Rockefeller were influenced by the vertically integrated, industrial economy they helped to create, Mr. Gates's philanthropic efforts are defined and effected by the less hierarchical, networked economy that he helped to create. With its small staff, strategy of creating partnerships and focus on research and development, the Bill and Melinda Gates Foundation more closely resembles a 21st-century software company than a 20th-century philanthropy.[12] [Copyright 2006 by *The New York Times Co.* Reprinted with permission.]

Much more information can be found at the foundation's web site: www.gatesfoundation.org.

Warren Buffett   In the summer of 2006, one of the richest men in the United States, Warren Buffett, age 75, stirred the philanthropic community by announcing the donation of his entire fortune, estimated at $37 billion, to charity—and specifically by giving the vast majority of it (80 percent) to the Gates Foundation. Mr. Buffett noted his belief in Andrew Carnegie's philosophy of giving back to society. And, while he wants to help his children, he notes:

> Our kids are great. But, I would argue that when your kids have all the advantages anyway . . . it's neither right nor rational to be flooding them

with money. . . . *a very rich person should leave his kids enough to do anything but not enough to do nothing.*[13]

Sandy Weill   Sanford I. (Sandy) Weill recently retired as chairman of CitiCorp. He and his wife have given generously over their lives (some $600 million over the last 15 years). Mr. Weill created the Sanford I. Weill Charitable Foundation in 1967 with assets of $47,746. Mrs. Weill's volunteer involvement includes Howard Smith's College and the Alvin Ailey Dance Theater, where her $20 million donation was recognized by the dance company's naming its new building in Manhattan The Joan Weill Center for Dance (2005). Mr. Weill is a long-time board member of Carnegie Hall. In 2003, he announced his own 70th birthday present—a challenge to other donors to contribute to Carnegie Hall. He would match their gifts from March to December of that year. By the end of the challenge he had donated nearly $30 million to endow the education programs at Carnegie Hall.

The Chronicle of Philanthropy recently quoted a few highlights of Sanford Weill's new book, *The Real Deal: My Life in Business and Philanthropy.* Sandy Weill's advice to aspiring philanthropists:

> First, it's important to make long-term commitments and accordingly select causes where one's passion will last. Second, one should look for organizations that can benefit from one's business expertise or relationships. Business executives typically excel at setting a vision and getting others to follow; therefore, institutions that are open to change in direction may be particularly fertile ground for involvement. Third, the person that runs the organization should be one that inspires confidence and who is open to strong cooperative partnerships with active board members. Finally, I believe it's essential to concentrate one's efforts on a manageable set of activities in order to maximize impact.[14] [Reprinted with permission of *The Chronicle of Philanthropy,* http://philanthropy.com.]

Mr. Weill was quoted in a recent article in the *Wall Street Journal:*

> . . . you can't take it with you. It's a lot better to do a lot of this philanthropy while you're still alive and you have the energy. We can use our brainpower to make the world a better place now . . . Being the biggest foundation doesn't interest us at all.[15]

The Seven Faces of Philanthropy

An important book on the values and motivations of donors is *The Seven Faces of Philanthropy*, by Russ Alan Prince and Karen Maru File.[16] Using social-science research techniques (File is an associate professor of marketing in the Graduate School of Business at the University of Connecticut), the authors conducted a three-phase research project that involved 476 donors in a quantitative study, 12 in-depth interviews with donors, an expanded questionnaire to 123 donors, and sampling the attitudes of 128 affluent donors. An affluent donor was defined as a person who maintained $1 million or more in a discretionary investment advisory account and who contributed $50,000 or more to a single nonprofit in the last two years. The rigor of their research is indeed commendable.

Prince and File found seven clusters of donor motivations for giving (see Exhibit 2.2). Some of the *Seven Faces* are intuitive while are others are surprising (as is the percentage of people in each category).

As you think through your own motivations for giving, and those of your friends and your donors, you can see patterns of donor motivation that match the list below. Of course, people are complex and they may have multiple motives in their philanthropy. And, couples and partners will combine and/or negotiate their motivations, making detecting gift strategies complicated.

Insights on the Faces   Most of my university faculty assumed that donors made gifts because they were *altruistic*, giving out of the kindness of their hearts. While you will find many kind-hearted people in the world, unfortunately, only 9 percent were found to operate from altruistic impulses

EXHIBIT 2.2   **THE SEVEN FACES OF PHILANTHROPY[17]**

• Altruists	Generosity and empathy	9%
• Communitarians	To improve the community	26%
• Repayers	Paying back a charity	10%
• Socialites	Social functions to have a good time	11%
• Dynasts	Family tradition of charitable giving	8%
• Devout	For religious issues	21%
• Investors	One eye on the cause, the other on tax benefits	15%

in the Prince and File study. As you talk to donors, those who give "just because" fit this category.

Through the 2,700 interviews I have conducted over the past 18 years of consulting, I have found that most people's philanthropy stems from *communitarian motives*. These donors feel blessed by their luck and good fortune in life. They express a willingness to help the community that supported their businesses and created their wealth. They want to give back. Many of these donors realize that strengthening their community helps improve society for everyone. At 26 percent, this is the largest group of donors.

Repayers are a surprisingly low 10 percent of donors. Reciprocation appears not to be a major factor in philanthropy, although I did experience one clear exception by an Episcopal priest:

> I got a scholarship from Yale to go to seminary. Even though I'm a minister who doesn't make much money I have been donating a couple of hundred dollars a year to the Yale seminary scholarship fund now for fifteen years. I intend to keep giving back for the rest of my life.

The low level of repayers may indicate that too many organizations are not seeking out people they have helped in the past to play the "pass it on" game.

The *socialites,* 11 percent of donors, brought a smile. They love special events and having a good time. Board members who are socialites will always lobby for having a ball, a dinner dance, a golf tournament—it is the social thing to do.

Dynasts, donors who give because there is a family tradition of giving (8 percent), were prevalent in Chicago, where my fundraising career started. Prominent families on the North Shore were expected to serve on nonprofit boards and to give generously.

When I moved to the West Coast a different pattern emerged. With most wealth created since the Second World War and with most donors the first generation of wealth, dynast giving was quite small. San Francisco is an exception given its generous, multigenerational families. We are starting to hear of many more families setting up community foundations and family-advised funds to stimulate family involvement in philanthropy. Nonprofits could do more work in asking donors how to stimulate family discussions around giving to the organization's capital campaign or annual fund efforts.

Given data from *Giving U.S.A.* that nearly half of all individual giving goes to religious causes, the *Seven Faces* 21 percent *devout* donors segment seems on the low side. This difference may suggest that additional research is needed to better connect these two statistics. Why is there a gap? Regional differences may also help to explain variations in the devout segment. In my client work in Utah, I find the Mormon tradition of tithing makes it the most generous state in America. The percentage of devout donors in Utah is probably far higher than the relatively unchurched Pacific Northwest states of Washington and Oregon.

The most surprising number of all belonged to the *investors,* at only 15 percent. These donors give because of the tax benefits of giving. To find that such a small number is motivated by tax saving is surprising. Everyone has assumed that almost all donors wanted tax advantages for giving. This research indicates the number is much smaller than suspected.

The Seven Faces of Philanthropy should be required reading for all major gift officers and volunteer campaign chairs. The insights and recommendations noted in the book are invaluable and come from solid research.

As you think through the *Seven Faces,* consider donors you have met. What are their values? Look at the top donors to your organization and ask each of them what is their motivation for giving. What factors do they consider as they look at making gifts?

To determine a donor's readiness to make a significant, transformational gift, explore his motivations for giving. If it takes 6 to 10 interactions to secure a big gift, dedicate one of those sessions to learn about the donor's values and motivations.

To keep your board members interested in fundraising and to keep educating them about fundraising, set up a short 10- to 15-minute exercise at each board meeting that follows a 5-minute training session. Go through the *Seven Faces* as a fundraising presentation to the board. Then ask them to pair up and ask each person to spend a few minutes telling the other person their motivations for giving. Allow time for each person to talk. Then gather the group back as a whole and debrief everyone on what they learned about their partner during the exercise. This will bring home the concepts and bring up complexities of motivations for giving.

Do Tax Incentives Drive Philanthropy?   The simple answer is mostly no. A good example is corporate philanthropy. Corporations are allowed a

10 percent tax deduction on their philanthropy. The national average for business giving is 1 percent. Some communities have tried to boost corporate philanthropy by creating 2 percent clubs to honor companies that give at this lofty level (even though it is only a fraction of what tax law allows). Obviously, tax incentives do not stimulate corporate philanthropy.

For individuals, the *Seven Faces* research shows the low number of investors who give because of tax reasons (15 percent) and suggests that tax incentives aren't a major driver for corporate giving, either. People give because of their belief in the mission and purpose of an organization and confidence in its management. In fact, over the past 30 years, the highest taxable rate for income tax fell from 78 percent to 38 percent while *Giving U.S.A.* data shows giving has grown throughout this time period. If tax incentives were driving philanthropy, giving should have fallen. Numerous donors interviewed for feasibility studies note that they are over their 50 percent deductible rate, yet they continue to be philanthropic. They do not care that they will not get a tax write-off. In fact, one of the biggest mistakes of philanthropic fundraising may be the overemphasis on tax breaks in encouraging gifts of appreciated securities and planned estate gifts.

In one of the follow-up stories about Warren Buffett's gift of $38 billion to charity, *Newsweek* (Sept. 4, 2006) writer Allan Sloan probed to determine if Mr. Buffett's gift was just about avoiding taxes or if he was truly being philanthropic. Sloan noted Mr. Buffett's 2006 donation of $1.9 billion and asked him how much of a tax deduction he would earn this year. Mr. Buffett replied that he would get nothing as he had several years of tax losses to carry forward into 2006. In 2008 he estimates he'll save $500,000 to $1,000,000— a 0.0005 percent savings on his taxes. Since he is making his gift to a foundation, he can shelter only 20 percent of his income instead of the 50 percent allowance if he gave directly to a charity.[18]

A constant theme throughout this book is to test these ideas by talking with your donors. If they are motivated by tax considerations, then you must address their values. But do not assume it is a philanthropic driver until the donor tells you so.

The Millionaire Next Door

The Millionaire Next Door, written by Thomas J. Stanley and William D. Danko and published in 1996, has just become common language in fundraising circles (for many nonprofits, it may still be a hidden asset).

The basic concept is that the average millionaire is not the person with the flashy car and big house but usually the person living in a normal neighborhood quietly saving and investing his way toward wealth. The author's research dating from the early 1990s showed that 80 percent of millionaires in the United States were first-generation wealth—they made the money versus inheriting it. And many of these millionaires didn't have big, fancy houses but rather disciplined themselves to save for the future.

Given that the following data is more than 10 years old, *The Millionaire Next Door* provides an interesting overall profile of the 3.5 million affluent households in the United States at that time:

1. 95 percent are married couples.
2. 67 percent are self-employed.
3. In 70 percent of the cases, the male head of household made 80 percent of the income.
4. Average net worth of $3.7 million (median $1.6 million)—6 percent averaged over $10 million in assets.
5. On average, total annual realized income is less than 7 percent of wealth; they live on less than 7 percent of their net worth.
6. 80 percent are first-generation affluent.
7. Most save at least 1 percent of earned income.
8. Well educated; 80 percent are college graduates.
9. As a group, feel that their daughters are financially handicapped in comparison with their sons, which is why most would not hesitate to share some wealth with their daughters.
10. Other key characteristic—they view themselves as tightwads.[19]

This is critically important information as it helps define the target audience for major philanthropic gifts. If these millionaires are conservative, well educated, and consider themselves "tightwads," fundraisers can tailor their approach to these potential donors. The fancy cultivation event may be a turnoff compared with the late-afternoon gathering with coffee, tea, and inexpensive cookies. Something I have recommended to staff and clients is "never give free food to rich people." If they are donating money to our organization, they want the funds to be used for charitable purposes, not feeding the affluent (the poor is fine, of course). And, if they are tightwads, then we need to exhibit similar values in our events by offering simple food, by collecting name badges at the end of events so we can recycle them for the next event, and by charging donors for the cost of their meals so their charitable donations can be fully used to further our mission in the community.

Here are some real-life stories:

Mary was a small donor to the historical society in a rural region of one of the Western states. She was volunteering at the museum and someone suggested I talk with her. Here is what she told me:

> My husband Joe and I were both school teachers. I started at age 18 in a one-room school house where I had to bring a bucket of hot embers from home to light the school stove each morning in the winter. We lived a nice, quiet life in town. We weren't big spenders but never had any real needs either. I'm 80 now; Joe just passed away a few months ago. Our attorney called me and said that I had a problem. Apparently Joe had taken my salary for my entire teaching career of 40-plus years and invested it in the stock market. He never told me a thing. Now, I find out I'm rich. In fact, I've got to start giving big gifts away or my attorney says Uncle Sam will take it all in estate taxes. Plus, we didn't have any kids so there's nobody really to leave it to except charity. I need some advice.

—DONOR INTERVIEW

A hospital client in the suburbs was starting a campaign to fund cancer research and asked me to interview one of its donors as part of the hospital's philanthropic market research study (feasibility study). Hank was to meet me at the education center at 11 A.M., so I waited for him outside the door. A guy in an old, beat-up pickup truck—at least 30 years old, rusted, and ready to fall apart—drove up. He got out and walked over in his faded, blue coveralls with patches on the knees. He stuck out his hand and introduced himself as Hank. He told me that when he was first married he had paid 10 dollars an acre for newly harvested timberland in the area. The land was worthless. He was amazed now, some 50-plus years later, that people wanted to live on that land and were willing to pay thousands of dollars an acre. Plus, they would let him harvest the mature timber, which was also worth a lot of money. I asked him about his truck. He said why buy a new one when it works fine. He said he had splurged and bought a big fancy television set and nice lounge chairs for his wife and himself, but otherwise they lived a quiet life in the woods. He didn't need a thing. A gift to the campaign? Sure, he'd give a major gift again (he had just given the hospital $600,000 for a new kidney dialysis center).

I met one of the wealthiest people in our town. He was a great guy. When we were almost through the meeting he looked at his watch—an orange, plastic digital watch that you might get out of cereal box. I asked him about it. He said he didn't care about material things. He enjoyed making money through his business and was now turning his attention to serving on our college board and philanthropy in our state.

A university was dedicating its new science building and invited all donors to the building to attend the ceremony and take a tour of the new building. One philanthropic foundation trustee, whose foundation had granted us $500,000 toward the project, was starting up the stairs to the second floor. He stopped a minute, knocked his knuckles against the metal hand railing, and smiled. "Hollow, that's great. You value-engineered the building and saved money on the hand railings so you could put money into the labs for the students and faculty. Way to go." Donor evaluations of how nonprofits deal with money and their gifts is subtle and constant. Remember, donors tend to be smart, tough-minded people. That's why they have the money.

Millionaire Next Door author Thomas Stanley expanded on his work in *The Millionaire Mind.*

How the unheralded, unflashy, build-their-wealth-slowly-over-time millionaires think and what value decisions they make throughout their lives. There are only a few pages dealing with philanthropy in the entire book, but it is fascinating as it was written by a nonfundraiser. In looking at common activities of millionaires, Stanley found:

> What high-income-producing young person today will probably become tomorrow's millionaire? . . . If this person plans to enhance his net worth in the future, he must become involved in certain outside activities. First, work closely with tax advisers and tax-advantaged investment consultants. Then, become active in your community. There is no nobler lifestyle than: Raising funds for charity. Note that nearly two-thirds of the millionaires (64 percent) engaged in this activity in the past 12 months, and there was a strong positive correlation between this activity and net worth.
>
> Some may note that fundraising is an activity of the affluent population. Or they suggest that raising funds for charity is an activity dominated by

people who inherited their wealth. In fact, volunteering time to raise funds for charity is not significantly related to age or inherited wealth, and it's not dominated by older multimillionaires. Nor is it purely the domain of those who are already wealthy. Most of today's millionaires were raising funds for good causes before they became financially independent, and most did it because of noble intent.

Good deeds do get rewarded even here on earth. Financially successful people and the next generation of economically productive people volunteer. When they cluster in various fundraising situations, they get to know and appreciate each other. People are always seen at their best when involved with noble causes, and their reputation and integrity are, in turn, enhanced.[20]

The message is: Don't judge a book by its cover or potential donors by the type of car they drive. You need to be careful how you qualify donors and how you talk about money.

Women in Philanthropy

Another significant, changing trend in philanthropy is the role of women. With any significant request for money you want to talk to the person who controls it, who has made it. Patterns of philanthropy have usually followed patterns in society. In the days when men were primary in the workforce, they made the money and they were asked for gifts. Naturally, women who controlled their late husbands' assets or fathers' assets were significant players.

As society has changed and so many more women have joined the workforce, become professionals, and created their own companies, they have made significant money in their own right. Their attitude toward giving away what they have made is different from that of women who have inherited their money from their husbands or fathers. Women are moving into the stratosphere of giving as they have created significant fortunes through serving as chief executive officers of Fortune 100 companies and as they have become successful in the financial world of stock market investment firms, venture capital partnerships, and hedge fund management companies. The CEO of eBay, Meg Whitman, recently gave $30 million to her alma mater, Princeton University.[21]

How are women donors different? How are they the same?

Women in their 70s, 80s, or older, who are in the "men-first" generation (their husbands made and controlled the money for their entire married lives), generally like to be partners in their husbands' philanthropy but are less apt to lead giving. This changes as their husbands pass away and they are forced to make financial decisions. These women realize that they are wealthy and can continue their lifestyles comfortably. However, they may not have a full understanding of their full asset base and their capacity to give money away to charity. Fundraisers should approach such women with gentle requests, stressing the need for funding to meet critical institutional needs. Fundraisers should be sensitive to these women's concerns for financial security for themselves and their families. They don't want to be a burden to their children and they want to help grandchildren go to college and get into their own homes. These women do not want to be poor so they tend to be conservative in their giving. One anecdotal survey indicates that women want three times the assets of men to feel financially secure. Encouraging women of this generation to speak to their financial advisors to help educate themselves about their assets and potential estate tax liabilities is helpful.

In *The Millionaire Next Door,* Stanley and Danko note that the unlimited marital deduction for estate asset transfers is particularly challenging for women as many will be married to the same spouse for more than 50 years, and because women live longer, on average marry a man two years older, and tend not to get remarried after being widowed, they have assets to manage on their own for nine years. Stanley and Danko surmise that these women will rely heavily upon their estate planning attorneys for advice during this time of financial loneliness.[22]

Here's a true story: Vic had made a $3.5-million donation to our university's capital campaign. He was glad to do so. We asked if his gift could be announced at the next trustees dinner where all of the board members and their spouses joined together on the evening before the board meeting. He agreed and we rehearsed the announcement from the board chair. As the gift was being announced I watched Vic to make sure he and his wife were enjoying the announcement. To my surprise, I saw his wife elbow him and lean in for some whispered conversations and laughter. After the dinner, I went up to Vic to thank him again for the gift and asked him about the little conversation. He just laughed and said that he had forgotten to tell his wife about the gift. I was shocked, but before I could say anything he said that was okay because she had made a million-dollar gift the week before without telling him. They had decided that each had half of the family empire to give away philanthropically and they were having fun doing it. So what's the point of this story? To start: It is surprising that a husband could give away $3.5-million without telling his spouse and surprising to hear that a couple in their 70s had thought through their philanthropic giving intentions and that they were both okay giving away million-dollar or more gifts without advising each other or asking permission. This was an enlightened couple and a philanthropically liberated woman.

Women are banding together to raise funds for women's causes and to help teach philanthropy. The Women's Funding Network, a San Francisco umbrella organization for more than 100 funds, is led by President and CEO Christine Grumm. She noted in a presentation that many wealthy women are reluctant to give their money away. They are afraid they will end up as "bag ladies" living on the street in poverty. Ms. Grumm indicated that women are more relationship based than men. They want a personal relationship with an organization's leaders and fundraising staff. If organizations do not thank women for gifts in a personal fashion, or if they become too aggressive in their fundraising tactics, women can get turned off. She also noted that getting a woman to start to give took a lot of time and nurturing, but once started in philanthropy a woman tends to enjoy the impact she can have on people in her community and throughout the world.

She noted that the whole area of women in philanthropy is changing dramatically. "We can expect future generations to be quite different," she said.

In a recent *Chronicle of Philanthropy* article on women in philanthropy, Ms. Grumm was quoted: "Women have the answers. It's not about handouts, it's about building assets and investing in your community."[23] When asking women for money, please use caution. A bold ask to a man feeds the ego. Even if he cannot grant the full amount of the gift request, the man feels important for having been asked for such an important gift. Women, being more relationship oriented, do not want to disappoint, so a bold ask could be a complete turnoff. They could shut down or feel like the relationship that was being fostered with the nonprofit is only financially driven and that they should go somewhere else. All fundraising is relationship based. In preparing to ask a woman donor to contribute, take the relationship model to a new level of sensitivity.

Millionaire Women Next Door   Another one of Stanley's books is the relatively new *Millionaire Women Next Door: The Many Journeys of Successful American Businesswomen*. In this book, Stanley specifically studied active businesswomen. The survey he used found the following statistics: average age, 49; average income, $413,960; responsible for 71 percent of household income; median household net worth, $2.9 million; 18 percent divorced (of those currently married, 50 percent had been divorced at least once); 60 percent college graduates with 26 percent holding an advanced degree; average donations, 70 percent of annual income (three and a half times the national average).[24]

Stanley states that high-income-producing women give significantly more than their male colleagues and that they tend to make donations to local causes.

> These women have a very strong sense of community, and they are locally oriented. Also, they see their role as helping certain types of noble causes—those that are understaffed, underfunded, underappreciated, non-elitist, and staffed or supported by women like themselves.[25]

Stanley found that few of the women he had surveyed had been asked to join charitable boards. He also found that these women wanted to be anonymous in their giving and tended to be conservative donors during their lifetimes. He noted that because they did not want to burden their families, they protected their assets to ensure for their own long-term care as well as their ability to provide for relatives. They tend to make bequests of considerable size to charitable organizations that they had little contact with.[26]

Co-trustee of the foundation she started with her husband, Melinda Gates was profiled in a recent *New York Times* article.

> [Ms. Gates] earned an M.B.A. degree from Duke University and then spent nine years rising in the managerial ranks at Microsoft. . . . Her favorite term of approval is "strategic" and smart philanthropy pursues "strategic intervention points". . . . And "charity," it seems, is not the business of the foundation. In a speech earlier this year, Ms. Gates characterized the strategic pitfall of philanthropy as succumbing to the temptation to "apply a thin layer of resources over a broad range of problems—and do a lot of charity but not effect much change."
>
> In explaining the Gates' growing commitments to philanthropy, Ms. Gates often points to the encouragement of Mr. Gates' mother, Mary,

who died of cancer shortly after the couple was married in 1994. Before the wedding, Mary Gates gave Melinda a letter about the marriage that ended, "From those to whom much is given, much is expected."[27] [Copyright 2006 by *The New York Times Co.* Reprinted with permission.]

Analytical Donors

With the rapid growth of technology companies in the United States, the company founders and early employees of Microsoft, Apple, Intel, Google, eBay, and countless other high-tech and Internet companies have built tremendous fortunes. At the same time, there has been a dramatic shift in the type of donor giving money away. Last generation's wealth tended to own and run raw materials companies or industrial companies, versus this new generation of engineering and quantifiably competent donors. Add to this group the other high-net-worth individuals who manage investments on Wall Street, run hedge funds, and invest in venture capital partnerships, and you have another group of high-net-worth, tough-minded philanthropic investors. These analytical donors were brought up on data, hard numbers, and pragmatic decision making in their professional lives.

In his comments on the difference between the philanthropy of Bill Gates and Andrew Carnegie, Daniel Gross of the *New York Times* noted:

> The foundation [Gates Foundation], which supports programs run by the World Bank and the World Health Organization, is also working with Path, an international nonprofit based in Seattle that was formerly known as the Program for the Appropriate Technology in Health, to finance malarial vaccine research. The outlook evident here is not that of a utopian like Carnegie, or of a moralist like Rockefeller, but of a practical engineer. Whether it's wiring libraries, stimulating the creation of smaller schools or paying for fundamental research, the Gates Foundation is trying to create products and systems that can be replicated and expanded with little marginal cost.[28] [Copyright 2006 by *The New York Times Co.* Reprinted with permission.]

While the efficient one-page request letter may never go away, this new generation of donors enjoys reviewing attachments (in hardcopy and/or online). Stock market analysts, angel investors (individuals of wealth who like to make strategic investments in small business startups), and venture capitalists are used to reading 10 to 20 business plans a day, research reports, and quantitative data analysis of business trends. They still want the executive summary, the 12-page PowerPoint overview, but they also want numerous background documents they can skim to do their own due diligence on the organization and the project they are being asked to fund.

Ask the background of your potential donors to see if this will be an issue for you. Ask them how they like to process information.

Family-Advised Funds

A variation of donor-advised funds managed by community foundations are the family-advised funds set up by commercial investment companies. *Giving U.S.A.* data shows that in 2004, $1.24 billion was contributed to the four largest corporate donor-advised funds (Fidelity, Schwab, Vanguard, and National Philanthropic Trust).

The Fidelity Charitable Gift Fund recently reduced the required minimum fund amount to $5,000. Their family-advised fund program has been so popular that in a few short years this idea has blossomed to the extent that Fidelity now has $3 billion under management for these funds and is one of the largest charities in the United States (this fund grew 30 percent in one year).

Universities and other nonprofits are now starting to offer family-advised funds. For example: Duke University will establish a family fund as long as 50 percent of the distribution is dedicated to projects on the Duke campus.

Just as with community foundations, finding out a person has set up a family fund is a good indicator of charitable intentions and gift capacity.

Leaving a Legacy

For many people, making a capital campaign donation to have a family name, a husband and wife's name, or another person's name on a room at a new building is a way of leaving a legacy. The family name will be there for future generations to see.

We talked earlier about women in philanthropy—a value heard from women donors is the need to memorialize the family name. Joan King marries John Henry and she becomes Joan King Henry. She is the last of the King family and now that she has married, the King family name has ended. Joan loves the idea of naming something at the new historical society building for the King family. They were early settlers in the valley and have a rich heritage of more than 100 years of wheat farming. Naming the new exhibit area for her family is an exciting idea—a way of leaving a legacy for future generations of grandchildren and great grandchildren.

Later in this book we'll look at the whole commemorative naming process that helps to stimulate donations. Be sensitive to donors as you approach them for a naming gift. Do they value it? For themselves? Their family name? Or, are you making them uncomfortable by suggesting they need an ego trip?

Foundation Values

Foundations are established to give money away. They are mandated by the U.S. Congress to spend a minimum of 5 percent of their market value on grant awards and the grant-making process.

To keep donor values and motivations simple, many fundraisers (and this book) treat corporate foundations as corporate donors. The major distinction is the company's decision to put some of its profits into an endowment for the foundation as well as to make annual gifts, thus ensuring a steady flow of giving over time rather than decreasing giving every time corporate profits dip. The basic motives of corporate donors and corporate foundation donors are the same: enlightened self-interest.

Likewise, for fundraising purposes, we will treat family foundations, community foundation–advised funds, family-advised funds (managed by corporate entities such as Fidelity Investments), just as we would individuals. To access funds from these family foundations you usually go to the founder or an immediate family member (about half of all foundation giving comes from foundations where the founder is still alive).

The balance of foundations, which many fundraisers label philanthropic foundations, are their own sector. What distinguishes these foundations is the presence of professional foundation staff officers that oversee grants. Most of the philanthropic foundations have published guidelines, applications processes, and a bureaucracy that you need to go through in order to receive foundation funding. In most cases the founder and immediate family members are not involved, or, because of the size of the foundation's assets, cannot be readily approached personally to seek funding. Examples would be the Kresge Foundation, the Ford Foundation, the

Kellogg Foundation, the David and Lucile Packard Foundation, the M.J. Murdock Charitable Trust, and so forth.

Some foundations are hybrids of family foundations and philanthropic foundations. The most prominent is the Bill & Melinda Gates Foundation (where staff handles all proposals but both Mr. and Mrs. Gates must both personally approve all grants of $10 million and higher). Many foundations are in transition from the founder(s), who were highly interested in giving, to second and third generations of the family who, of course, want to carry on the tradition but who may now be spread geographically across the country. We know of one such foundation in the third and fourth generations of the family where 34 cousins help make foundation decisions. It has gotten so complex that staff was hired to referee family discussions and bring discipline to the foundation's giving.

As the Gates Foundation, with its enormous resources, has dwarfed some of the traditional foundation leaders, they have started to think differently about their role in philanthropy:

> We have learned that impact is what really, really matters. . . . We aren't going to be remembered for how big we are, how smart we are, how hard we tried or even how much we cared. We're going to be remembered for what we accomplish.[29]

— JUDITH RODIN, PRESIDENT, ROCKEFELLER FOUNDATION

If you can help a foundation make an impact, they will be willing to fund your programs:

> Please do your homework. Look at the foundation's web site. Understand their process. Call with questions. We want to help you. Talk to other organizations we have funded. What did they learn in the process? Remember, as a foundation we like to help, but understand we are episodic; we don't do general operations or endowments.
>
> Just as with individuals remember fundraising is all about relationship building. The best time to build the relationship with a foundation is when you're not asking for money.

— JOHN CASTLES, TRUSTEE, M.J. MURDOCK CHARITABLE TRUST

Community Foundations

One of the fastest growing trends in philanthropy in the past few decades is the asset growth and philanthropic impact of community foundations. With their focus on community, all are defined to a specific geographic scope. Some community foundations are statewide: Rhode Island and Oregon; others are city oriented, such as the Chicago Community Trust and Seattle Foundation; and other states have a patchwork quilt of localized foundations as well as statewide community foundations such as the California Community Foundation along with the San Francisco Foundation and the Santa Barbara Foundation (for the entire county):

> In 2005, U.S. community foundation grants totaled $3 billion, up 14 percent and $371 million more than the previous year's total of $2.6 billion. Annual grant distributions have tripled since 1996, the first year community foundation grants totaled $1 billion nationally.[30]

Donors can give to the community foundation directly or set up an advised fund within the community foundation by transferring assets irrevocably while retaining advisory rights as to where the distribution of the endowment proceeds go each year. Many times families involve their children in this advisory role to help teach them the values of giving back to the community.

Obviously community foundations tap into the communitarian motivation of giving as well as encouraging dynastic giving through the involvement of family members. Community foundations are usually a combination of funds—undesignated gifts that build the community foundation's own endowment fund, family-advised funds that donors can help direct giving, and managed endowments for small and mid-size nonprofit organizations in the community.

Community foundations were started in 1914 through the formation of the Cleveland Foundation by visionary banker Frederick Goff. He was frustrated by some of the bequests from wealthy people that were so tightly written that court orders were needed to keep the residual funds useful to society. Ironically, one of these problem trusts was set up by Benjamin Franklin's bequest to support apprenticeships. One hundred years after Franklin's death the apprenticeship system in the United States was no more and his trust was sued to dissolve this restriction. Goff's concept was to divide the administration of the foundation into two parts: a group of banks and trust companies would invest the funds while a group of citizens would form a distribution committee to make grants. Donors could leave restricted endowments with the understanding that future boards could adjust the funds to meet changing conditions.[31]

Community foundations market themselves to families with modest fortunes as many of the tax and investment chores of a small family foundation are avoided. For other people of substantial wealth who do not wish to deal with the setup costs of a philanthropic foundation, community foundations are also attractive.

Most community foundations adhere to the 5 percent of assets distribution rule, and they must ensure that family-advised funds are making donations to qualified charities and that evaluation reports are filled out after the grant.

Staff members at community foundations indicate their lists of advised fund donors are important and should be closely watched by nonprofit fundraisers. Setting up an advised fund speaks to a person's values regarding philanthropy and giving back to the community. In addition, most people setting up a fund will not put their entire asset base into the fund—this is usually done upon their death—thus, much philanthropic capacity remains with the individual and family.

CORPORATE MOTIVATIONS FOR GIVING

Corporations don't give money away just to be nice and generous. They see philanthropy as an investment in their community and a way to help boost their image as good citizens. While federal tax law allows corporations to donate up to 10 percent of their profits, most don't even reach a 1 percent level. The Twin Cities in Minnesota have tried to encourage corporate philanthropy through promotion of a 5 percent club to honor companies donating at least that amount of their profits. Other cities have tried to copy this model at a more modest 2 percent level and have failed. When you think of corporate giving, think of community reinvestment and enlightened self-interest.

As one senior-level corporate executive in charge of his company's international social responsibility budget said:

We don't really give money away; we invest it in the communities where our employees live and in areas that will improve society so more people can afford to purchase our products. We can't have a world of "haves" and "have nots." We need to build an educated workforce and to be profitable. In the long term we want everyone to be part of the American dream . . . and now the global dream. We believe in enlightened self-interest.

This sentiment is echoed throughout corporate philanthropy in the United States. As we saw in the *Giving U.S.A.* data, corporations are not a major philanthropic resource. However, they are a noisy one. They like lots of attention for their giving. They want full credit for their community investments; that visibility is part of the return on these investments in charitable causes. To be fair, companies have responded generously to times of national and international crisis—9/11, the tsunami crisis in 2004, and Katrina hurricane relief efforts in 2005.

For many nonprofits, the real path to corporate support is through the marketing budget and corporate sponsorships. These aren't philanthropic investments at all, but rather advertising purchases and cause-related marketing to help sell corporate products.

Enlightened self-interest is the mantra for corporate giving. To work the corporate giving marketplace, meet with your potential business donors to find out what they value in a relationship with you. For example— our university focused on graduate work in science and technology offering masters and doctoral degrees. In talking to potential corporate donors about the possibility of securing scholarships for our students, we learned that the corporate world was very interested in master's degree technology students. Providing them with scholarships and paid internships was of high interest. As soon as the students graduated from our two-year graduate program, the companies were eager to hire them. However, corporations were less interested in providing support for doctoral students because these programs can take six to eight years to complete, and most of the students want to go into academia rather than the corporate workforce in our community. We set up a master's scholarship and internship philanthropy program and had great success.

Many corporations tend to be communitarian in their giving programs. Some will contribute 1 percent of a capital campaign's goal so they can be seen as good corporate citizens, supporting their local communities. After the initial Hurricane Katrina relief efforts, many companies were seeking ways to become more strategic in their response to disasters to ensure their generosity provided more bottom-line impact.

The Chronicle of Philanthropy reported in 2006 on a survey of 62 large companies by the Committee to Encourage Corporate Philanthropy. Companies reported that their giving increased 14 percent in 2005, which tracked the median increase in corporate revenues of 17 percent and pre-tax profits of 15 percent. However, in the same article, *The Chronicle* noted that in a separate survey of 800 adults by the National Consumers League to assess the way consumers view corporate social responsibility, 76 percent said they strongly or somewhat strongly agreed that a company should place salary and wage increases above making charitable contributions. Fifty-three percent said it was extremely important or very important that companies make donations to charities that are relevant to their businesses.[32]

Providing your corporate donors with high visibility and exposure for their giving will go a long way toward meeting their needs for community visibility.

WHY IS ALL OF THIS IMPORTANT?

If you take a winning-gifts attitude and a marketing approach to philanthropic fundraising, then you must be sensitive to the values and motivations of your donors. In Chapter 3, Listen, we'll discuss techniques to detect more specific values of your donor marketplace. But this chapter on general donor values should motivate you to start reading books and scan local and national newspapers for articles about donors' values about philanthropy.

Two critically important national newspapers to read are the *New York Times* and the *Wall Street Journal*. Both are widely read nationally by your best donors. And, while each paper has a political tone (the *New York Times* is perceived as liberal and the *Wall Street Journal* as conservative), between the two you will get a balanced view of the world through the eyes of your donors. Both papers highlight major philanthropy stories in the news and will provide you with conversation items for meetings with donors, volunteers, and nonprofit leaders.

For more specific information about philanthropic fundraising, look to *The Chronicle of Philanthropy* as a key source of the latest news for fundraising and the nonprofit world. It will also lead you to many other sources of information. For information check the magazine's web site at www.

philanthropy.com. I encourage you to take 30 minutes a day to read books on fundraising and the nonprofit sector. While some disciplined, academic research has started to take place in the last 10 to 15 years, most of the literature is written by practitioners educated in the school of hard knocks. The information tends to be pragmatic, practice based, and highly useful in moving your philanthropic fundraising program forward quickly.

APPLY WHAT YOU'VE LEARNED

1. *Best and worst gifts.* Do this exercise by yourself. Then repeat it with your fundraising staff and then with your volunteer fundraising team and then your board. Ask everyone to write their names on sheets of paper so you can collect the information at the end of the exercise. Then answer the following:

   a. What financial gift have you made to a nonprofit that made you feel really good? Why?

   b. Think about the most dissatisfying gift you have made to a charity. Why did it make you feel bad?

      As you do this exercise, ask each person to spend 5 or 10 minutes filling out their own sheet of paper; then have them pick a partner and trade stories for 10 more minutes. Use a final 5 minutes to ask for participants to share what they learned about each other and the gift-making process. Set up a flipchart with the following categories: Best Practices and Worst Practices.

      Write up these findings in a brief whitepaper that you read every three months. Share it with your senior management team, physicians if you're working in a hospital, faculty members if you are working in a college or school setting, and others so they can understand donors' values around giving.

2. *Pick a book.* Skim through this chapter again looking for one of the books mentioned here that would be of most interest to you. Go to your local library to check it out, or ideally order it online so you can highlight and mark up your copy as you read. What else can you learn from this source?

3. *An "aha" moment.* Which part of this chapter hit you as an *aha* moment? What new idea can you use today? This week? This month?

This year? Send me your ideas by e-mailing me at Tom.Wilson@
WinningGifts.INFO. I'm curious.

NOTES

1. The Drucker Foundation, *Self-Assessment Tool Participant Workbook*, p 32.
2. Alexis de Tocqueville, *Democracy in America*, edited and abridged by Richard D. Heffner (New York: Signet Classic published by Penguin Group, 1956, 1984).
3. Ibid., 198.
4. Ibid., 199.
5. Ibid., 200–201.
6. Sally Beatty, "Giving Back: The Global Giving Gap," *Wall Street Journal*, Friday, September 8, 2006, W2.
7. "Giving U.S.A. 2007: The Annual Report on Philanthropy for the Year 2006," 52nd Annual Issue (researched and written at The Center on Philanthropy at Indiana University, Giving U.S.A. Foundation, 2007).
8. Gail Sheehy, *New Passages* (New York: Ballatine Books, a division of Random House, G. Merritt Corporation, 1995).
9. Andrew Carnegie, "Gospel of Wealth," *North American Review* No. CCCXCI, June 1989, www.swarthmore.edu/CocSci/rbannis1/AIHI9th/Carnegie.html.
10. Waldemar A. Nielsen, *The Golden Donors: A New Anatomy of the Great Foundations* (New York: Truman Talley Books/E.P. Dutton, 1985, 1989), 134–135.
11. Sally Beatty, "Giving Back," *Wall Street Journal*, Friday, September. 8, 2006, W2.
12. Daniel Gross, "Giving It Away, Then and Now," *New York Times*, July 2, 2006, 4.
13. Carol J. Loomis, "Warren Buffett Gives It Away," *Fortune*, July 10, 2006, vol. 154, no. 1, 60.
14. Nicole Lewis, "Weills' Philanthropy Emphasizes Collaboration and Bridging Cultures," *The Chronicle of Philanthropy*, October 12, 2006, 10.
15. John Hechinger and Daniel Golden, "The Great Giveaway: Like Warren Buffett, a New Wave of Philanthropists Are Rushing to Spend Their Money before They Die," *Wall Street Journal*, Saturday/Sunday, July 8–9, 2006, A8.
16. Russ Alan Prince and Karen Maru File, *The Seven Faces of Philanthropy: A New Approach to Cultivating Major Donors* (San Francisco: Jossey-Bass, 1994), 9.
17. Ibid., 14.
18. Allan Sloan, "The Truth about Buffett's Tax Bill," *Newsweek*, September 4, 2006, 16.
19. Thomas J. Stanley, Ph.D., and William D. Danko, Ph.D., *The Millionaire Next Door: The Surprising Secrets of America's Wealth* (New York: Pocket Books, 1996), 8–11.
20. Thomas J. Stanley, Ph.D., *The Millionaire Mind* (Kansas City: Andrews McMeel Publishing, 2001), 376–377.
21. Holly Hall, "Giving: Power of the Purse—Self-Made Women Are Making Their Mark on Philanthropy," *The Chronicle of Philanthropy*, February 11, 2005, 7.
22. *The Millionaire Next Door*, 215.
23. "Power of the Purse," 10.

24. Thomas J. Stanley, Ph.D., *Millionaire Women Next Door: The Many Journeys of Successful American Businesswomen* (Kansas City: Andrews McMeel Publishing, 2004), 8–10.

25. Ibid., 17.

26. Ibid., 18–19.

27. Steve Lohr and Stephanie Strom, "No Longer in Shadow, Melinda Gates Puts Her Mark on Foundation," *New York Times*, Thursday, July 6, 2006, A12.

28. Daniel Gross, "Giving It Away, Then and Now," *New York Times*, July 2, 2006, 4.

29. Stephanie Strom, "Charities Try to Keep Up with the Gateses," *New York Times*, Sunday, January 14, 2007, 14.

30. "New Standards for Community Foundations," *Advancing Philanthropy*, November/December 2006, 12.

31. *The Golden Donors: A New Anatomy of the Great Foundations*, 242–247.

32. Suzanne Perry, "Giving by Companies Rose 14% Last Year, Study Finds," *The Chronicle of Philanthropy*, June 15, 2006, 10. A summary of the survey can be found at www.corporatephilanthropy.org; poll on corporate responsibility can be found at www.csrresults.com.

CHAPTER 3

Listen

Taking notes during your meeting with the prospect helps you listen, puts you in a position of authority, encourages your prospect to open up, and sends positive signals. . . . There's something about having an empty sheet of paper in front of you that really tunes you in to what is being said, and makes it more difficult for you to miss important points.[1]

—STEPHAN SCHIFFMAN, *THE 25 SALES HABITS OF HIGHLY SUCCESSFUL SALESPEOPLE*

In Chapter 1, People Centered Fundraising, we sensitized you to the necessity of becoming customer oriented rather than institutionally oriented. In Chapter 2, Donor Values, we described philanthropic motivations as found in fundraising literature and the media. In this chapter, we will look at three important listening techniques:

1. How to become a deep listener—someone who is an active and empathetic listener.

2. Ways to collectively listen to donors, constituents, and potential donors.

3. How to listen to a specific donor to determine that person's interests, values, and motivations for giving so you can develop a sense of the giving potential to your organization.

One of the great lessons of philanthropic fundraising is to take each new donor as a new experience. No matter how many years in the business you have, no matter how many books and articles you've read, donors will continue to surprise you with their complexity and their individual motivations for giving.

But be careful with your time. These techniques will work in listening to anyone and everyone. Make sure you are doing this with qualified donors so that your listening is cultivating a major gift, not just a major friend (qualified donors are what your organization would consider to be the biggest donors; for some this may be all annual donors $5,000 or higher, for others $25,000 or more—this should be no more than the top 100 of your donors that you can personally see each year). You'll learn in this chapter the amount of thinking, training, energy, and discipline that it takes to be a deep listener, a world-class listener.

BECOME A DEEP LISTENER

What does it mean to be a good listener? We all can think back to our school days and the different ways we listened (or didn't). Remember the droning professor who restated everything that you had already read in the textbook? In real life we know it's critically important to listen—like the careful listening I did prior to doing 100-yard zipline, canopy tours in the jungles of Costa Rica (where, if I didn't learn how to stop myself with the leather glove they had given me, I would have slammed into a tree trunk at an exciting velocity).

All of us listen every day. Hopefully we're paying attention, but frequently we don't have to, want to, or need to. Usually we only listen to the news with half a mind, or go to meetings and daydream until something important comes up. Remember your last job interview? Every word was critical. What was the person asking? What did she really want to know? What clarifying questions could I ask to understand where this person was coming from? Now, that was deep listening.

How do you show active, deep listening? You take notes, you nod your head in agreement, you ask clarifying, follow-up questions to gather additional information, and you restate to see if you heard correctly.

The next time you're in a one-on-one meeting, look to see how active are your partner's listening skills. Does he have a notepad to write down what you are saying? If not, maybe he's not a listener. How can you tell if he heard you? A nod, a smile . . . that's something. A restatement of what you said to see if he got it correctly is the best. Reflect on whether you felt listened to. Did you walk away feeling the other person understood what you were trying to say? Did the person perceive the emotion and energy behind your words? Was the listening empathetic? A tape machine can be accurate in recording what you say, but is it sympathetic to you? Of course not.

Can you empathize with a donor? Sure, just remember to seek the emotions and affect behind the words and facts you are hearing. For example: You meet with Mary, one of many mid-level donors who someday might become a major donor at your new job. During your conversation you ask how the fundraising department has done in the past year and what could be done better in the future. She comments that her gift last year was made in memory of her late husband, but her name was put in the annual report instead of his. She thought she had made her wishes clear to your predecessor and is not so much mad as disappointed. The good news is you were there to listen. You were able to find out there was a problem and note her angst. Clarify the situation by restating what you heard in terms of the facts and her advice on resolving the situation. Take good notes so Mary knows you have listened intently. The real issue here is memorializing her husband. You need to admit your organization blew it. Be sure to slow down and ask for some stories about her husband. How did they meet? Why was he so special? Show interest in the person at the empathetic level, where feelings are expressed. Be genuine about your interest. This is easy as many of the stories you will hear are fascinating.

One way to practice your listening skills is take a notepad with you wherever you go. Take as detailed notes as you can during a one-on-one meeting. It's a fine balance to take notes but keep tightly focused on the person's facial expressions and body language. It's critical that before 24 hours are up, you type up your notes, adding as much detail as you can remember. Include any follow-up promises that were made by either side. In fund-raising, these contact reports are vital.

Why is note taking so important and why are contact reports so critical to fundraising success? While you can listen intently in the moment, if you take no notes your surface memory will keep shifting to the next topic and you will forget the last one—that's the job of surface memory. If you take some simple notes, you can jog your short-term memory later that day. To help cement your memories of the meeting, write complete notes. Just the exercise of fleshing out your notes helps you to remember them. Turning in this complete contact report is critical to your organization as you are establishing institutional memory of the interaction. Reflecting on the meeting during the contact report writing process will put the person's comments into perspective and add background meaning to some of her comments.

With frequent turnover of fundraising staff, the only way for an organization to truly get its money's worth from its fundraisers is to insist on contact reports for every call. If you are a star fundraiser or you want to be, you should be having 5 to 10 face-to-face meetings a week with donors (15 is okay, too). That's an average of 30 per month. There's no way to remember all of those meetings and discussions if you do not write down notes. If you build the habit of taking good notes and writing thorough interview contact reports, you will be able to scan them before the next meeting with a donor and appear to have a photographic memory. You will find that the very fact of writing them up, of reflecting on the meeting and looking for meaning, helps to burn the experience into your memory.

In addition to what you heard, what did you see? Experience? If you were in an office, were there diplomas on the wall? If so, from where? Any family pictures? Hobbies (golf, sailing, etc.)? How big was the office? Where did you sit? At a desk? At a conference table? Next to the donor or across the table? Did the donor smile? How was her sense of humor? Were there any mementos of your organization on the desk or in the office? Mementos of other organizations? Was the donor dressed formally or informally? Was there an administrative assistant? What is the assistant's name? Did you make a connection with the assistant?

Similar observations can be made if you are meeting in someone's home. What type of neighborhood is it? What style of home? How new is it? How is it decorated? Is there art on the walls? Sculpture in the yard? Did you meet in the living room or the kitchen? Is there a dog or cat?

Will you need all of this information later? Who knows? Being observant can provide clues that are useful later. And your notes certainly provide topics of conversation during this visit or future visits.

A caution on listening—sometimes as people tell you their stories it brings up memories from your life. This is the good news. You are empathizing with the person you are listening to. But, as quickly as you can, store away your memories for later. Don't share them right now. If you are not careful, it may feel like you are trying to one-up the donor's story with your own. Keep the focus on the donor and her story and save your story for your spouse/partner or your journal. If you start trading stories to top each other then you become ships in the night talking past each other rather than really communicating.

If you have accepted the concept that your first job is not to sell, but rather to listen, you will be fine. You do not have to worry about making a pitch at your first meeting. It's a discovery call, not a solicitation call. Yes, you should be ready to respond if the donor tells you he wants to discuss making a gift. But that is not your goal today. You want to find out about the person and his connections to your organization.

What Others Advise on Listening

In reviewing business and management books for advice on listening in preparation for this book, I was amazed to find so little information.

In *Interviewing Techniques for Managers,* author Carolyn Thompson devotes a chapter to interviewing techniques for hiring new employees. Some of her concepts are specific to the job applicant interview process, but many ideas translate well to fundraising listening. She reminds us that effective interviewers talk only 25 percent of the time. Your mission on an interview is to draw out the other person and listen intently rather than present your organization too much. She attributes "overtalking" to nervousness, lack of planning (a solution is to use a formal interview tool to guide your listening), or a naturally verbose communication style."[2]

Thompson goes on to describe active listening behaviors. In Exhibit 3.1 you can see her CHEER method of listening:[3]

EXHIBIT 3.1   CHEER METHOD OF LISTENING

C Concentrate (get rid of distractions and other barriers to listening so you can focus).
H Hear totally (people communicate 7% through words, 38% through voice, and 55% through facial and body language).
E Empathize (think of a time you were in the same situation).
E Elicit information (ask questions and paraphrase).
R Remember (take notes in your interview tool).

Thompson's statement about the percentages of how people communicate is critically important. This is why face-to-face interviewing is so effective. With telephone interviews you are losing more than half of the communication; remember 55 percent is nonverbal. And, because the person you are interviewing cannot see your facial expressions, it is hard to encourage discussions on the phone. Miscommunications are easy. Do not assume a telephone interview is sufficient to help build a relationship for fundraising. Nothing takes the place of a face-to-face meeting.

Later is this chapter we will provide some interviewing tools you can use out in the field talking to donors. Having a questionnaire written prior to your interview process is critical to good listening. The tool allows you to actively listen rather than think of new questions. Referring to your interview questionnaire keeps you on track and prevents you from leaving critical questions out.

In his latest book, *The 8th Habit: From Effectiveness to Greatness,*[4] Stephen R. Covey reflects on the importance of communications in our lives. He notes that people communicate through reading, writing, speaking, and listening. Ironically, the most used of these is listening, even though the least school training and lifelong training is devoted to listening. He notes the following five levels of listening: 1) ignoring, 2) pretend listening, 3) selective listening, 4) attentive listening, and 5) empathetic listening.

Covey views empathetic listening as the highest level because you put yourself within the other person's frame of reference. To successfully listen, you need to turn off your inner reaction voice, to stop worrying about the next question, to shut down the judgments about what the other person is saying to really listen for understanding, and to go to where the speaker is, not where you are.[5]

Peter Drucker, in his *Self-Assessment Tool* workbook, prepares planning and retreat participants to become involved by "empowering constructive dissent." You want to encourage board members, volunteers, and donors to share their questions and concerns with you rather than with each other in the parking lot after the meeting. While not presented in the context of listening, this notion of encouraging lively discussions and debate has proved a powerful listening tool in my work. Adults learn by questioning, debating, and suggesting. You can't listen until you encourage someone to talk. Too often we adults are too polite for our own good. As you start interacting with donors in groups and individually, you need to reinforce the importance of candid, constructive feedback and comment. That is the only way you can improve your organization, your fundraising systems, and the care of your donors.

In a similar vein, the total quality management (TQM) movement of the 1990s and Japanese *Kaizen* practices (continuous quality improvement) are all about listening. W. Edwards Deming developed the concept of encouraging employee feedback to improve manufacturing processes. He taught it to the Japanese in the 1970s and 1980s as they were developing their manufacturing systems. Now the Japanese lead the way in *Kaizen* by encouraging their workers to continuously give constructive advice on how to improve business systems. Toyota, about to become the world's largest automobile company, is a master of organizational *Kaizen*. For more information on Deming's methods, read *Dr. Deming: The American Who Taught the Japanese about Quality.*[6]

Civil engineers, the people who design bridges, tunnels, and earthworks, hold failure analysis meetings when something goes wrong. If a new bridge breaks apart because of a design flaw, they don't fire the design engineer. Instead they form a failure-analysis discussion group to learn from the mistakes made. The issues are not personal but systems oriented—they are seeking to identify the failure so they can correct problems and assure success in the future. Encouraging this systems improvement type of thinking frees you to *listen* when critical remarks are made about you, your ideas, your programs, and your plans.

My graduate university was located in the heart of the high-tech, Silicon Forest of suburban Portland, Oregon. In fact, within a 10-mile radius of campus we had more than 12,000 Intel engineers and another 5,000 engineers working at other high-tech companies. Working with Intel in the early 1990s, I found out the company had a new-employee class (I assume it still does) that taught employees how to argue, listen, and actively discuss issues with their fellow employees. The goal was to maintain the engineering culture of forthright discussions rather than allow new employees to adopt a passive-aggressive communications style.

In *The Zen of Listening*, Rebecca Shafir notes that people feel listened to when their concerns are adopted by the listener, when their feelings are understood, when days or weeks later the listener comments on their previous conversation, and "when they act on what I said."[7] She also notes that good listening builds trust. If you have any type of sales position, be a good listener.

Remembering what was said by a donor and acting on it are critical to philanthropic fundraisers. The best way to remember is to write detailed contact reports. According to Douglas J. Herrman, author of *Super Memory*, anything given less than a minute of thought will fade from memory—occasional rehearsal of your new memories keeps the information in long-term storage.[8] This is why taking notes during an interview is important—you're capturing surface memory to short-term memory that can be jogged by reviewing your scribbled notes. The next step is taking your rough notes and completing a full, detailed, permanent record in the form of a contact report. By taking the time to do this within 24 hours of your interview, you take a three-word phrase that might not make sense three months from now and turn it into a coherent thought for you or someone else. It is important that your personal intelligence from these meetings gets turned into institutional intelligence so that your successor can pick up your notes and keep the donor moving forward with the organization. The real relationship is between donors and the nonprofits they are investing in. You are just the short-term steward and communications channel between the two (whether it's 18 months or 10 years). At the end of your contact report think through your listening session and restate the action items you heard during the meeting; also include action items that have come to you as you reflect on the meeting. What is the right next step with this relationship? If you write everything down, your donors will be amazed at your great memory.

Note in Exhibit 3.2 the graphic elements of capturing your information from a meeting. If you do not take good notes, the wispy tendrils of the cloud of your meeting will dissipate in the morning air. Use your notepad at the meeting and then commit your notes to institutional memory on your laptop (or a dictating machine for someone else to transcribe).

The Zen of Listening describes two sets of listening response types:

1. Encouragers—silence, reassurance, open-ended questions, paraphrasing
2. Stoppers—denial, interrogation, advice giving (unless asked, and if asked, keep your answer short), psychoanalysis (without a license)

The most effective encourager is affirmative silence—one of the most powerful and least used techniques.

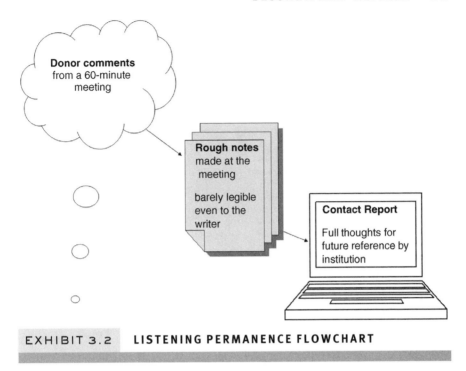

EXHIBIT 3.2   LISTENING PERMANENCE FLOWCHART

Silence is virtuous in its ability to make your speaker feel good about himself. Silence allows the speaker's deeper thoughts to surface, thoughts that often contain solutions to problems. When you allow your speaker the time to think out loud in a supportive environment, you set the stage for her empowerment, and she will want to be in your company more often.[9]

In *Listen Up*, by Larry Barker and Kitty Watson, four personal listening preferences are identified: 1) people oriented, 2) action oriented, 3) content oriented, and 4) time oriented.

While many people will exhibit two preferences, under pressure or when tired one style will predominate. They note that listening styles can be detected through watching speaking and presenting styles, as we tend to present as we like to listen. Here is the description of each listening style and some of its advantages:

- **People-Oriented Listener**—listens to understand the emotions of others, cares for others, nonjudgmental, and provides clear feedback signals; interested in building relationships, notices moods, and may get too involved with others' issues.

- **Action-Oriented Listener**—concentrates on tasks, prefers to listen in outline form, finds it difficult to listen to disorganized speakers, gets to the heart of the matter quickly, and helps others focus on what is important, encourages others to be organized, concise, and identifies inconsistencies in messages.

- **Content-Oriented Listener**—carefully evaluates everything he hears, enjoys listening to details and digging below the surface to explore all aspects of a problem, prefers listening to experts, tries to see all sides of an issue, enjoys listening to complex and challenging information, values technical information, is detail oriented.

- **Time-Oriented Listener**—clock watcher; encourages time efficiency, which may stifle creativity; may interrupt or discount relationships with others; manages and saves time effectively; lets others know time guidelines for meetings; discourages wordy speakers; gives cues to others when time is being wasted.[10]

It is challenging to present to an audience composed of different types of listeners. You need to have enough information in your presentation so that the content-oriented listeners are satisfied. State your conclusions and then go back and build your arguments to support these conclusions. If you build a chain of logic and then present a conclusion, any break in the chain (a person who does not buy one of your assumptions or statements) and your whole presentation can be discounted. For action-oriented listeners, use an outline presentation style (PowerPoint lends itself well to this type of person). For the people-oriented listener, have stories about people and situations that make your general points concrete and specific. People stories are powerful for all types of listeners. And, for time-oriented listeners, keep to your agreed-upon time limits for presentation. If you agreed to 15 minutes, keep your promise. If you told them 25 minutes, do it. It is always better to leave your audience wanting more than being bored because you presented too long.

Matt Oechsli, author of *The Art of Selling to the Affluent,* emphasizes the importance of listening by using interviewing techniques to build a relationship:

> You must replace your "sales pitch" with a questioning process that provides you with vital information about your customers and their families while helping them discover how what you offer can successfully satisfy their needs and desires.

Keep asking questions to get others to tell you more about themselves. Keep probing so you can begin developing a relationship based on what they enjoy most—talking about themselves. Asking the right question and then listening carefully in order to ask other questions is the key to your success. . . . You can tell whether a man is wise by his questions.[11]

Oechsli's quote is in the context of selling high-end cars, investments, and other material items to the affluent. However, he is also right on with the approach you need for philanthropic fundraising.

In *Listening: The Forgotten Skill*, Madelyn Burley-Allen lists 12 methods for improving your listening skills:

1. Search for something you can use personally—listen for ideas that broaden your perspective and that will be worthwhile later.
2. Take the initiative—reach out for the idea that is being communicated. Stimulate the talker with your attention.
3. Work at listening—listening takes energy, listen energetically.
4. Focus your attention on ideas—listen for central ideas, examples, facts, principles, evidence, and opinions.
5. Make meaningful notes—improve your ability to learn and remember by making a brief record of the speaker's main points.
6. Resist external distractions—sit where you can see and hear well.
7. Hold your rebuttal—do not react to emotion-laden words.
8. Keep an open mind and ask questions to clarify for understanding.
9. Capitalize on thought speed—summarize what you've heard.
10. Practice regularly by listening and taking notes.
11. Analyze what is being said nonverbally—be patient and sensitive to the talker's feelings.
12. Evaluate and be critical of content, not the speaker's delivery.[12]

Share Yourself

As you strive to become a great listener, you can be so attentive that you disappear as a person. This isn't fair to your partner in communications. It should be a two-way interactive process. Don't be so professional that you don't share information about yourself. Yes, you should be cautious as it is not about you, it is about your organization and its mission, and the donor. But, as you listen carefully you will find people asking questions about you, your family, and your background.

Share and be open. Keep your answers simple and quick. What you studied in college, your kids, your spouse's work, your hobbies, and why you like fundraising are all safe ground. It's a good idea to read national newspapers like the *New York Times* and the *Wall Street Journal* to keep current on trends and items of interest for smalltalk with people that you interview and for larger talk of major issues of the day. Be a good conversationalist.

COLLECTIVE LISTENING

We participate in collective listening exercises all of the time. When your hotel asks that every guest fill out a comment card, it is trying to listen to its customers. Good, proactive, customer-focused businesses constantly seek feedback from the collective voices of their customers.

Nonprofits do some of this but could do more. What are some examples? Every time you hold a cultivation event, put a feedback form under the plate and ask attendees to give you quick responses to three or four simple questions about the quality of the evening's program, food, schedule, location, and suggestions for future events. This may seem strange to do at a social event for your organization. However, when your volunteer chair thanks everyone for coming and asks for two minutes to fill out the survey you will find people appreciative that you care enough to listen to them. This is good listening but it also makes sense. You can gain some wonderful information about future events from suggestions made on the feedback form. You can also spot potential volunteers through critical comments that show an experienced event participant (ask that people print their names on their forms so you can follow up). A feedback evaluation form can be useful after board meetings, fundraising committee meetings, or any other setting where collective listening can help. Create an attitude of continuous learning and improvement in all of your events, publications, and activities.

The first groups to listen to are your board members and fundraising volunteers. Debrief last month's dinner auction. Ask for constructive criticism that will make next year's annual fund drive even more successful. Empower depersonalized discussions of how to raise more money at the event, make it more elegant, the schedule more efficient, and the room more gorgeous. As a good facilitator you want to capture all of these ideas in brainstorming mode without necessarily agreeing to implement any or all of them for next year's event. First listen; capture the essence of what people are saying. This is a good opportunity to review the feedback forms. Based on your committee discussion and the feedback forms, you may want to hold a further feedback session with sponsors or with table sponsors to further involve them in redesigning next year's event.

But, one caution—if you tell people you are there to listen to them, please do so. You can create more problems than you solve if you conduct less than authentic collective listening exercises.

> This nonprofit asked me to their offices to learn about their plans and to give them feedback. I listened to them but when it came time to give them advice nobody at the organization wanted to listen to me. I was shocked and now I'm just mad. If they don't want to listen to me, fine. I know people can have their plans set, but be honest if that's where you're at. Don't try to fool me into thinking you'll listen. I'll never go back there again for a meeting. I'm done with that group.
>
> —MARKET RESEARCH STUDY INTERVIEWEE

Listening to Create a Major Gifts Club

As you come to a new organization to take its fundraising to the next level, it is exciting to put new programs in place. Or, if you have been at an organization for five or six years, it is time to renew the organization by re-engineering your program—from new concepts to work learned at your last conference or book.

How can you take an idea from somewhere else and ensure it is successful in your current situation? Use collective listening.

Because major gifts require 6 to 10 contacts to build the relationship before asking for gift support, it is wonderful to have authentic reasons to meet with donors to listen for feedback on your events, publications, and gift clubs.

One university wanted to start a $1,000 annual giving club to provide unrestricted support. What should it be called? What should the benefits of membership be? How should it be marketed? The fundraiser put together a standard president's club with 10 benefits modeled on similar clubs at other institutions. After revising the draft several times based upon internal feedback from colleagues, the club description was field tested with board members. Potential donors were asked for 30 minutes to review the gift club description, name, types of activities, and benefits. Each exposure draft was formally labeled as a draft with a version and date. After each interview information was considered and a new draft created. By interview number 12 the results were amazing. The name changed from President's Club to Quantum Society to better express the high-tech nature of the university. Of the 10 benefits of club membership that were developed in draft one and then tested, the donors threw out 7 of them (a sobering experience). The donors were consistent in their opinion that getting the university's newsletter, while important for the organization, was not a benefit to the donor. A coffee mug? It was okay but not a motivator. A dinner (described as typically mediocre) on campus to hear propaganda from the administration would be okay, but not really a benefit. However, if a star faculty member were to present his or her latest research (in layman's language, please) and donors happened to eat dinner while listening, well, that would be fun and something to look forward to. And the number-one benefit to them? Understanding the impact of their gift in helping to make the university a top-notch institution for students and helping it to bring the latest research to local industry. The best news—of the 12 people interviewed, all of them became charter members within the first 30 days of the announcement of the club. After one year there were 100 members of the club giving $1,000 annually and within three years 250 with a 90 percent renewal rate. The market research, listening to the donor, helped to launch this annual fund program to success.

Written Surveys

Another way to quickly gather collective data is to conduct a written survey. Once data is gathered it can be used later for individual follow-up. Written survey work is also helpful in informing strategic planning efforts to gather customer value statements about a nonprofit organization. For one church where the pastor and church board needed to determine whether to expand the number of services or the size of the sanctuary, we conducted a simple one-page (front and back) written survey during a morning worship service.

We asked the pastor to introduce the topic and turn the podium over to the planning leader. Only five minutes were needed in the service to complete the survey. For the next three Sundays, they announced that additional surveys were available at the back of the sanctuary and asked parishioners to fill them out before leaving. In addition to gathering reactions as to when additional services could be offered (Saturday evening or earlier on Sunday morning), the church sought feedback on how large a sanctuary parishioners wanted, the quality of the Sunday School program, and the effectiveness of the small-group program for adults, and included an open-ended section for any comments a person was interested in making. The poor volunteer who had offered to tally the surveys and present the results was flooded with information. It was so rich and detailed that the planning committee was tickled pink. Parishioners appreciated being asked for their opinions and suggestions and the planning committee was delighted to have real data and feedback to base their decisions on.

Several years ago, I expanded the traditional philanthropic market research study process to include a written survey component. It is still critically important to conduct 35 to 200 face-to-face interviews with the organization's best donors (the number of interviews is usually based on the size of the goal being tested in the study). But, we know that for a campaign that will need 50 to 75 key gifts to be successful, 250 to 500 prospective donors need to be involved in the personal cultivation and solicitation process of the campaign. If we can only interview 100 of the 500 potential donors, how do we start to engage the other 400? How do we gather information from them sooner rather than later? How do we let unknown prospects come forward to us?

The written survey turned out to be the answer. For an organization with a contained constituency of relatively small numbers you can mail the survey to everybody. See who responds and who self-identifies their interest in helping your fundraising program. No matter how much prospect research you do, some donors remain hidden within your different levels of constituencies.

Here are some examples. To test the campaign case and goal for an organization of 500 donors, the top 35 prospects were identified and interviewed in the philanthropic market research study. The balance of the list was sent the written survey. One survey was returned with indications of a $500,000 gift. When personally interviewed, this couple confirmed their interest in a three-year challenge gift to the campaign. But, they wished to remain totally anonymous and asked a trust attorney 100 miles out of town to route their donation and challenge conditions. The survey enabled us to detect a totally unknown prospect. This gift turned out to be the largest of the campaign.

For another organization of 40,000 members testing an $8 million goal the challenge was different. Once the top 100 prospects were identified for personal interviewing, the organization decided to review the database of members with the goal of describing the top 5 percent of its list. The survey was mailed to 2,000 people and resulted in a 15 percent response rate. This is about average. You can increase this rate to 40 percent by mailing the survey five to seven times to nonresponders. You can further boost responses by offering a free latte certificate ahead of time or by weekly drawings for donated prizes. The results? Some gifts indications of $5,000, $10,000, and even one $25,000 prospect. The real win? On the question asking if they had included the charity in their estate plans, more than 100 people indicated they had or were willing to. Exciting.

What's the process? You adapt the standard request for a personal interview letter into a request to review the enclosed case statement and ask the recipient to take the time to complete the one-page (front and back), five-minute written survey. Include a stamped return envelope, or you can use a business reply envelope where postage is paid by the organization when the mail is picked up to save money. Ideally the request-for-participation letter is signed by one of your prominent fundraising volunteers (a board member or donor who has significant name impact in the community). The response envelope should be sent to an objective outside party (e.g., a fundraising consultant). See Appendix B for a sample survey form that you can adapt.

Many e-mail tools are available now that enable you to do simple e-mail surveys to supplement a traditional mailed survey. Using a combination of mail and e-mail approaches can be effective in boosting your response rate while keeping your survey costs reasonable. Of course, you need to have the e-mail addresses of the people you want to survey.

You should always ask for permission to follow up the survey response if the participant agrees. Ask for volunteers—for your annual fund, for a special event, or for a marketing committee. See who would like to take a campus tour—and abide by a rigid, no-ask rule for the tour participants.

Participative Focus Groups

You can use an exciting technique to gather intelligence from the philanthropic marketplace while at the same time engaging donors personally—the participative focus group. A variation of the traditional one-way mirror, hidden-microphone, and videotaped corporate focus group sessions that Madison Avenue marketing firms have used for decades, the participative focus group techniques for nonprofits were first articulated in Richard A. Krueger's *Focus Groups: A Practical Guide for Applied Research*.[13] Krueger adapted traditional focus group techniques to find a way for nonprofits and government agencies on limited budgets to reap the benefits of the process on a shoestring budget. Rather than excluding clients from the focus group meetings, Krueger advocates for their participation to help speed the learning curve from the information gleaned at the meetings.

Having practiced participative focus group techniques with nonprofit organizations in a fundraising setting for more than 10 years, I have found them to be robust and powerful for the organization, its leaders, and the participants. The participants hear from the nonprofit leaders' voice and personality describe the case statement, and the nonprofit leaders hear from participants their authentic reactions to the case. This two-way information exchange is facilitated by an objective third party to help encourage constructive dissent and suggestions for case improvements. It is a highly organized listening session of several levels of complexity.

The process unfolds as follows. Determine the total number of people you would like to engage in the process. The ideal number of people at any one session is 15. Sessions of 30 or 40 are doable (I had one at 100 and that was a little *too* exciting). You lose energy in the room if you go below 10 people.

You also need to determine how many sessions to offer. Consider multiple options so the flexibility in your scheduling will encourage attendance by your best donors. Offer more than one meeting day and time to provide flexibility. When you send the invitation letter to attend the meeting, list all of the dates and times to show your willingness to meet the schedule of your target audience. For example, for one hospital that wanted to be inclusive but go through the process quickly, we sent out 250 invitations offering the following meeting options:

- Week one—Wednesday, 7 A.M. or 3 P.M.
- Week two—Thursday, 1 P.M. or 4:30 P.M.
- Week three—Tuesday, 6:30 A.M. or 7 P.M.

A return postcard let participants select any one of these six meeting times. The early-morning times were important to physicians who could attend prior to making their rounds at the hospital. We have found that late-afternoon times work well for business leaders who usually start their office day early and are willing to come to a late-afternoon event as long as they are done in time to go home for dinner. The early-evening time is helpful to people who can't get off work midafternoon but are willing to come after dinner.

Look at the geographical distribution of your donors and prospects. Take your meetings to the geographical focal points of your organization. If all your donors are in the metropolitan area, you can hold meetings downtown at your office location. However, at many large organizations donors can be spread out over the country (college alumni, for example) or across the state (organizations with satellite operations—hospital clinics or university campuses). If the prospective donor has to drive more than 30 minutes to attend your focus group meeting, consider offering optional geographical sites. For one organization in the Seattle, Washington, area we did four sessions, two in downtown Seattle, one in north Seattle, and one in Bellevue. For an organization in California with a statewide base of 3,000 potential donors, we held 22 focus group sessions throughout the state over a four-month time period.

Please note: Offer light refreshments at meetings, but avoid serving meals as this lengthens the session and makes it awkward to break into small discussion groups at the appropriate time during the meeting. You can offer meals if your volunteer host insists, but appreciate that meal meetings present logistical challenges (you should also extend the meeting from 90 minutes to 120 minutes to allow for food chaos).

Please don't forget to offer multiple options for meeting times and days. You are trying to engage busy, important people with many other calls on their time. For one organization, we offered six sets of three meeting options to prospective donors. At the last one, number 18, one of our best prospects showed up. At the end of the meeting as he was preparing to leave, I thanked him for coming and asked, "Just out of curiosity, why didn't you come to any of our earlier sessions?"

"Oh, I was interested, I was just busy," he answered. By the way, he eventually contributed $100,000 to that campaign.

To invite people to the participative focus group meetings, ask your volunteer hosts to sign invitation letters asking their friends to attend a special listening session on your organization's upcoming fundraising program. Summarize your case in one paragraph so invitees can begin to understand your impact on the community. Announce the multiple dates, times, and locations and ask people to send in the enclosed postcard to save volunteers from making too many follow-up phone calls. Add a postscript assuring recipients that this is a no-ask session—they can leave their checkbooks at home.

To ensure good attendance, each volunteer host should call the three to five people they know best on the invitation list. Staff should call everyone else to encourage attendance. Leaving messages is not considered a call. Leave one message and then keep calling daily until you talk to a real person.

So how does the meeting work? As you send out the invitations, race to get the case outline done. This compelling story of your organization, its impact on society, its challenges, and the solutions that philanthropy can provide needs to be improved internally before being shown to prospective donors (see Chapter 4, Make Your Case). Get the board of trustees to go through a focus group session of its own to learn the case and the process of participative focus groups and encourage their involvement as meeting hosts. You want the board members' feedback on the case and their understanding of the participative focus group process.

Please note: A narrative case can be developed for use in the market research study; however, we have found that for focus group meetings a case outline presented on PowerPoint through a computer projector or outline style on an overhead projector has more impact.

At the focus group meetings the organization's president will spend 20 to 25 minutes presenting the case outline to participants (absolutely no longer).

In your recruitment letter, promise focus group meetings of no more than 90 minutes (if you have a meal involved, you will need two-plus hours). Also, assure people of the no-ask policy in effect for these meetings. While it is a fundraising discussion, no requests for funding will be made. This is a listening event, not an asking event. This must be clear to participants or they will be shy about coming. In your phone follow-up calls to encourage attendance, make sure to reinforce the no-ask rule.

Here is a sample agenda:

SAMPLE AGENDA	
4:00 P.M.	Welcome, purpose of the meeting, and personal testimonial—Volunteer Host
4:05 P.M.	Second testimonial (if a cohost)—Volunteer Host How our meeting will work—Facilitator
4:10 P.M.	Case for support—CEO
4:30 P.M.	Complete personal feedback form—Facilitator
4:40 P.M.	Small group discussions (two to three people)—Everyone
5:10 P.M.	Report out to the entire group—Facilitator
5:25 P.M.	Closing remarks—CEO, Host(s)
5:30 P.M.	Meeting ends

You should hand out the meeting agenda to everyone with times listed to keep everyone on schedule (or you can print a large poster of the schedule and put it on an easel at the front of the room). Having everyone aware of the schedule will help to keep the case presenter on schedule.

The volunteer host (or cohosts) opens the meeting by welcoming everyone, stating the overall purpose of the meeting, and then giving a one-minute, from the heart, testimonial about why this organization is so important to the community. Having cohosts for each meeting is ideal as you have two invitation-letter signers, two networkers to build the invitation list, and two testimonial speakers to describe their commitment to the organization and their passion about the need for funding to solve the organization's challenges. Together, they can help to fire up the meeting and build a sense of excitement that will last the entire session.

The facilitator should then take the participants through the meeting agenda so everyone understands what will happen and the intent to complete the meeting on time. Stress this is a listening session. Empower and encourage questions, comments, and suggestions. Tell people there may not be time to address all of them and still keep on schedule. But capturing the questions is critical to the success of the fundraising process. You need to hear from your best customers, these potential donors attending the focus group meeting.

Ideally, the facilitator should be an outside-the-organization person who can listen objectively and who has gone through this process in a variety of settings (a consultant or a volunteer who has this professional skill set).

Where can you make mistakes? By overpresenting the case and using up all of the meeting time selling rather than listening. The magic of this process is capturing thoughtful information from each attendee on the feedback forms (which you will collect at the end of the evening—by having people write impressions down individually you gather one set of data and small group discussions expand this information for later reflection; for a sample set of feedback questions, see the Audition Externally section of Chapter 4, Make Your Case) and the energy released in the small group discussions. Things will happen at the beginning of the meeting to delay you—people will show up late, the host's testimonial may go long, and so on. The key is making sure you start the feedback form process 30 minutes after the start. This will put pressure on the case presenter (your president) to be succinct. The facilitator needs to be firm in enforcing the schedule. The schedule should be announced during the orientation (the facilitator has the prior approval of the presenter to close the presentation if it heads into overtime). Practice will be needed. It is a real challenge to describe your organization, its impact on the community, its challenges, and the solutions that money can buy in 20 minutes. But if you take longer you will lose the attention of your audience, your donors.

In facilitating more than 100 participative focus group processes over the years, I have made some modifications for fundraising purposes. One important one was use of the feedback form before the small group discussions so that individual reflections could be captured earlier in the process. I had always used a feedback form but came to realize it was important to capture individual impressions prior to mixing up reactions with group discussion. Quiet time is hard. It is important to monitor the clock to make sure you give a minimum of five minutes for personal reflection; ideally you want to provide 10 minutes. Watch the room. If more than a third of the people have finished the feedback form in seven minutes, it's time to move to small group discussions.

In setting up the small groups, ask that the executive director and fundraising staff not participate. They can go meet as a group in the hallway. Their participation will hamper free communication among the group participants. The organization staff should come back into the room as the small groups report out—not to answer questions or objections but to listen and observe.

As the small groups are forming, ask that each one pick a person to report out to the entire group. Encourage people to think of questions you will get on the fundraising trail. Draw out constructive dissent.

The ideal small group size is three. Based on room logistics going up to five people is okay. Do not let groups of larger size stay intact. You want everyone to participate; as soon as the group gets too large you have talkers and listeners. We want everyone to share equally in discussing and absorbing.

During the reporting-out session, a good facilitation technique is to ask one of the staff to capture highlights on a flipchart so the participants know you are listening. Ask each group to report out one idea—and only one so they don't steal all the great stuff from the other groups (if another group has this same idea captured, ask them to applaud to help show this is a common theme across groups). Rotate around until each group has completed its comments on a question. Then move to the next question on the feedback form.

Once the report-out group comments are completed, end this portion of the meeting by asking each participant in the room for a final comment or observation. This enables a few quiet people to comment. The focus group session concludes with closing remarks by the president and the host(s).

After each meeting and before the next one, debrief with the organization's presentation team members. What did they learn from observing the discussion? How can the case be presented with the same outline but with more emphasis on language and information donors need? It is so much fun to watch the growth process through four or six focus group meetings as the CEO listens to donors, changes his stump speech, and makes the case more compelling.

Each organizational participant should fill out a simple "lessons learned" process sheet at the end of your cycle of focus group meetings. All of the feedback forms should be collected and someone at the organization charged with keying in all of the information by question number (so we can see 45 participant responses to question number one, number two, etc.).

The facilitator should write up a summary report of findings and recommendations for case adjustments based on this collective listening process.

While essential to preparing for capital campaigns, the focus group techniques outlined here will work just as well for taking your annual fund program to the next level or to begin a concerted planned estate-giving effort.

Board and Strategic Planning Retreats

Board and strategic planning retreats can be powerful listening exercises for organizations. The whole purpose of a retreat is to carve out the extra time for people to reflect, interact, and listen to each other. Breakout discussions, social time over meals, and group processing all lend themselves to collective listening and organizational team building.

You may only need a formal strategic planning retreat every three years, but you should have a board retreat yearly for a day or two. Include board members, their spouses or partners, the senior administrative team, and program leaders from your organization so you add depth to the discussion from all areas. Invite emeritus board members to join you. They help to keep the heritage of the organization alive for new board and staff members.

A good facilitator will capture many items on flipcharts throughout the retreat. You should document information from these charts by typing them up and distributing them to all retreat participants after your session to show you have listened. Bring one of your support staff to the retreat as the formal listener. That person should be writing continuously throughout the meeting to capture general comments and specific reactions from key people in the room.

Strategic planning retreats do have some limits. They involve your leadership team and board—the insiders of your organization. To the extent your board represents key constituent groups, including major gift donors, you will have good community comments from the board. Some of the most challenging retreats result from the nonprofit's board not representing major segments of the donor universe. Board members without the personal resources to make significant gifts may want to steer the organization into car raffles and dinner auctions (transactional and social fundraising) rather than face-to-face philanthropic investment discussions needed for major gift fundraising.

LISTENING TO A SPECIFIC DONOR

With all of the collective listening exercises discussed, you can learn a great deal about the philanthropic marketplace in your community. But, you can't stop there. Nothing replaces the one-on-one, face-to-face, personal interview. Taking the time to get to know your donors, to probe their understanding of your organization, and to get a snapshot of their lives is invaluable. In the following sections a variety of listening settings are described. Each one can be used for the setting you are in and where you are in the life cycle of fundraising for your organization.

While I developed many of these techniques in my career as a professional consultant, all of them can be applied by organizational fundraising staff. Nothing here is brain surgery, just hard work.

Start by listening to your board members—why do they give their time and money to you? What motivates them? Then move to your top 10 donors for this year, then the top 25, and then the top 100 cumulative donors to your organization. For all of these interviews don't worry about raising money. If they offer it, take it, but that's not why you are there.

Just listen.

Discovery Calls

If you are new on the job, discovery calls are relatively easy. You are going out to meet your new organization's best donors to understand why they support it and to get acquainted. Be ready with your short organizational elevator speech. People will want to listen to you. Why did you take the new job? What does your university really do anyway? What happened to that building they donated to 10 years ago? Be ready for skeletons to come out of the closet. You may be the first person in a long time—if ever—to be willing to listen and learn.

If you are a longtimer in your job, you can still go out on a new listening expedition with your donors. Tell them you are establishing a new giving club or taking your existing one to a new level. Find out what donors want. Go out with a sense of openness and wonder—wonder what new volunteers you will detect and wonder what new ideas you will uncover.

On one foundation discovery call with a university president we found the foundation angry at our organization for a misstep of 10 years ago. The first 30 minutes of the meeting were an introduction to hell. But then, as the meeting progressed and the foundation staff found that we were listening, they asked about our new sense of direction. We ended up our two hours together with a ray of hope—if this was a new management team, if the organization now had its act together, then the foundation would be receptive to a major proposal. But, we had better have our act together and keep it together. We eventually secured two rounds of multimillion-dollar grants from this foundation. If the person has energy and history on an issue, let him talk it out. That may be the only thing that will happen at this first meeting—listening.

In another discovery call, this time on the phone, we had the spouse of the donor grabbing the phone to talk to us, as she had so many things to tell someone who was finally listening after 30 years of their major gift involvement with the organization.

If there has been no organized, institutional listening, you will get an earful on your first set of discussions. And, you will be thanked for listening.

As you hear things from the fundraiser's chair, you have to assure people they have been listened to but you cannot overpromise solutions. If you are working for a hospital and hear about a billing problem, you can't solve the problem. You can ask the person's permission to forward the specific complaint to the right department for follow-up. Would she like someone to get back to her? Or does he wish to remain anonymous with you reporting in some general information? Get specific information and enough details so someone on staff can fix the problem.

As fundraisers become good listeners, one of their big challenges is trying to bridge the communication gap between what they have heard on the outside and an organization's internal culture and attitude systems toward feedback from outsiders. An engaged board of directors helps to set the tone. Fundraisers need to be patient and do what they can to bring in senior administrators to collective listening sessions so they can hear directly from the community.

Requesting the Interview   If you know the donor well enough, calling on the phone to set up a discovery interview will work fine. For many people, however, it is more effective to send a preapproach letter (one page only) letting the person know why you will be calling and what the agenda will be. Then make the follow-up call restating points in the letter to request an appointment. You may find some donors resistant to seeing you, as other organizations (certainly not you) have taught them that a visit from a fundraiser means a gift request. Knowing this objection is out there, add a postscript to your letters assuring people this is not a gift request meeting. Restate your intentions to listen and not ask for money during your appointment-setting phone call—do this as early in the call as possible. Have some dates in the next few weeks when you are available ready to negotiate when you make your appointment-setting telephone call; be flexible as to day, time, and meeting place. Offer to meet them at their office, home, or a convenient coffeeshop (while you would love to go into their home or office to look for cues, some people may feel invaded or feel major housework is required for your visit; the meeting is more important than the setting).

Be prepared at the meeting to cover your agenda and your specific questions in no more than 30 minutes. But, be ready to stay for 90 minutes if the potential donor has a lot to say. When asked in the appointment-setting phone call how much time you need for the meeting, a good response is: "I need 15 to 20 minutes of your time, but you may want to budget some additional time for the meeting based on how much you have to tell me."

Thank-You Visits

Another way to systematically stay in touch with donors and to get to know them better is to establish a pattern of thank-you visits. For the donors you have personally solicited and have gotten to know, you can pick up the phone to say thank you as well as send a written acknowledgment letter. But, what do you do for donors who respond to your direct mailing by giving $1,000? Of course, you will send them a thank-you note. But is that enough? No.

Two significant reasons strongly recommend that you personally visit every new donor who gives at what you consider a major gift level for your organization (for some groups that is $1,000, for others $500, for others $10,000): 1) to cement the donor relationship for the future, and 2) to conduct personal prospect research to find out who this person is.

Research has shown the benchmark renewal rate for multiyear donors is about 80 percent; for first-year donors it is 50 percent. Many first-time donors are experimenting with an investment in your organization, or something appealed to them in that one request letter, or a friend encouraged the gift just at the right time. They made a gift. But they may not understand the organization well. Unless you do an extraordinary job of connecting with first-time donors you, too, will experience a 50 percent renewal rate. So the first reason for a personal thank-you visit is to make the personal connection and to fill in this new donor's knowledge gaps about your organization. Give the donor a coffee mug to provide a memento of your organization (remember *memento* means "mind jog"—you want donors to look at your coffee mug and think of your dental outreach clinics for the working poor and to enjoy the investment they have made in your organization).

Prospect research techniques have grown in sophistication over the last quarter-century from nothing to highly elaborate, web-based information searches. But, the best source of information is the simple request of a donor: "Tell me about yourself and your career." If people are not corporate officers or holders of at least 5 percent of one corporation's public stock, it is still very difficult to find out much information about them through Internet prospect research. The best way is to talk to the donor. Use the personal touch.

A true story: An organization was getting ready for a capital campaign. It had an aggressive annual funding need and was short staffed. A first-time $10,000 gift showed up in an envelope. Everyone cheered. The standard thank you was upgraded by including a personal note from the music director. To take a more personal approach to this mystery donor it was suggested that a representative of the organization conduct a personal thank-you visit. Maybe this person would be a good prospect for the upcoming capital campaign. A senior fundraiser made the personal visit and found out Martha was new to town. She came from a prominent East Coast real estate family with a tradition of philanthropy. She loved the arts. She came to town, and made seven $10,000 gifts to let the organizations know she had arrived. She would be glad to help in the future. She eventually made a $250,000 gift to the campaign. She had been signaling the community of her interest in supporting philanthropic causes. We're not sure how many of the groups tried to listen to her.

The thank-you visit with a coffee mug or some other simple thank-you item is a great time to get acquainted and to get to know the person and his reasons for investing in your organization. Put away your asking hat and put on your listening hat.

If you are a staff of one, you will only have time to thank your very top donors. If you have multiple staff members, you can divide the work up by gift level. For example, as a vice president of a university you can handle all donors of $10,000-plus gifts, the associate vice president can handle gifts of $2,500 to $9,999, and the annual fund director all $1,000 donors. At your weekly staff meetings you can share findings and listening techniques that work for each of you in different settings.

Make sure to document what you learned about donors' reasons for giving, their base of knowledge, and who they are so your organization can continue to build its warehouse of knowledge about its donors.

Philanthropic Market Research Studies

Fundraising-consulting firms have been conducting feasibility study interviews for decades. Whether the process is called a philanthropic market research study, a planning study, or a feasibility study, most of the techniques of the study have become standardized.

This book will not spend a great deal of time talking about these studies except to say "do it." The organized listening that is done in a short period of time by objective ears is critical to your eventual campaign success. Can you win a campaign without a study? Sure. Will you raise more money and raise it more quickly with a study? Absolutely.

Just remember to send your consultants to the best donors you have. Don't hold back names and work closely as teammates with your consultants for a mutually successful study process.

Listening Tools   A preapproach letter to a listening interview is critical. Soften the ground before you call to set up the appointment. Include with the letter something for your interviewee to react to—campaign case statement, annual fund case, gift-club description and benefits, or dinner auction plans for next year. This will provide a focal point for your discussion.

When you get ready to go on the interview, take extra copies of what you mailed. Most people will have read the materials in advance but not have a copy readily available; some people know they got it but did not read it; and others will claim never to have seen it. You also want to have a copy you can read as they react to their copy.

Create a list of standard questions that you plan to ask during the interview. By having the interview questionnaire handy you can listen intently without worrying about your next question. Here is a sample list of questions:

1. What do you do for a living? (Or ask, What *did* you do, if the person is retired.)

2. How did you get involved with our organization?

3. What other nonprofits are you involved with?

4. Where do we rate in your philanthropic causes?

5. What does your spouse or partner do?

6. Any children? What are they up to?

7. Tell me about a charitable gift that makes you smile. Why was it important to you?

8. What questions do you have about our organization?

9. Have you been on a site visit? What are your impressions?

10. Why do you think our organization needs gift support?

11. I'm all done with my questions; before I leave, do you have any advice for me?

Make copies of your questions and write on a blank questionnaire form. Or, use a notepad or bring a laptop and write notes as they talk. Please adapt these questions to fit your own style. There is no right or wrong order to the questions. Just remember that people love to talk about themselves and you are eager to gain this perspective.

Another useful tool for market research interviews is the reaction list. Take a highly selective list of your best 250 prospects for your interviewee to review and rate (including interviewees' names on the list is fine; it's always interesting to see what they say about themselves). Put the list in nonglare sheet protectors (along with your copy of the case document) both to protect the documents from the wear and tear of interview travel and to prevent people from writing on the donor list itself. Number the list so interviewees can call out the numbers, speeding up the time it takes to the review the list and the accuracy of capturing names (numbers are easier to write down than phonetic spellings). It is interesting to see how many names people react to and how many they list for us.

If you are in the prospective donor's home or office space, take note of details in the meeting room. Also record the person's style of dress, energy around your cause, and what steps (if any) you should take in the near future.

Whatever technique you use for taking notes during the meeting, sit down and fully write out a detailed contact report within 24 hours to institutionalize your meeting and burn the meeting into your long-term memory. If you are busy, take a tape recorder with you and talk into it on the way to your next appointment. Have your assistant transcribe your dictation and let you edit the final version.

Supplemental Interviews by Staff   Philanthropic market research study (feasibility study) interviews have traditionally been done exclusively by an outside consulting firm. This is still a best practice. Knowing the listener is an objective outsider who will maintain confidentiality sets the interviewee at ease and makes consultant interviews highly effective. However, you and your fundraising staff don't have to miss out on all of the fun of interviewing. The study interview process is a wonderful cultivation process. Develop a "B" list of potential donors that the consultants won't have the time (or you the budget) to interview, and you and your staff can go out to gather information to supplement the "A" list consultant interviews. Join the fun.

Turn over the interview reports to the consulting team so your information can enrich their data. Your organization will interact with two to three times as many people by combining consultant and staff interviewing as part of your study; this can help jump start your capital campaign. Be mindful that when using organizational staff to interview donors, you cannot assure the donors of confidentiality. But you can be careful that your team is going out in listening mode—in marketing mode—rather than sales mode.

What Is Different with Corporations and Foundations?

We noted in *Giving U.S.A.* data in Chapter 2, Donor Values, that individuals are responsible for 80 percent of the charitable contributions in the United States. Most of the listening techniques and tools in this chapter are focused on individuals. How do you modify listening techniques for corporate and foundation donors?

First of all, do your homework. We mentioned corporate and foundation donor values in Chapter 1, People Centered Fundraising. Be sensitive to their motivations for giving before going into an interview with them. Getting appointments with individuals is work; getting meetings at corporations and foundations is a professional challenge.

Listening to Corporations   Always remember that a corporation's reason for being is to make a profit. There can be no donations without profits. So make sure you are interviewing profitable companies. Do your research.

Which companies are giving donations to everyone else in town except you? Which ones are giving big dollars to other organizations but only a modest amount to you?

How do you get the interview? It won't be easy. Corporate people are busy. In doing your research develop a top corporate prospect list of 50 to 100 names. Then look in your local business magazine's book of lists to find names of the chief executive officers and members of their senior management teams. At your next board meeting, ask for some time to review the list on a projection screen to find out if your board members have any connections. A request from a board member or a member of your fundraising committee can open the door for your interview. Unless your organization is very prominent in the community, cold calling for interviews can be a waste of time. As you begin networking with companies, ask which ones have giving officers (company staff who handle all gift requests). Ideally you want an interview with the chief executive officer of the company and the giving officer.

Because time is so precious to corporate leaders, be ready for a whirlwind interview. Be able to tell your story and ask your questions in 15 minutes. If they want to talk longer, fine; but be organized and ready to listen quickly, ask pertinent follow-up questions, and leave. Also be prepared for the chief executive officer who has an unknown, deep connection to your cause and who may be ready for a break from business to talk about your more enlightening issues. Can you keep up your presentation for an hour? Be ready.

Because of busy schedules and the high volume of reading required of business leaders, assume they have not read the materials you sent with the letter requesting the interview. As you orient them to your organization at the beginning of the interview, point out the three highlights that you would like them to remember about your organization.

Some common questions for a corporate interview (for nondonors) are:

1. In reviewing our materials (which they probably have not done ahead of time, so bring an extra copy so they can review it with you), what strikes you about our organization compared with other nonprofits that you support in the community?

2. When your company makes gifts in the community, which investments are winners in your mind? Why?

3. How do we get on your annual giving list for $1,000 (or whatever your major gift club level is)?

4. Is our major gift request of $ appropriate? If not, what would be?

5. In what form should we make our request? Who should we send it to? When should we send it? What should we send in terms of support materials?

6. Does your company support nonprofit sponsorships out of your marketing budget?

7. Here are types of events we have . . . would any of them be a fit for you?

8. (After clearing this question before leaving your organization) Do you or anyone in the top management of your company have an interest in joining our board? Annual fund committee? Special-event steering committee?

9. Who else at your company should I talk to? May I use your name?

The last question is really important as many companies have a group process for making gift decisions. And, companies have turnover and promotions that keep fundraisers on their toes. To protect a corporate donor relationship long term, seek at least two, ideally three corporate connections within any one company.

Listening to Foundations Many foundation program officers are gracious with their time for informational interviews. Others have no patience for them. Many of the larger, staffed foundations have written guidelines, annual reports, and information listed on their web sites and/or in *The Foundation Directory*. It is critical that you read all of this information before attempting a request for interview meeting. If their guidelines say no meetings, respect their guidance (although you can try for a board-member-to-board-member contact if you have the right volunteer). Before you start serious foundation fundraising, read the entire 30-plus-page introduction of *The Foundation Directory*. It contains some good advice for all grant seekers. It helps sensitize you to the foundation world from their viewpoint.

Be ready to conduct the interview on the phone when you call to set up the appointment or within the next week if they give you a personal meeting time. Many times the program officers want to be helpful but are overworked in reviewing proposals already submitted to the foundation. They may be willing to provide information but will do so only on the phone when you call in for the appointment. So be ready for the interview when you call in— it could happen right then.

If you do get a face-to-face appointment, realize the program officer's job is to help organizations present winning proposals to the foundation trustees. If you are ready with a specific set of questions, the program officer will see that you have done your research, have a project or two in mind, and are ready to get down to brass tacks.

Some sample foundation questions are:

1. Do you know how our organization impacts the community?

2. I notice in your guidelines that you have funded X in the past. We do something in that area, would you consider project Y?

3. In reviewing the pattern of your grants, I see you give a range of A dollars to B dollars. We are considering asking for C dollars. Is that appropriate?

4. Your application process talks about this type of proposal. What else should I know about your application process?

5. When would be a good time to submit our proposal?

6. What common mistakes do you see when organizations apply to your foundation for funding?

7. What other advice would you give me?

Readiness Interviews after the Study

The market research study process is so robust as a data gathering and cultivation activity with potential donors that you should continue interviewing after your study is officially completed. Either your consultant and/or you and your staff can keep contacting people for discovery and "readiness" interviews for several months after the official end of the study. In a market research study your prospect list building will continue because of the names generated and qualified through the study interviews. You should end up with more names by the end of the study than when you started it. As your campaign effort gets started, be ready to experience the busy, but quiet, preparation phase of the campaign. Leadership needs to be recruited, insider family gifts solicited, and pacesetting gifts secured.

The first few months of any capital campaign are just like the beginning of any major endeavor—a lot of preparation work before the action. Volunteer leaders need to be recruited, campaign materials written, the campaign DVD produced, and the presentation books put together. This preparation phase of the campaign is an ideal time to do readiness interviews.

Almost all of the questions used in a market research study can be used in readiness interviews, except for the ones asking for feedback on whether a certain project should be in or out of the campaign project list. You need to be honest with people regarding whether the campaign is moving forward with the projects as described. You still need volunteers, project champions, and reactions to lists of names of other potential donors. You should feel a real urgency to get these readiness interviews completed in the first three to four months of the preparation phase of your campaign. As the campaign marketing materials solidify, it is harder to promise donors that their feedback on the case is meaningful input that will sharpen the case. At a certain point, you need to stop these interviews and move forward with cultivation events and specific action plans for each of your lead donors.

Listening during the Ask

We will talk more in future chapters about the role of the chief executive officer and volunteers in the fundraising process and about the ideal calling team of these two people plus the philanthropic fundraiser. The volunteer is the door opener who ideally has the preexisting personal relationship with the prospective donor and who provides the voice of enthusiasm for the organization and its need for project funding. The executive director relates the vision of the organization and is there to answer specific questions of the prospective donor. Ideally, the volunteer makes the gift request. So what is the fundraiser's job? To listen.

Sometimes, of course, the volunteer is not comfortable with the gift request or needs help at the last minute in asking for the gift. The fundraiser can certainly help here. But, the fundraiser's major job is to be the prompter of lines for the volunteer and the president, and most importantly to be the listener and observer. In solicitation training, everyone will be cautioned about overpresenting and the importance of listening to donor questions and comments. The fundraiser is the listening monitor, the person who may need to gently interrupt the presenters to draw out the prospective donor's reactions, opinions, and questions. The fundraiser should be taking notes throughout the ask to capture questions that need follow-up later and objections that may not have been fully addressed. The fundraiser should also watch the donor's facial expressions and body language.

After solicitation training at a child services organization, the executive director commented that this listener role for the fundraiser in the ask is very similar to the observer role in a crisis intervention team. If a teenager threatens suicide in the middle of the night and the parents call in an intervention team, three people usually arrive. Two members are active in the intervention and the third person acts as the observer and recorder. In order for the two active team members to continually improve their crisis management process, they want a listener along to capture the situation for later debriefing and to occasionally remind the two active members of a way to make the solution process go more smoothly.

LISTEN FOR GIFTING NOISES

Remember, through deep listening you have a wonderful way of connecting with donors, to build an authentic relationship, and to develop a winning gift for the donor, yourself, and your organization.

Be sensitive to listening for "gifting noises"—an indication that a donor is ahead of you in the cultivation process and is more ready to give than you are to ask. Let the donor lead the way.

Here are some examples of gifting noises:

- "My college sends me planned giving materials. Is an estate gift something your organization can handle?"
- "I don't think I can make the *lead* gift."
- "Is your organization interested in challenge gifts?"
- "I'm seeking a naming opportunity for my parents who both passed away recently."
- "Your organization fits our foundation guidelines well. Don't be too aggressive with your first request as we are just getting to know you."

- "Our company is very interested in disadvantaged youth. Your organization seems to be making a big difference in this area."
- "Getting a first gift from our company is really hard."
- "I just gave my alma mater a million-dollar gift. It was a lot of fun."

Not all of these may be signals for immediate action and a request. But, they are indicators of a willingness to get closer to your organization, a history of giving and/or an intent to learn more about charitable giving, a desire to start negotiating a potential gift, and a potential mutually beneficial relationship—a winning gift. Use these openings for follow-up discussions later in the same meeting in which the person made the comment if possible. Or, more realistically, refer to them in the next meeting you have together. Use the prospective donor's comment to extend the conversation. "At our last meeting, what did you mean when you said . . . ?"

When You're Invited to Listen

Sometimes donors call you up and ask for a meeting. They might be making gifting noises by doing that. So what should you do? Slow down and listen first. Find out why they are calling. What are their needs? What is their agenda? Yes, you always need money and here is someone ready to offer it, but don't blow the deal by being too aggressive; listen first.

Comply with the request for a meeting. Bring your notepad and ask how you can help. The donor may have a concern over a recent thank-you note or may want your advice on another charity project she is working on. No matter what the reason, it is wonderful to have a donor seeking your input. Be ready for the prospect to move into a gift discussion but don't jump to conclusions. Hear the donor out. Take good notes. Restate what you have heard. Try to find out if the donor wants advice or just to talk. Either way is fine, but let the donor communicate first.

Sometimes you will only get partway through the discussion and questions. The donor may start a gift discussion, get some information from you, and then stop. The meeting is over. Hopefully another meeting will follow as the donor thinks through your responses and their implications on the gift-making decision process.

George was nearing 80 and in frail health, but he had a razor sharp mind. He had supported four organizations in the community regularly and at a significant annual level. He called the four organizations and requested meetings. Here is what happened. The first two organizations lost the message or it did not get to the right person. Nobody responded; nothing happened. The next organization met with him, learned he was trying to put his estate in order, and requested he consider a $100,000 bequest. He agreed that the organization would get the money upon his death. The last organization wanted to ask him for $250,000, but upon advice of fundraising counsel decided to have a lunch meeting and listen to him first to see what he was thinking. What did he have in mind? When the organization asked why he had called and what his plans were, he indicated that he knew he was dying. He had had a full life so he was at peace, but now it was time to get his estate in order. He strongly believed in this organization and wanted to strengthen it long term. What did that mean to him? He wanted to give them a million-dollar challenge grant restricted to endowment. With the matching funds, this would give the organization a $2 million endowment, which would provide $100,000 every year—his legacy to the organization. And, he wanted the challenge met quickly after his death. George and the organization agreed that within five years of the announcement of his estate gift the organization would raise the matching one million dollars or his gift would go to the local community foundation (George had wanted the matching funds raised in two years, but the organization reminded him it still had annual fundraising to do and that a million dollars from other donors for endowment was a big challenge for this relatively modest organization). George did pass away a year later and the endowment challenge was announced. The rest of the story? I don't know the details except to say this organization is still active in pursuing its mission 10 years after the gift.

The power of deep listening is wonderful. Take some time and slow down to listen and understand what donors are trying to accomplish through their giving. They're telling you what the winning proposition is if you listen deep enough.

APPLY WHAT YOU'VE LEARNED

Here are some ideas you can use to implement the concepts in this Chapter. Feel free to adapt them to fit your needs.

1. *Program feedback.* Find one program you want feedback on from your donors. Pick a modest program if you want a low-risk experiment or a select a big one so it's worth spending your time on this listening exercise. You can select from an annual fund gift club, your annual ball, golf tournament, recent direct mailing, or newsletter.

    Spend the next month using the one-a-day plan of seeing at least one donor every working day to discuss this program. Your job is to capture 20 voices giving you advice on how to make this program more people friendly and more responsive to what your donors are expecting from you and your organization.

    When setting up the appointments for these meetings tell the donor your objective of listening and learning and that the no-ask rule is in effect for this meeting.

    Write up each contact report in two sections: (1) feedback on the project and (2) observations about the donor's thinking style, perceptions, and opinions of your organization.

    Gather all of the project feedback data into one document. What did you hear? What changes in the program do your customers want? What did you learn about listening? How did it feel to follow the one-a-day listening plan?

2. *Top-25 listening.* Research the top 25 cumulative donors in the history of your organization. Ask them to tell you their sense of the history of the organization, how they started giving, and how you should relate the heritage of your organization in your case statement and printed materials. Complete the interviews within 60 days and write a summary report for yourself, your staff, and/or your boss.

3. *Board thank-you calls.* Select a level of major giving in your organization and ask that board members make three thank-you calls to donors. Encourage them to listen and to just say thanks. Debrief each board member so you can write down what they heard on each call. Present a summary report at your next board meeting and ask board members to reflect on what they heard on the phone.

NOTES

1. Stephan Schiffman, *The 25 Sales Habits of Highly Successful Salespeople* (Holbrook, MA: Bob Adams, Inc., 1994), 125, 57–59.

2. Carolyn B. Thompson, *Interviewing Techniques for Managers* (New York: McGraw-Hill, 2002), 131–132.

3. Ibid., 140.

4. Stephen R. Covey, *The 8th Habit: From Effectiveness to Greatness* (New York: Free Press, 2004).

5. Ibid., 191–192.

6. Rafael Aguayo, *Dr. Deming: The American Who Taught the Japanese about Quality* (New York: A Fireside Book, Simon & Schuster, 1990).

7. Rebecca Z. Shafir, *The Zen of Listening: Mindful Communication in the Age of Distraction* (Wheaton, IL: Quest Books Theosophical Publishing House, 2000), 90–91.

8. Ibid., 206.

9. Ibid., 122–134.

10. Larry Barker, Ph.D. and Kitty Watson, Ph.D., *Listen Up: At Home, at Work, in Relationships: How to Harness the Power of Effective Listening* (New York: St. Martin's Griffin, 2000), 24–31.

11. Matt Oechsli, *The Art of Selling to the Affluent* (New York: John Wiley & Sons, 2005), 43, 85, 115.

12. Madelyn Burley-Allen, *Listening: The Forgotten Skill*, Second Edition (New York: John Wiley & Sons, 1995), 120–123.

13. Richard A. Krueger, *Focus Groups: A Practical Guide for Applied Research,* Second Edition (Thousand Oaks: Sage Publications, 1994).

Seek Winning Gifts for Your Organization

A ll of the philosophy and good intentions of a people centered, winning-gifts approach to philanthropic fundraising sounds nice, even enlightened. But, will it help you to raise money? Will it result in successful annual fund drives and capital campaigns that achieve their goals? In Part II of this book, we will take the background information about donor values and listening presented in Part I, A Winning Gift for Your Donor, and combine it with fundraising techniques (traditional and innovative) to help you meet your fundraising goals.

Chapter 4, Make Your Case, will present ideas on how to create a compelling case statement for your organization—what stories can you use to motivate donors to contribute money? Chapter 5, The Win-Win Ask, examines roles for members of the ideal ask team (volunteer, executive director, and fundraiser) along with steps to prepare for the ask, make the ask, and follow up the gift request in order to close the deal. Chapter 6, After Winning the Gift, focuses on what happens after the gift decision—thank-you systems, donor-recognition programs, and stewardship to provide accountability back to donors to prove your organization is a good steward of donated funds.

Before moving to these specific asking tools and tactics for requesting winning gifts, two other important sets of concepts will be introduced right now:

1. How to bring together the story of your cause (the case statement), the right people (volunteers and staff), in the right setting to reach a point of synergistic success, a tipping point, where your fundraising program takes off and achieves success

2. Techniques for influencing donors to make gifts to your institutions that are proven not only in the fundraising world but also in society in general

One of the exciting aspects of philanthropic fundraising is taking our field's pragmatic approach to raising dollars and finding outside-the-field resources that reaffirm and enlighten our practices. Until recently, nobody went to school to be a philanthropic fundraiser; our profession developed in the school of hard knocks. Behavioral and social-science research has just begun studying philanthropic motives and techniques. We still need to beg, borrow, and steal research study information from the social sciences and psychology to help inform fundraising.

Two such sources will be reviewed here in Part II—Malcolm Gladwell's *The Tipping Point*[1] and Robert Cialdini's *Ethical Influence.*[2] They are must-reads for fundraising professionals. They both are well written, reinforce pragmatic approaches we have taken in fundraising over the decades, and show us how we could be more effective in the future.

For many years, we have known that the winning elements of a successful capital campaign are a strong and urgent case for support, visionary institutional leaders, committed volunteers with respect and relationships in the community, hardworking fundraising staff, small-group cultivation events, and face-to-face asking. *The Tipping Point* talks about how societal trends gain momentum through many of these same elements.

In a parallel way, we as philanthropic fundraisers have developed a common set of ethical practices to help raise money for our nonprofits. Robert Cialdini, a psychologist, has studied influence from an academic viewpoint of rigorous behavioral research. His work has nothing to do with fundraising and yet the principles he has developed around ethical influence make sense in a philanthropic fundraising setting.

After reviewing these two important sources of outside-the-box thinking and research, we'll look at how to secure winning gifts for your organization in Chapters 4 through 6.

GLADWELL—*THE TIPPING POINT*

Throughout this book, sources for fundraising ideas will be mentioned and best practice ideas presented and interpreted. To keep expanding philanthropic fundraising's field of knowledge, I continuously hunt for articles, books, and research totally unrelated to fundraising that can improve our thought processes and practices. As I wander the universe of interesting and wonderful people who volunteer their time for nonprofits, common chords are struck and conversations started that range far beyond the initial scope of our fundraising meeting. One such new friend was Stephen in the San Francisco Bay Area. After meeting with him and discussing a broad range of topics in our focused interview for the client, he sent me a follow-up e-mail suggesting that I read a great new book. It was all about my business of fundraising, even though it wasn't a fundraising book. In getting ready for our next meeting we touched base and he asked how I liked the new book—the airport bookstore helped me start reading on the plane on the way to my next appointment with him. Stephen was right. The new book is all about fundraising, in an indirect way. It was a real eye opener.

Why it this book so important? To take a modest program and take it to the next level or to take a long-term annual fundraising program and help the organization to succeed at a major capital campaign takes a marshaling of forces, a synergy that helps tip the donor marketplace to embrace the nonprofit's mission, its vision for the future, and its need for funding to meet community needs.

Each of Gladwell's three major ideas in *The Tipping Point* will be reviewed here and then referenced throughout this book as they apply to philanthropic fundraising. Exhibit II.1 is a summary slide that you can use to describe these points in meetings with your staff and volunteers.

The Law of the Few

In philanthropic fundraising, we have always known that a small core group of people can make a big difference. The nonprofit's board of directors (trustees) can number 15 to 50, may only meet quarterly for a couple of hours, and yet can run organizations that save hundreds of lives yearly in a hospital, educate thousands of students for an entire lifetime at a university, and have numerous other profound impacts on society.

The Tipping Point
Malcolm Gladwell

1. The Law of the Few
   - Mavens–people who accumulate knowledge
   - Connectors–know lots of people and
     spread the message
   - Salespeople–skills to persuade

2. The Stickiness Factor
   - A message with a memorable impact

3. The Power of Context
   - The setting and small factors can make big difference

EXHIBIT II.I   THE TIPPING POINT

As you form a capital campaign or annual fund volunteer committee, seek the one or two people to chair the campaign that have the leadership and vision to raise the $1 million required for the annual fund, the $5 million for the new science building, or the $100 million for the new hospital wing. Once your leaders are in place, seek the 10 to 20 people to join the campaign chairs to lead divisions of the campaign to success.

We have all experienced that one inspired volunteer who is not afraid to ask for money, has the time to devote to the cause, and is willing to work with other volunteers to win the campaign. How can only a handful of people perform all of the miracles needed for a major fundraising campaign to succeed?

The answer is, *The Tipping Point*'s The Law of the Few.

Champions Champions of your nonprofit organization (*mavens,* in Gladwell's terminology) are people who take the lead in thinking through an organization's issues. They are the early visionaries who see the future of the organization and who are the true believers. Nonprofit organizations tend to have two types of champions: (1) those that are on staff and are the natural leaders (e.g., the visionary university president, the inspired cancer

GLADWELL—*THE TIPPING POINT*   131

researcher, or the star faculty member), and (2) board members and other volunteers who really "get" the organization and who seek change and new paths for the future (sometimes the volunteers who push for change even when the staff is comfortable with the status quo).

These idea leaders become the mavens for elements of the strategic plan, they become the advocates of endowed funds or they serve on the building committee to ensure it meets the needs of the organization now and in the future.

These champions and early promoters may not be great fundraisers or storytellers of the ideas but they are the people with the detailed knowledge who are inspired by the concepts of the plan. For example, at one college seeking a new library, the president wanted a state-of-the-art digital learning center and the librarian wanted dramatically expanded space for library books and journals and online databases to help faculty and students. Both were mavens for the project—the president articulate and able to succinctly state his vision and the librarian passionate, with every detail on all of the elements needed for a first-rate modern library, both real assets in making sure that solid planning for the library would take place. There was also the volunteer champion who agreed to chair the campaign because he believed in the importance of the library for the community, his children, and his future grandchildren. All three are champions and mavens for the cause.

Connectors   Many people who aren't the early champions for the cause (mavens) still may be willing to volunteer as *connectors*, to help open doors for your organization to people with money to donate. The connectors may know the message only in general terms, but they know a lot of people and can help spread your message to their vast network. Having their help is essential to your cause. It would be great for them to ask for gifts, but because of their networking skills you may not care if they ask. They are the "people magnets" of your cause.

In our college library example, another volunteer offered to help. He was frankly bored by the discussions of the digital library versus traditional library. He accepted the president's vision that a new library was needed. He wanted to get on with the list work. Who could he visit to tell the story? Who should be invited to the groundbreaking to get the story out? He was willing to open doors and use his connections in the community to help the university. His story of the library was done in two to three minutes (while the president could talk for 30 minutes and the librarian for three days . . . just kidding). This volunteer's real asset was his ability to connect with many of his colleagues in the real estate development and business world and to carry a simple, impactful message to them from a credible source.

On philanthropic market research study interviews, we always ask people to react to the case statement (the story of the organization, its impact on the community, its plans for the future, and its proposal for fundraising). On one interview a gentleman said that, yes, he had glanced at the case statement document, knew all about the college, and was in favor of the campaign—one minute and we were done with the case part of the interview. He asked if we had a list of names to review (he obviously had done an interview like this before) and proceeded to spend the next hour talking about all of the people who would be good to talk to and why. He was a classic connector. The good news? He agreed to serve on the campaign committee to help open doors for the campaign.

One of the biggest mistakes you can make with your volunteers is insisting that all of them be gift askers. It is easier to distinguish between the roles of the connector and the salesperson. Ideally you want the volunteers to play all three roles, but the connector may be the most important role a volunteer can play—they open the doors to money. In fact, when you sit down and really probe your board members' feelings about fundraising, you will find that you have three to four times the number of connectors as salespeople.

Salespeople   For fundraising to be successful, you have to ask for the order; you need to solicit the gift, and close the deal. This book will cover many philosophies, strategies, and tactics for the ask. Nonprofits generally have two types of *salespeople*: internal and external.

The philanthropic fundraiser, the chief philanthropy officer (CPO), of your nonprofit is, of course, the first-line internal salesperson. In private higher education, the president is hired with the expectation that 50 percent or more of his time will be spent fundraising. The highly successful college presidents and other nonprofit executive directors are fearless, relentless (but in a nice way) askers and salespeople. Other nonprofit leaders are apprehensive about asking and fall back to the maven role relying upon the fundraising volunteer or staff fundraiser to be the asker. That is fine. We will cover more on the ideal ask team in Chapter 5, The Win-Win Ask.

Some large organizations can do all of their fundraising with internal salespeople—the president, the chief philanthropy officer, major gift officers, and annual fund staff. Most nonprofits rely upon a combination of internal salespeople and external ones—volunteers. Again, don't assume every board member is a salesperson. They all need to play a role in fundraising. But the reality is a few will be excellent mavens and champions, most will be connectors, and only a couple will be comfortable selling. That's okay. One great fundraising volunteer can make an entire capital campaign succeed or help an annual fund to reach its goal ahead of schedule. Hopefully, over time other volunteers will watch the ace salesperson and pick up tips that will expand the sales talent pool.

You can develop salespeople through training and by removing some of the ask-reluctance barriers that will be discussed in Chapter 5, The Win-Win Ask.

The Stickiness Factor

The case statement, the story of your organization's heritage, future vision, and financial needs, is a message to potential donors. For years, I have advocated for an in-depth case development process to produce a powerful, compelling message to help motivate volunteers and inspire donors. You need to be the seeker of stickiness factors to strengthen your case. In Chapter 4, Make Your Case, we will look at ways to develop and test your case for support to create this sticky message critical to your success.

Gladwell talks about the second key factor of *The Tipping Point*—the stickiness factor of the memorable message. He relates the history of how *Sesame Street* was developed 30 years ago by testing shows with kids to see how easily they could be distracted—how sticky each episode was. They found out during this early testing that having only puppets on the show wasn't working enough. When they combined the puppets with real people, the show became sticky and the kids paid attention. It is a fascinating story and relates in many ways as we try to get our prospective donors to attend to the story of our organization, its benefits to the community, the challenges it is having, and the need for financial investments (gifts).

For philanthropic fundraisers remember the sticky part of this concept. You want a professional brochure, but don't go for the superslick brochure. Make your materials organic with quotes, charts, pictures, and stories that show your organization's impact. Pick funky over elegant if that helps donors remember your case. Think of your case statement like a strong piece of Velcro™—relatively smooth to the touch but if you look closely you see a series of small hooks that really grab on and hold fast.

In Chapter 4, Make Your Case, we will look at techniques for building a sticky, memorable case statement for your organization, for your annual fund, for your capital campaign, for your planned estate-giving and endowment program.

The Power of Context

In philanthropic fundraising, we have known about the principle of contextual power for a long time. The right cultivation meeting with a significant group of peers usually has more storytelling impact than just a one-on-one meeting. The cultivation event in the museum's dinosaur hall or the tour of the surgery suite by the open-heart surgeon is always more interesting than a dinner in a restaurant. In our world, you can talk to someone one-on-one to review a list of prospective donors—you get information and it works fine. You have this same discussion with eight to ten people in the room and the synergy of the group creates 20 times the information. It is the power of context.

Having a student talk about the impact of her scholarship is more powerful than you telling the story on her behalf. The power of the group, the context of the session, the personal testimonials by key donors and leaders all create a power and energy that you can never replicate in a different setting.

Think through how you are delivering the sticky message of your organization and its fundraising needs—how can you boost the impact of the message through the power of context?

Here's an example: A public radio and television station needed a new broadcast center. Of course, potential donors were aware of National Public Radio (NPR) and the Public Broadcasting System (PBS) programs, and many were members of the public broadcasting entity. But, our market research indicated that these donors had no idea there was a local organization sending out the signals, that there was a broadcast studio, and why a local organization was important. They didn't know who operated the local station and why they should give to it. This presented a big challenge. We started putting together a case statement, a sticky message, but decided we needed the power of context to bring the message home. We hosted 20 cultivation events at the old, run-down studio. The same list of 500 potential donors was invited quarterly to one of three upcoming monthly studio tours and campaign briefing meetings. We assured donors they would not be asked for a gift. The purpose of the event was to tell the donors the public broadcasting station's story. We had the prominent community leaders who had volunteered to lead the capital campaign tell why they were involved. We had small group tours of the old broadcast center so donors could see firsthand how antiquated it was. We showed a video at dinner describing the impact of the station on the city and the state and described the vision for the new broadcast center. And that was it . . . no ask . . . just sticky messaging in the context of the old run-down studio.

The rest of the story: The $12 million campaign goal was exceeded with $15 million raised. The campaign was more about finding the sticky message, using our connectors to invite people to hear the message, and using the power of context to drive the message home. And yes, we needed a few salespeople to close the deals to raise the money.

Implications for Philanthropic Fundraising

Read *The Tipping Point* to glean additional ideas that you can use. It is clear that nonprofit fundraisers intuitively understand many of Gladwell's concepts. By reading the book you will be more consciously aware of them and therefore you will be able to apply them even more effectively in your fundraising program.

The use of volunteers in fundraising can be refined, as it is clear not everyone will be a salesperson and that the social connecting networks of board members are critically important to reaching out to new donor audiences (therefore, a larger board is better). A few people on your board and fundraising campaigns can make a big difference, especially when they are staffed for success.

The importance of your case statement, your sticky message, is clear. Look for ways to make your case memorable (more to come in Chapter 4, Make Your Case).

And finally, the context of presenting your story is reaffirmed. Site visits, personal meetings with students or grateful patients, home cultivation events, will all make a difference in helping to tip your organization toward fundraising success.

CIALDINI—ETHICAL INFLUENCE

Another book with indirect, yet profound insights into philanthropic fundraising is Robert Cialdini's *Influence*.

Top-notch philanthropic fundraisers have good people skills and can sell. They probably could go into any type of high-end sales work like insurance or the stock market and make more money than working for nonprofit organizations. But fundraisers have a mission drive, an interest in helping society through their nonprofit organizations that binds them to "the cause." In a similar fashion, board members and other fundraising volunteers have many calls on their time and energy. They don't need to work for free raising money for nonprofit organizations. They are mission driven and community-service oriented.

Therefore, when it comes time to use sales techniques to raise money, using ethical practices matches the high purposes of the nonprofit, service orientation of volunteers and philanthropic fundraisers. This is why major fundraising associations created a Donor Bill of Rights, a code of ethics for individual philanthropic fundraisers through the Association of Fundraising Professionals (AFP), a code of ethics for grantwriters (www.grantprofessionals.org), and a code of ethics for consulting firms to nonprofits through the Giving Institute, the trade association of nonprofit consulting firms. Please see Appendix C for the Donor Bill of Rights and Appendix D for the AFP ethical code or check out the AFP web site at www.afpnet.org, "Ethics."

As a psychologist, Dr. Robert Cialdini was interested in doing in-depth, academic research on influence in sales situations in American society. What made some practices ethical and others unethical? What was the basis and distinction between these two sets of somewhat vague behaviors? In addition to setting up traditional psychological testing, he did on-the-job analysis by training and working as a car salesman. Why do they have such a terrible reputation for unethical practices? What distinguishes the many ethical car dealers from the bad apples?

1. Reciprocation—be the first to give.
2. Scarcity—unique features, exclusive information.
3. Authority—show knowing, admit weakness first.
4. Commitments—from public positions (small and build).
5. Liking—make friends to influence people.
6. Consensus—unleash people power by showing responses of many others, testimonials of others.

We'll look at each of his principles to see how they fit in a context of philanthropic fundraising. Authenticity may be the hallmark of all of these ethical influence techniques. Each technique can be false and unethical if it is being used inappropriately. You have to look at all six techniques to see which fit your organization at the right time and the right place. They are food for thought, not hard-and-fast rules that you have to implement to be successful.

#1 Reciprocation—Be the First to Give

Doing favors for people before asking anything of them builds a sense of responsibility to reciprocate, to respond back positively. Cialdini thinks this is an ingrained human capacity that builds a sense of community and mutual help.

How have we used this principle in fundraising? In a couple of areas: For years direct-mail fundraisers have sent a request-for-funding letter along with a gift of a calendar or address labels. Both items are useful and help build a sense of owing the charity something in return. You want to reciprocate so you send in a $25 gift to the charity. It worked. The 50-cent investment in the calendar resulted in a $25 donation. Direct-mail responses are higher if a small, token gift is enclosed in the request letter.

For major gift fundraising, a less overt technique has been the practice of inviting donors to a free lunch to learn about the organization. At the end of the meeting the organization calls for donations. You don't have to make a gift in response to your free meal and heart-rending luncheon stories (the power of context), but the request is hard to turn down. You want to reciprocate for the organization's free meal and more importantly for the wonderful services it has been providing to the community.

You can ethically apply this technique in many ways to help build influence with your donors—the free estate-planning seminar, the free healthy-living brochure from your local hospital, the investment tips your broker sends to you quarterly—all are subtle ways of influencing you by offering a favor first.

#2 Scarcity—Unique Features, Exclusive Information

One of the consistent messages to all nonprofits in positioning their organization with donors is to share your unique aspects. Why are you different from other organizations in the community? Why should a person give to your organization versus the United Way? For many corporate and foundation donors this discussion is critical. Are there 10 other organizations just as worthy and just the same as yours? If so, then, if they give to you, they should give to all of them. You need to provide them some ammunition as to why you are so special—why giving to you does *not* set a precedent for other organizations to approach them.

The exclusive information part of this principle can be a lot of fun. Most organizations have insights that fascinate donors. For example, one organization had more than 100 years of experience in adoptions and working with troubled youth. At their cultivation events they shared information that had been developed during this history of practical work with families and children. This inside information was fascinating to the donors; they felt like more knowledgeable citizens of the state.

Hospitals have a wonderful advantage using this fascination with inside information. Sure you can read about the latest in cardiac care, but the context of hearing a nationally recognized cardiologist provide you with the latest research findings on stents and noninvasive cardiology procedures is so exclusive, so special, that you will never forget the experience of that evening's presentation.

Scarcity can also relate to attendance restrictions—only eight people can attend our upcoming behind-the-scenes tour of the art museum's collections in storage. Hurry, don't miss this once-in-a-lifetime opportunity.

#3 Authority—Show Knowing, Admit Weakness First

If you are a recognized authority, people listen to you more intently; they take your information as solid and reputable. If you are a college, identify some of your most prominent faculty members who are national or international authorities in their field. Quote them in your publications. Show them off at your cultivation events. Their presence gives your entire organization credibility.

Admitting weakness may seem like a strange thing for an authority to do. But, it makes sense. If you are an authority, you are secure enough to admit what you don't know. This gives more credibility to your other statements. Only rookies tell people they know everything. Real experts acknowledge the limits of their knowledge.

For example, in writing grants always look for an opportunity or two to admit that your organization still has some weaknesses that need addressing. That's why you need the foundation's assistance. Your project plan is well thought out but only by implementing the program will you be able to work out the questions that need to be answered. Be honest and direct in telling the story of your organization to the grant-making organization. Having learned of your honesty in sharing your weaknesses, the grant reviewer will believe more of the rest of your grant proposal. Your honesty is refreshing and builds trust.

The computer software industry came up with an interesting saying many years ago. *If you have a bug in the software and can't fix it, then feature it.* Nonprofits should be honest with themselves about their weaknesses and admit them to potential donors. One of the reasons donors have money to give away is that they are so smart. For example: If you are raising money for the state university in your town, it is fine to talk about your wonderful local students, some of your star faculty, but also admit that in the latest *U.S. News & World Report* rankings you came out at the top of tier III institutions and that fundraising is needed to get you into tier II. Some of your programs are at tier II now and should be taken to tier I for the benefit of the state's economy.

#4 Commitments—From Public Positions (Small and Build)

Public testimonials from not-yet donors are a classic fundraising technique. Asking your key volunteers to make a personal testimonial at a cultivation event inspires other donors who respect the speaker. The testimonial also works wonders on the person asked to make it. By coming forward in public to share his enthusiasm for the cause, he is selling himself as well as the audience. This is such a powerful double-impact way to influence the speaker and the audience that you should seek to use it at every board meeting, every cultivation event, and every committee meeting. Ask your best donors to make public testimonials at your cultivation events. Even a 30-second statement of why they believe in you makes them more committed to you. Many times they haven't articulated this commitment to themselves, so for them to hear themselves telling others in public is powerful and authentic.

The traditional fundraising technique of getting donors to start their giving with a small donation to help the annual fund, then increasing their gift to a midrange gift, and therefore gradually building their allegiance to your organization works. Over time, the person often increases his support to a major annual gift, then a capital gift, and then an estate gift.

This starting-small-and-build path is well-established fundraising. Now, we have found that you can speed up this process and start with a larger commitment as a first gift, but Cialdini's principle still works for many people.

#5 Liking—Make Friends to Influence People

Being likable is a natural influence technique that all of us use every day. If people like us, we have a better chance of convincing them about what we need. This is a common way to influence people. This is one reason that philanthropic fundraisers are hired for their people skills, their likeability, and their sociability.

Part of being liked involves good listening habits (please revisit Chapter 3, Listen). Listening for common interests, backgrounds, and activities can help build a sense of friendship and commonality, which are at the heart of relationship building.

In liking someone you also have to get past their public position, private wealth, and potential to you and your organization as a major donor. First, be a friend.

#6 Consensus—Unleash People Power by Showing Responses of Others

Showing the long list of donors to your organization in your concert program book or annual report is a common fundraising technique. This is another intuitive influencing technique that nonprofits have been using for decades. This is why nonprofit organizations constantly show lists of their donors on donor walls, honor rolls of donors, commemorative plaques, and so on. Sure, it is to thank the donors for giving, but more important, it is to show the not-yet donors the power of the people who believe, the responses of others.

Earlier we talked about the power of the testimonial speech on the speaker. In the consensus influence factor, we see the double power of the testimonial: It also impacts people who are not yet committed. If Joe is a friend and a respected person and he is speaking for your organization, then I need to get with the program and join him. In seeing my friends' names on the donor list I start to feel bad that I am not on board yet.

Throughout this book, we will speak to the importance of involving volunteers in your fundraising program. One can see in Cialdini's ethical influence factors several places where the power of the volunteer can really help your fundraising program. Have volunteers vouch for the authority of your president or a physician on your medical staff. They show the power of others and through their public statements deepen their own sense of commitment to your organization.

SUMMARY

Hopefully, you will find these two books to be useful in providing you with tools to train yourself, your staff, and your fundraising volunteers on how to seek philanthropic gifts. I encourage you to buy them and read them in depth.

In the next three chapters, you will see how the concepts in Part II are used to build your case for support (your sticky message), how to make the ask using the ideal team (the law of the few), and how ethical principles can guide your philanthropic fundraising in order to win gifts for your organization. The inherent power of the concepts of *The Tipping Point* and, *Influence* are their ability to prepare you, your volunteers, and your organization for a successful gift request in Step #6 of the Six I's.

■ NOTES

1. Malcolm Gladwell, *The Tipping Point: How Little Things Can Make a Big Difference* (New York: Little, Brown, 2000, 2002).
2. Robert B. Cialdini, *Influence: Science and Practice*, Fourth Edition (Boston: Allyn and Bacon, 2001).

CHAPTER 4

Make Your Case

*I don't like fundraising, but if the cause is important, I can ask any
amount of money. I'm not asking for me, I'm asking for the cause.*

The case statement (case for support) is the story of your organization
and its need for funding. One assumes the concept of the case
statement comes from lawyers (don't all good things? Ha-ha). Lawyers make
their legal case in court to a judge and jury. They win or lose their case based
on compelling arguments, on exhibits, evidence, diagrams, and stories—
anything that helps convince a jury.

Making the case for your organization to a donor is very similar. You
want gifts from donors by convincing them that their gift will make an
impact in the world, that your organization is worthy of a financial
investment, and that your institution really needs the money. In a winning-
gifts approach you want the case statement to be so strong and memorable
that making a gift in response is obvious. You also need to make your case
clear, concise, concrete, and understandable. For many organizations this
may be easy; for others involving technical information, cancer treatment,
or complex scientific issues getting the case to be understandable to the lay
donor is not easy. If you have made your case, the donor should thank you
for asking for the gift. A powerful case for support inspires the donor's joy of
philanthropy.

The importance of a compelling and urgent case statement is well accepted for capital campaigns. To raise $10 million for a new building takes large gifts and a thorough explanation of the location of the building, the floor plan, and how the new rooms will help the organization fulfill its mission.

Good case statements aren't just for capital campaigns. They can be just as effective for special-project funding, annual funding, endowment funding, or planned estate-gift funding. All aspects of philanthropic fundraising will be assured of greater success if you make your case. Of course you can get by with the traditional annual fund case—we need the money to balance the budget, or give this year because you gave last year. But that is not very motivating for the donor, the volunteer, or the fundraising staff. It's not a winning-gifts strategy.

In *The One Minute Sales Person,* Spencer Johnson and Larry Wilson state:

> The fact is, with a product or service you believe in, selling is inherently purposeful. You do add value. You help people solve problems, seize opportunities, and, by acting, feel better about themselves.[1]

In *The Art of Selling to the Affluent,* Matt Oechsli comments on the importance of product and service descriptions and service delivery (see the stewardship section of Chapter 6, After Winning the Gift):

> You must make everything clear and easily understood, remembering that affluent prospects normally have already done their homework. Everything must work exactly as intended.[2]

This chapter, Make Your Case, will cover three major items:

1. How to make your case memorable so that it inspires donors, volunteers, and staff to achieve success

2. The process of case refinement that builds ownership in the case by all of the nonprofit's staff, affiliated professionals, and board

3. Ways to achieve top-of-mind understanding of your case through using a variety of communication channels with your donors

MAKE YOUR CASE MEMORABLE

As you prepare to write your case for support, start with the assumption that the reader does not know anything about your organization. Do not write for the board chair who has known the organization for 10 years, or the college president who has known academia for a lifetime, but rather for that millionaire next door who is smart, willing to learn, but ignorant of the organization's very existence. Your case needs to be flexible so that the consistent $10,000-a-year donor learns something from it just as the periodic $500 donor, the $100 donor who gave for the first time this year, or the wealthy community member who might be enticed to make a donation if she really understood your organization. Be concise and brief in making your case. New people don't want all of the detail—capture their imagination quickly.

When preparing an organization for a capital campaign one often hears people in the organization say: "We are the best-kept secret in town." The organization does great work but has not communicated it well or broadly to its target audience of donors. So many organizations are so focused on delivering their services that they forget to position themselves in the philanthropic marketplace. So start with the assumption that donors do not have a clear and concise knowledge of your organization.

The eventual goal of the entire case creation process is to present a clear, memorable case in 15 minutes on 12 PowerPoint slides, a two-page executive summary of narrative text, or eight minutes on a DVD movie. Getting your case short and sweet is hard work. Mark Twain once quipped: "I would have written a shorter letter but I didn't have the time." Brevity, conciseness, and essential truths will all seem obvious to everyone after you toil for many months and countless hours on your case statement. Be patient. It takes time, energy, 10 to 15 drafts, and testing with target audiences to get down to the 30-second elevator speech that you need to win gifts.

Case statements have been evolving over the last quarter-century. The standard used to be a 20-page narrative case statement full of facts, details, and all of the information about the organization that anyone would want to know. When you start writing your case, that's what your first draft will look like. Keep it. Some foundations will want every shred of information in this draft plus more.

Through testing we have found that many donors will not read this type of document. They do not have the time or the interest. But, there can be exceptions, so if somebody asks for every detail you can be ready to give it to them (I've only had one request like that in more than 25 years of fundraising; the gentlemen read everything and made a $100,000 gift back in 1989—there must be another person out there like that somewhere).

To make your case memorable, take a visual, magazine approach (see Exhibit 4.1). Don't bore your donor with thousands of words and pages and pages of gray text. The goal of your case statement is to use all of the tricks of the communications trade to get your story across, to intrigue the donors with your story so they are interested in making a gift to your organization. The case prepares the prospective donor to be receptive to a request for gift support.

Take a moment right now to go back and reread the section of Part II, Seek Winning Gifts for Your Organization, that describes *The Tipping Point's* reference to a sticky, memorable story as one of the key elements for successfully tipping an idea or product in society. That's what you're after in a fundraising case statement—something sticky rather than slick. Use clear, memorable words rather than fancy, sophisticated ones. Time after time, in testing traditional case statements we hear donors comment: "I don't get it." Or, they don't take the time to read it so they have no chance of getting it. Make your case attractive and inviting to your potential customers, the donors. Keep things basic. Make your problem statement clear and compelling.

We were taping a DVD for a church one rainy day. The film crew happened to capture on tape a bucket catching water leaking out of the church ceiling. When church members watched the movie they would gasp in horror at their poor church falling apart. They were literally shocked into action to make sure repairs were made. If you have a problem, you need to

EXHIBIT 4.1   A MAGAZINE APPROACH

I must admit a personal bias. I have a graphics dependency. I must have graphics in my documents. I am a former magazine editor (I served as an editor for a national music publication for a company located in Evanston, Illinois, where I worked part-time as I worked on my doctoral studies at Northwestern University).

I learned to use magazine-style layout and graphics to make my magazine articles attractive to readers. I like my case statements the same way—lots of photos with captions, graphs, white space, sidebars, and so on.

I have read research articles that describe how major magazine companies observed subscribers reading their magazines. First, readers skim through looking at the pictures and reading their captions; then they notice graphs, shaded areas of text, headlines, and if they get really bored, they finally read the articles. Think about how editors put together *USA Today* and how revolutionary it was when they first started their graphical approach. I take to heart the old saying that a picture is worth a thousand words.

demonstrate it starkly. You share challenges and problems with your friends in life. Treat your donors as friends and be open with them about the issues your organization is facing. Honest, direct communications will help them to understand your need and your vision for the future so they will be willing to make a gift to you.

Also in Part II, Seek Winning Gifts for Your Organization, we discussed Robert Cialdini's ethical influence principles. Apply some of these principles in your case statement. Use authority to make your points. Don't just use yourself, the faceless author of the case statement, to try to convince donors; go to respected people in the community. For a food bank located in the state capitol, the governor was recruited to write a letter of support to foundations and to appear in the campaign movie talking about the importance of solving hunger problems so children from poor families could go to school having eaten a full breakfast and ready to learn.

Use prominent donors that people respect to tell why they support your cause. They are making your case in their own words from an outside perspective. This can be very powerful as they sell others on the importance of your case for support.

Photos can be powerful grabbers of attention (see Exhibit 4.2 for an extreme example). A dental association foundation wanted its case to show

A Case Statement with Impact

Before
This is me before I started listening to classical music. Overweight, poor, unhappy, and alone.

After
This is me after 16 short years as a classical music listener. Rich, trim, and sexy.

EXHIBIT 4.2   A CASE STATEMENT WITH IMPACT

how the foundation helped children from underserved areas with bad tooth decay. Yet, the early draft showed smiling kids with no tooth problems. After getting feedback, we replaced the photos of smiling children with rather ugly, but dramatic pictures of young children with rotted, "baby-bottle teeth" that cried out for help. Check your latest *Time* magazine for the nonprofit that is fixing cleft palettes in third-world countries. They show children ages 3, 5, and 10 with terrible facial disfigurements that we would never see in the United States. The organization asks for your donation to help these children get a normal, smiling face. It makes its case with sticky, memorable photos.

The Annual Fund Case

Stating your case for the annual fund seems obvious, but it is rarely done. What is the usual rationale for annual giving? "Money is needed to balance the organization's operating budget, so please help close the gap by making a gift." At least this type of case statement is truthful, even if it isn't very motivating. It focuses on an internal need rather than an external benefit. Where is the positive, impact-on-people statement? How can donors feel like they've made a winning gift when their donation falls into the black abyss of the operating budget? Instead of helping students get educated, they're helping the chief financial officer get his job done.

One diversionary tactic around the urgent need for undesignated operating funds is the use of an annual fund major gift club. This solution is selling the "join the other enlightened community leaders who support this fine organization" concept rather than the financial needs of the organization. For many organizations, all of the operational details are a lot like making sausage. The product is wonderful as long as you don't look too closely at what goes into making it.

Set a basic level of club affiliation for your organization—$500, or $1,000, or $2,500. Your goal is to seek undesignated gifts from as many gift club members as you can to build a community of donors to support your organization. One of the benefits to donors is listing their names as active, gift-club members alongside other insightful people in the community who are enlightened enough to support your organization. In building your club you can describe some tangible benefits to encourage membership (coffee mug, key chain, invitation to presidential luncheons, etc.). Your basic case proposal for the annual fund gift club is strengthening your organization to serve its basic mission. If annual fund donors appreciate your mission and the impact you have on society, they will make general, undesignated gifts for the good of the cause. If you are a college, you need many president's club members to provide ongoing scholarship support for students in need. For a hospital, the gift club can have a project of the year (funds will go to a digital mammography machine this year); the theater company's gift club might support payment for the set designer, carpenters, costume designers, and seamstresses (all of the mundane budget items that help the show go on).

When you are seeking special gifts to the annual fund above your basic major-gifts club membership level, look at your organization's operating budget for exciting projects that can be funded through donor contributions. You can develop designated fund proposals that are budget relieving. Through writing short letters of proposal around these special projects, you can help donors to understand the impact of their gifts. For example, a university needed operating funds. In reviewing the budget, we noticed the *library periodicals* line item. We explored this budget item with the head librarian and discovered that some of the biological sciences department's periodicals were highly specialized and cost $1,000 or $2,000 a year. Why so expensive? Only 500 people subscribe worldwide. The special-project appeal of the library was compelling, and donors were eager to support this specific, tangible project even though it was part of the ongoing operating budget.

Not everything in the operating budget lends itself to special project funding. Very few people are interested in sponsoring the yearly costs of the finance office or the fundraising department. But, donors will support a students' travel fund, which the university always budgets minimally, to enable the winning debate club to go to a national competition or the math team to compete in the Southeast regionals. And, of course, at K–12 private schools, colleges, and universities, student scholarships are awarded first and funded later (if at all). The institution is already committed to making a certain level of grants. Any donations that come in to offset this budget commitment are an annual fund win.

As you present tangible projects to your donors, you may get into the gray area of budget-relieving gifts versus new project funding. Be clear and honest with people that the project you are presenting is not new but a recurring, unfunded operating expense. While covering this operating expense is a win for your organization, the donor's gift is not making a difference in the community. A better winning-gifts strategy is to ask the donor to cover the unfunded operating expense plus take the project to the next level of impact. For example: The museum's visiting exhibit budget is $105,000, and therefore a gift of $105,000 to sponsor special exhibits would be exciting to the organization. Some savvy donor may push harder for what is really needed for the organization to be successful—what will take it to the next level of service to the community? Here is where your strategic plan, comes to the rescue. You check the plan (or, instead of reviewing the plan, you go to the person in charge of special exhibits) and you find out that what is really needed is $150,000 this year plus a discretionary fund of another $50,000 so that deposits can be made on exhibits for two or three years out. Your donor may not be able to cover all of this, but he may become a champion for giving $125,000 and working with you to raise another $75,000 to meet the true institutional need of $200,000.

Test your annual fund case with your board members and other friendly donors. Do they buy the case? Empower their questions and comments. If they keep bringing up an issue consistently, then you need to put the answer to that issue in your case statement. For example, an organization that works with hearing-impaired children focuses on effecting profound changes in a few children rather than modest changes in thousands of children. That's just the way the organization works. Don't hide it—feature it, and be proud of your impact.

Developing an annual fund case statement that has impact and that helps donors make a difference in peoples' lives in your community can be powerful because so many of your competitors in the nonprofit world do not take the time to do this. You can really stand out by doing some work on your annual fund case statement.

The Case for Building Campaigns

As mentioned earlier, capital campaigns came about because nonprofits needed to raise extraordinary funds from donors to pay for building construction projects. Making the building case still needs to be based on your mission and impact on society. A reminder—the building is just a tool to help you achieve your mission. The building is not an end in itself. Be careful of the edifice complex (falling in love with the building instead of its impact on your organization).

After describing your mission and how buildings help serve your constituents, please do not jump to the new, beautiful building plans. You have skipped a step. You need to articulate the problem statement. Describe what is wrong with your current facilities: too small, outdated design, wrong location, whatever it may be. You and your staff have lived with the problems of the facilities for years, so you are well aware of the challenges. Your job as the case writer is to assume that the donor thinks all of your buildings are just fine. You need to prove a new building is needed. You need to make the case about why your current building is inadequate, broken, and in need of replacement.

Sometimes you get the opportunity not only to make the case for a building but to participate in the planning charrettes facilitated by the architects (small group meetings that architects hold with various constituencies of the organization to understand how a building will be used in the future). Being able to listen to the needs of your program staff helps you to share with donors during the cultivation and solicitation process. You know why aspects of the building are so important to program delivery. It is helpful to have you, the fundraiser, participate in these meetings as a "donors' representative" to ask questions donors are likely to ask. Such questions might include: Is there a potential for performance space in the classical public radio studio so that small ensembles could perform? Does the executive director's office really need to be larger than the chair of the board's?

A food bank wanted a new building. After some thinking, its leaders were able to describe the shortcomings of their current overcrowded warehouse. Several times of the year (especially before Thanksgiving and Christmas), the food bank's warehouse was so full, volunteers couldn't move pallets of food around and had to turn food donations away. There was no room for volunteers to work, so helping hands were told to stay home. Food delivery trucks had no room to turn around as the parking lot was too small for trailer trucks and residential neighbors were complaining about trucks jockeying for position by their homes. When a major food drive took place, assembly tables had to be set up in the parking lot in the rain and cold as there was no room in the warehouse. Projections for families needing food assistance showed the need for a distribution center twice as large as the current one. As they began planning their new space, they included a nutrition education classroom. They had made their case to the community and were highly successful in the building campaign.

A private high school needed a student activities center adjacent to the gymnasium. In trying to understand why this student center was needed, we learned that the school's plans had called for such a building 25 years ago when the gym was built, but money was tight so the second phase of the project, the student center, was deferred until "later." Because this space was missing, there was no room for a school lunchroom and classes had to be juggled in four 20-minute shifts to enable students to eat in the hallway outside the gym. Food was served out of a converted closet using a hot plate. Student and family social activities had to be held in the gym or scheduled for an open area in the library, which meant the library couldn't be used by classes or students for study and reference purposes (the cheerleaders had to practice in the library after school, so it was closed for student study use). The architect's plan was developed and the campaign was getting under way when a new principal and fundraising consultant arrived. In reviewing plans one more time to make sure the new principal was on board, we noticed that a movable stage was planned that could shift between the student activity center and the gym when a larger assembly or all-family program was scheduled. The principal walked into the gym, looked at the plans, and realized the architect had a made a mistake in the design. The movable stage was going right through one of the basketball stanchions. In probing further with the architects, the principal found that the movable stage was not needed often enough to warrant the extra $50,000 expense and this aspect of the plan was scrapped. The lesson? As you build your case, keep asking tough questions to make sure the designs have been well thought out. You are going to be spending donated dollars, so follow the old carpenter's adage— "Measure twice and cut once." Pretend your mom and dad were giving their lifetime assets to make a special family donation; would this be a good investment for them?

Architects are the best friends of fundraisers in helping to make a building case. They are masters of vision and eloquence about the look of the new building and how it will help the organization. They come up with conceptual floor plans, exterior artist renderings, and even scale models that make the building real. All of this costs money, of course, but to make your building case strong ask the architects to go beyond the conceptual floor plans, as most people cannot envision the final building from just those plans.

EXHIBIT 4.3   ARCHITECT'S MODEL

SOURCE: Used with Permission WRNS Studio, Architects.

An exterior drawing of the building and two or three significant spaces bring the new building to life. Scale models that allow the roof to be removed to view inside rooms are fun (architects can take closeup photos with their cameras to show you what the building will feel like in real life). Exhibit 4.3 is a photo of a scale model created for a school's performing arts building project.

For some projects, architects go to the extra level of planning by creating a virtual-reality, three-dimensional computer tour of the building. By touring the building in this way, the architects can confirm with the client exactly how things will look in the finished building. For fundraising, these tours can be exciting for donors as you can walk the halls of the new hospital, look at nurses' stations and patient rooms, and even look out lobby windows.

Building Budget Planning for Fundraising   When donated philanthropic dollars are the source of building construction funding, you have a special responsibility to accurately plan the project so it comes in on budget. Nothing discourages fundraising volunteers and staff more than selling a campaign case that the building will cost $5 million, working for three years to raise the money, declaring victory, and then, in the glow of exhausted exhilaration, being told, "*Oops*—the budget is really $6 million and you need to start up the campaign again." Yes, this really has happened.

For some organizations, cost overruns are not a huge problem; reserve funds can cover missed building budget items. It's covered and everyone is fine. But for many others, if the campaign does not raise the money, organization leaders have few options: Stop construction (usually not possible), borrow money (but how do they pay it back?), or increase the campaign goal.

For fundraisers who have worked hard to motivate volunteers to raise campaign dollars, and for donors who have stretched their giving to achieve the goal, bad building budgets can be devastating. They imply poor planning on the part of the nonprofit and poor budgeting controls by senior management. When years of case presentations have been spent building up the credibility of the leadership's vision and management expertise, cost overruns imply poor stewardship of donated dollars. This is bad, bad news all the way around.

So what causes these accidental budget overruns, and is there a way to look for potential problems sooner so they can be prevented?

One can detect a pattern for many of the misbudgetings for building capital campaigns. Most of these issues are inadvertent and can be anticipated. One important thing to realize is the architect's budget is not the fundraising campaign goal. These are two entirely different numbers. Why?

Many times the lack of good project planning is the result of the usual lack of accountability of construction projects. Corporate and governmental projects can go over budget, but this type of client has deep pockets. The contractor and architect just go back for more money to complete the project. A recent classic example is the new U.S. Capitol Visitor Center in Washington, D.C. This three-level underground complex adjacent to the Capitol had to be expanded in scope in response to 9/11 security issues and an ever-increasing vision for the project. The "open checkbook" approach of our federal government has led the visitor center to end up costing taxpayers $600 million, well more than double the initial $265 million estimate. At an airport project, the new connector roof between the terminal and parking garage was $30 million over budget before anybody realized the problem. A city's aerial tram ballooned from $15 million to $55 million because of design flaws. While the newspapers cover some of the problems of these overruns, we faceless taxpayers foot the bill.

When cost overruns of even a fraction of this magnitude happen at a nonprofit organization, it is a major scandal and the president can be fired and a capital campaign totally derailed.

So, to help prevent problems, understand that most architects provide project estimates based on rough conceptual floor plans and rough square-footage estimates from subcontractors with expertise in buildings like yours. If it is a library project, they will bring in a library consultant who has done many of these buildings and knows some of the special needs. But, the key word here is *estimate*. Contractors have explained to me that these estimates are like weather forecasts. They can easily be 10 percent or more off even after detailed construction drawings are completed, so be careful with that preliminary number. Be sure to label these budgets *forecasts,* not estimates. Remind people that these preliminary figures are like weather forecasts; their accuracy is always somewhat debatable—manage expectations.

Also realize that architects tend to give their budget estimates in today's dollars. They assume you will start construction now, not three years from now after your campaign is completed. Ask them to include construction inflation factors in the budget to account for this. When architects design buildings they do not focus on total project needs. That's not really their job. Their contract is based on the hard construction dollars. Their work ends five feet outside the building. If you want landscaping, new trees, benches, and so forth you need to ask the architect to team up with a landscape architect to get these estimates into your budget. In addition to the already-mentioned construction inflation and landscaping factors that should be included in the budget, the cost of fundraising is always missing. As a placeholder until your philanthropic market research study is done, budget 10 percent of the building cost for fundraising (if you are a new organization with little fundraising infrastructure, this cost could go as high as 15 percent; if you are a highly sophisticated fundraising institution and your building is budgeted at $50 million, you may have only a 5 percent cost of fundraising, but it is never zero).

You also need to factor in pledge financing. If you run a two-year campaign that offers five-year pledges, you will have cash flow going out seven years. Even if you do not start construction until your pledge goal is reached, you want to start building before all of the pledges are paid. You can take pledges to the bank and get a loan, but interest will be owed on the loan. Budget at least 5 percent of project cost for pledge financing (if you want to

EXHIBIT 4.4   BUILDING BUDGET MODEL

Land Acquisition	$750,000
Building	$10,000,000
Contingency @ 10%	$1,000,000
Soft costs @ 20%	$2,200,000
Construction inflation of 15%, 2 to 3 years	$1,980,000
Pledge financing @ 5%	$660,000
Fundraising @ 10%	$1,386,000
Landscaping	$350,000
Total Building	$17,576,000
Total Campaign Including Land	$18,326,000

be conservative you can always budget 10 percent). Generally, we see about 50 percent of the cash in hand before construction starts, because you never, *ever*, want to start construction before the pledge goal of the campaign is achieved. We have learned the hard way that once the building is open and in use the capital campaign is over. You now have a management problem, not a capital campaign on your hands.

Exhibit 4.4 shows a chart of a fully loaded budget based on what the architect said was a $10 million building project (which in an architect's world is correct).

You can see how the $10 million building project grows into an $18.3 million capital campaign. And please realize in this example that the construction inflation, soft costs, fundraising, and pledge financing assumptions are all relatively conservative. Unfortunately, getting organizations to look at this fully loaded fundraising objective so scares everyone that they want to take the loading factors out. Luckily, once we share some horror stories about organizations that have gone into bankruptcy, had executive directors fired, board members sued, and so on, reality begins to set in. Either the fully loaded number is accepted or the organization goes back to the architect to cut back the scale of the project to reduce the $10 million base budget to a more realistic $6 million or $8 million or to see if a phased-construction approach could work.

Be sure to check your local community's situation and the type of building project you are working on. The percentage assumptions for each of the soft cost factors may be too conservative for your situation. For example, in the Los Angeles basin from 2004 through 2006, construction inflation was averaging 25 percent for all construction and 65 percent for hospital construction. Soft costs for furnishings and equipment can be much higher for a science classroom than for an English classroom. Construction contingency for a building renovation should be much higher than for a new construction. (On one kitchen remodel for a 100-year-old building, one of the campaign volunteers who was an industrial kitchen design consultant warned us we might need a 75 percent contingency. We scoffed but listened—costs came out at 65 percent over budget; we thanked her profusely.)

It is important for the philanthropic fundraiser to push for realistic, not-to-exceed numbers, even if they seem painfully high to everyone else. Make sure the case shows the organization has planned carefully and that budget projections will not be exceeded. It's not insurmountable when actual costs come in higher than the budget, but it hurts the case for fundraising and breaks the trust with donors we have worked so hard to cultivate throughout the campaign.

If your project finishes under budget, tell donors you will put the unspent funds in a building maintenance fund to care for your facilities in the future. By the way, it would be nice to build this into your building budget, but the numbers get so high that this is usually impossible.

To help prevent some of the budget planning issues, hire an experienced owner's representative who is independent from the architect and contractor. The owner's representative's job is to manage all of the players in the project to ensure that architectural plans have been reviewed by an outside expert, and that someone meets regularly with the contractor to help make the frequent decisions needed during construction, and to advise the owner (you, the nonprofit) to avoid costly change orders. The owner's representative helps to manage the project contingency and to present decision options to the owner during the construction project on how best to spend the contingency when unexpected issues come up (which they always do).

The Case for Endowment

Just like a person can never be too rich or too thin, it seems like nonprofit organizations can never have too much endowment.

Why are endowments so important to nonprofit organizations? Why does Harvard University with a $26 billion endowment still raise special-project funds, seek more endowment gifts, and aggressively invest its endowment so it will grow ever larger? What is the magic of endowment?

A strong endowment for a nonprofit organization is like a large trust fund for an individual. Wouldn't it be nice to have a quarter of your income show up unearned, untaxed, and able to be used for whatever project you would like to tackle—giving you time to exercise, learn a new skill, start a new business, or expand your house? Harvard, for example, uses part of its endowment to offer all incoming freshman whose annual family incomes are $60,000 or less a totally debt-free education. If you are admitted, and you meet the income guidelines, you get a free ride at Harvard. The university feels that commitment to economically diverse students is critical to its mission.

Benchmarking indicates that vital, financially healthy nonprofit organizations receive somewhere in the range of 20 to 30 percent of their operating budget from their endowment funds. For a $5 million organization, 20 percent of the operating budget is $1 million. At a 5 percent distribution rate that would require a $20 million endowment fund. For many nonprofit organizations with an average earned income of 65 percent, raising the other 35 percent of the budget each year is a big challenge. If 20 percent of this unearned income revenue can be derived from the endowment fund and 15 percent from the annual fund, nonprofit life is no longer a budget crisis every year.

In benchmarking higher education endowments, one can see a range from Harvard's $26 billion through top-20 University of Southern California's $2.7 billion. For private schools, Phillips Exeter Academy in New Hampshire leads the list with an endowment of $706 million, and number 50, the Pingry School in New Jersey, has an endowment of $51 million. It is interesting to note that for private schools the nine with the highest endowments are all in the Northeast. The school with the largest endowment west of the Mississippi is St. Mark's School of Texas, which, with a $98 million endowment, is number 23 on the list.[3] One can see that endowments for higher education are significantly larger than for private schools and that endowment traditions for private schools are much stronger in the Northeast than in the rest of the United States.

In a 2003 study, The Advisory Board noted that the median margin for hospitals in the United States was one-and-a-half percent (excess revenues over expenses) but the capital needs for these same hospitals required a four-and-a-half percent margin. The three percent difference needs to be made up from fundraising and endowment. For a hospital with $100 million operating budget, this means $3 million of endowment proceeds and a $60 million endowment (assuming a 5 percent distribution; $75 million if you assume a 4 percent distribution).

Ah, but there's an inherent challenge for the endowment case. It cannot imply that this extra funding will enable the organization to take it easy by resting upon its endowment funding. Many donors like to reward hard work, not relaxation. Just like our individual trust fund example—20 percent of your income coming from this magic fund is kind of nice; if it were 50 percent you would probably quit your job and be lazy. For nonprofits, too much endowment can enable an organization to drift, to become unresponsive to members and donors. Generally, receiving more than 30 percent of your operating revenues from endowment can be a bad thing.

In making the case for endowment, it does help to show national benchmarks. In tough economic times, when a nonprofit is needed most by its community, contributed and earned income could be down. The endowment fund can protect the organization's budget and enable it to continue fulfilling its mission despite a challenging economy.

How Endowment Works   Here are a few tips to understand endowment and how it really works. It may not be as simple and straightforward as you think.

The general concept of endowment is the donor gives the organization a sum of money (the gift principal) that is kept intact for perpetuity with a certain percentage going to operations each year. It is the gift that keeps on giving. The power of endowment is its permanence and assurance of ongoing funding. The biggest challenge with endowment is that it takes a large sum of money to produce enough yearly distribution to fund projects.

For example, let's consider a donor's new gift to endowment of $100,000. Because the donor restricted his gift to endowment, the $100,000 is called "permanently restricted funds" in your financial statements and is combined with other true endowment funds to show the size of your total endowment fund. If the donor simply restricts the gift to the general endowment of the organization, you can track this endowment gift with your other donor-designated endowment gifts. If the donor further restricts to a specific project, the organization needs to be able to prove that the distribution from the endowment to the project takes place each year. For example, what is the impact of an endowed research fund?

The power of endowment is its endurance, its permanence. Assuming you set an endowment guideline of a 5 percent distribution, the $100,000 endowment gift will provide your organization with $5,000 a year—next year, 10 years from now, 100 years from now, forever.

Nonprofits frequently have another type of endowment—"temporarily restricted funds." These are endowments established by the organization's board from undesignated dollars. Most frequently, these temporarily restricted funds come from unrestricted bequests made to the organization that the board votes into the endowment fund. These "quasi-endowment" funds are commingled with true endowment (permanently restricted endowment) for investment purposes. While the board's intention may be to never touch these board-designated endowment funds, accounting principles mean that these funds will always be temporarily restricted even if they are not touched for 50 years. Any future board can unrestrict the funds and use these dollars for any purpose. For many boards serious about endowment, significant hurdles are put in place to prevent the casual taking of board-restricted endowment funds by any future board. One organization requires a two-thirds vote by two different boards in order to move any temporarily restricted funds (by two different boards the bylaws mean that a board election must take place between votes so that a new class of board members must reaffirm the first vote of the old board).

Another interesting thing about endowment is that it isn't quite correct to say that interest and dividends from the endowment are distributed to the organization each year. What really happens is an asset distribution based on an agreed-upon market valuation of the endowment. Some organizations take the average market valuation over 13 trailing quarters to determine the asset value, and then take 5 percent to distribute to operations. Others do a three-year average or the value on the last day of the fiscal year. The 13 trailing quarters is the conservative standard so that asset values in your endowment are protected against wild up and down swings in the investment marketplace. You may want to check with your local community foundation to understand its guidelines. Community foundations usually have a strong, fiscally conservative set of financial advisors that can set excellent benchmarking for all nonprofits. The 5 percent distribution to operations is not set in stone, either. For many years, this was the standard as it matched the federal requirement of a 5 percent distribution by charitable foundations to maintain their charitable status. We have seen distributions as aggressive as six-and-a-half percent and as low as two percent. As of the writing of this book, a new benchmark of four-and-a-half percent distribution has been generally agreed upon (interest rates and stock market returns have been low for several years).

A new endowment distribution policy will be needed during endowment campaigns as new outright gifts and multiyear pledges to endowment start coming into your endowment fund. Even though you may have a market valuation policy of 13 trailing quarters, you don't have to wait that long for new additions to your endowment to begin making distributions for general operating or special-project funding.

Here are a few items to consider. The new endowment funds should be invested for a minimum of four complete quarters before distributions can begin. You have already established the quarter timing for your market valuation (e.g., January, April, July, and October). Your new endowment should go through at least four of these cycles before you consider a distribution. For example, a $250,000 endowment gift is donated in November 2006. After four complete cycles (which would start January 2007 and run through December, 31, 2007), this new endowment would begin distributions effective January 2008. You can apply the 13-trailing quarter averaging that you are applying to your long-term endowment to this new addition at that time. For a fiscal year starting July 1, with a general endowment 13-quarter trailing average of 7 percent growth, you can apply this effective rate to the $250,000 of new endowment as of January 2008 and budget for two quarters of distribution during this first partial fiscal year of endowment impact. If you want to be ultraconservative, you can check the last four quarters, averaging for the initial cycle of this new endowment addition to see how this valuation compares with the 13-quarter trailing average. You can certainly take the lower of those two values to preserve capital. Please note that you can take endowment distributions annually or quarterly with only a small difference in rate of return. For organizations with cash flow needs, quarterly distributions are fine as long as your investment advisors are aware of this need for cash distributions from your endowment funds.

Another discovery—one client's chief financial officer who wanted to assure the success of an endowment campaign asked that the campaign pledge form include the language "This gift and all of its future asset appreciation is restricted to endowment." He said that accounting standards require this language to assure that both the principal and its future appreciation are permanently restricted. Unless the donor stipulated the asset appreciation as part of the endowment, accounting rules state that this appreciation is unrestricted money and can be used anytime in the future. Donors assume you are saving excess asset appreciation with the endowment and/or their restricted project fund. With restricted asset appreciation the endowment grows over time as the asset grows (e.g., while 5 percent is taken out after year one, if the fund grows 7 percent, then in year two the new asset basis is $102,000—$100,000 principal plus $7,000 asset appreciation minus $5,000 distribution). Most donors assume this is what the organization will do. But unless the donor restricts the asset appreciation in writing, the growth is really board-designated endowment and can be used by future boards if they so wish.

Another endowment fundraising fact: Because endowment needs to be invested before a distribution can be made, any endowment pledges must be completely paid and the entire sum invested for one year before they can help your organization. This means the $100,000 five-year pledge will wait until year six to produce that $5,000 so greatly needed by your program. Donors and organizations have developed solutions to this problem. David Rockefeller, a member of the board of trustees, recently made a wonderful $100 million endowment pledge to the Museum of Modern Art. He made this gift a five-year pledge backed by his estate (he was 92 at the time, so if he died during the pledge period his estate would pay the balance of the pledge). Understanding endowment as he does, Rockefeller also made an announcement that he would donate an additional $5 million per year during his endowment pledge period, effectively letting the organization have the endowment proceeds as he fulfilled his pledge.

One donor who liked endowment wanted to see the impact of his scholarship gift immediately. He directed his university to take two-thirds of each of his pledges during the five-year pledge period and place it into endowment. The other one-third was used to provide immediate scholarship support for students. As he said: "By the time my pledge was paid up and my scholarship fully endowed I had already helped five students." This is a great winning-gifts strategy.

Endowment Examples   Endowing aspects of an operating budget can protect these programs from future budget cuts. For example, in one hospital campaign, the four-person chaplain's office was endowed by raising $6 million. Since chaplain services were critically important to this hospital's faith-based mission, there was a philosophical commitment to continuing a robust chaplain's service in spite of the lack of any medical reimbursements. The only way for the hospital's administration to protect the chaplain's office permanently was by endowing its budget through a capital campaign (yes, an endowment campaign is a capital campaign, too; you are seeking gifts of capital assets to be transferred from the donor to your organization).

For a symphony orchestra, raising an endowment for a statewide touring program helped to lock in this mission-critical aspect of its season given the state name of the orchestra. This is another interesting aspect of the perpetuity aspect of endowment. If a donor wants to assure an organization continues an activity long-term, then endow the program; by doing so the donor can force the organization to maintain the program.

As you think about what programs to endow in your organization, look at budget items that will always be with your organization. Universities endow professorships in core disciplines; they seek endowment of scholarships, of graduate research fellowships, any ongoing budget item that can be secured by a steady stream of income. For a hospital, one can look to endow the continuing nursing education program, a new equipment fund, a physician loan-forgiveness fund, and other items that appear in the budget year in and year out (just make sure you have a compelling story for how funding this item benefits the mission of the hospital, of the university, of the organization). Be careful, because donors can force you to continue a program by endowing it and be sure to review all endowment gifts to be sure you have a long-term (in-perpetuity) commitment to continuing the program to be endowed.

Endowments are helpful to the organization; they shore up finances and help provide fiscal stability. A pleasant by-product of many endowments is the positive impact on individual staff members within the organization. To be appointed to a named endowed chair is a high honor for a faculty member. This appointment will go on the faculty member's resume, be touted among colleagues throughout the country, and listed on any publications written by that faculty member in research journals. It raises the prestige of the faculty appointment because there are only a handful of endowed chairs on campus. Likewise, an endowed chair in a symphony orchestra is an honor to the musician holding the chair. It is a win for the organization, a win for the musician, as well as for the donor.

Why do donors like endowed chairs? What makes them so special? Some of the prestige may come because of the rarity of endowed chairs. It is a big deal for an institution to receive an endowed chair. The college's honest and authentic celebration of the donor and faculty member is fun. Both the institution and the staff member are honored by the distinction as well as rewarded financially from the cash distributions each year from the endowment. Many organizations recognize the donor of an endowed chair by giving the donor a real chair with a plaque listing the donor's name along with the name of the first professor holding the title. Recipient organizations issue press releases announcing the endowments, take photos of the professors holding the newly endowed chairs, and often host yearly lunch meetings for the donors and the chair holders. Donors can build personal relationships with the faculty members, and become acquainted with their teaching and research focus, their students, and their departmental aspirations. An endowed chair can be a winning gift for everyone.

What are some other endowment examples? At one college the strategic plan called for more undergraduate student research projects with faculty members. An implementation plan was developed and several faculty members were eager to participate. To figure out the project budget, we took an average senior faculty salary of $100,000 for 10 months of work. To take on a six-week summer student research team, the faculty has agreed to be paid $15,000. The first students who would be invited to participate in a potential program are willing to be paid $1,500 for the six-week research project along with the prestige of listing the undergraduate research fellowship on their resumes. The faculty would like at least two students per team; three would be ideal. The budget, then, is $15,000 plus $4,500 plus $500 for expenses and miscellaneous for a total of $20,000 for one program for one summer. The strategic plan called for ramping up the program from one research team in year one to 10 teams across the curriculum in year five. Exhibit 4.5 shows the budget.

To endow the program at 5 percent (to keep the math simple) would take $400,000 per research team or $10 million for the campuswide program. A foundation might want to test pilot the first three years of the program through an investment of $180,000. An individual could sponsor one year for the department of his choice for $20,000 or ideally commit to a five-year sponsorship of $100,000. A family could endow one team for $400,000 or a visionary family foundation could endow the campus program for $10

		Immediate	5-year	Endowed
Year 1	1 team	$20,000	$100,000	$400,000
Year 2	3 teams	$60,000	$300,000	$1,200,000
Year 3	5 teams	$100,000	$500,000	$2,000,000
Year 4	7 teams	$140,000	$700,000	$2,800,000
Year 5	10 teams	$200,000	$1,000,000	$4,000,000
TOTAL		$520,000	$2,600,000	$10,400,000

EXHIBIT 4.5   PROJECT FUNDING — IMMEDIATE AND ENDOWED

million. Donors would receive copies of research reports from the teams, meet the teams to hear what the students have learned over the summer, and talk to the faculty member about future research ideas. To make the case even stronger, quote the faculty member and students who are willing to be the first to implement the program. Bring them to a presentation with a potential donor and allow their excitement and plans for the research program to come alive for the donor.

For a library endowment, think through the various types of acquisitions a librarian would make out of her budget each year. For a small community library, we developed the following endowment packages:

$15,000 endowment—$675 a year

Adult Fiction Fund

$25,000—$1,125 every year

Periodical Fund

Adult Nonfiction Fund

Children's Books Acquisition Fund

$50,000—$2,250 a year

Technology Endowment

Medical and Healthcare Collections

Historical Collections

Young Adult Acquisition Fund

$100,000—$4,500 a year

Children's Hour

Reference Endowment

$250,000—$12,500 a year

Endowed Associate Librarian's Chair

$500,000—$25,000 a year

Endowed Head Librarian's Chair

Please note: For all of these examples the total endowment is listed along with the yearly distribution. It is important that we make the endowment math easy for both the donor and the organization. In the library example, look at the cost of the endowed chairs. For the head librarian, $500,000 is needed to produce $25,000 a year from the 5 percent distribution from endowment. Clearly the librarian is being paid more than this amount, so the endowment is only partially covering the true expense of the position. Because the position is covered by the library's tax levy, full coverage is not necessary—and, if listed at full value, the request might be out of the range of donors interested in endowing the chair. You can see this type of partial endowment funding at public universities, where the cost of endowing a chair may be one-third to one-half of doing so at a private college.

To set endowment targets, start with the budget amount and then think of donors, the pricing of other endowments in your community (including any educational institutions community members graduated from), and your ability to raise the endowment funds. This is part of the art of fundraising.

The whole point of any endowed program is to make endowment concrete, exciting, tangible, and desirable.

What to Do for Financially Fragile Organizations   Endowment's purpose is to provide for ongoing streams of revenue that an organization can use in perpetuity. But what if the organization is so financially weak (either in reality or by perception of the donors) that an endowment gift may not seem appropriate since the organization may not be around in the future? How do you motivate a donor to make a risky investment in this type of organization?

This is a puzzle. One elegant solution is a variation on financial modeling developed by the National Arts Stabilization Fund (NAS, which has since focused on different issues under new staff leadership). NAS was founded as a spinoff of the Ford Foundation and the Kellogg Foundation in the 1970s. NAS was created out of the realization that just adding endowment funds to organizations did not automatically result in financial health as everyone had assumed. In the late 1960s and early 1970s, the Ford Foundation initiated a series of endowment challenge grants for arts organizations in the United States. With the Ford Foundation grants and matching funds from local donors, it was assumed that endowment funds would dramatically increase, thus assuring long-term financial health for the organizations they supported. Almost all of the challenge campaigns were successful and the Ford Foundation went away feeling good about its victory. However, to its dismay, most of these arts organizations found themselves in financial trouble once again (some almost immediately and others within a few years).

What went wrong? A staff member of the Ford Foundation dug into the problem and discovered that having a large endowment fund was not the financial magic bullet everyone had expected it to be. The lack of budget discipline or unexpected financial shortfalls led to operating deficits, which led to borrowing against the endowment fund. As soon as the interest on the borrowing became as large as the yearly distribution from the endowment, the organization had basically zeroed out the economic impact of the endowment fund. The asset was there, but only as collateral for loans whose interest gobbled up all of the endowment distributions.

This led to further investigation. Why were the budgets frequently running in the red? Couldn't these organizations budget for future years? Yes, they could, but the budgeting was so tight that any single budgetary variance could put the organization into peril. If there was an unexpected operating expense or a revenue shortfall, a deficit resulted because there was never a contingency fund in the operating budget. This happened year after year, even though a review of previous years' budgets showed consistent deficits because of unforeseen circumstances or overly optimistic projections for ticket sales or fundraising.

The following six-step financial stabilization fundraising model has been modified from NAS principles to fit all nonprofit organizations. We thank NAS for its pioneering work in this area.

Step 1 of financial stabilization was crystal clear: Organizations must balance their operating budget each year and should strive to include a 5 percent contingency in their budgets to provide a cushion against changes in operational life over which they have no control. For example, most ballet companies and some symphonies perform the *Nutcracker* ballet around the December holiday season. Audiences love the performances and the *Nutcracker* becomes a real cash cow for the organization. But, what if a major ice storm hits the city, forcing the cancellation of five shows over three days? This could take the *Nutcracker* from a moneymaker with a net positive impact of $250,000 to a money loser of $100,000—a $350,000 swing in the budget. Without a contingency fund, the organization would suffer a $350,000 deficit and need to borrow against its endowment fund.

Steps to Financially Healthy Nonprofits

Step #1   Balance operating budgets with 5% contingency line.

Step #2   Eliminate debt.

Step #3   Develop cash reserves equal to 25% of operating budget.

Step #4   Establish a risk venture fund equal to 10% of budget.

Step #5   Ensure endowment provides 20% of operating budget.

Step #6   Assess building and capital equipment needs.

Debt is an albatross around the neck of an organization. Debt creates cash flow challenges and forces borrowing with no revenue to cover interest (except endowment proceeds). Debt must go, so Step 2 of the six-step model is to eliminate debt. Because debt is so hard to retire, when NAS came to communities to help bring financial stability, it would offer a challenge grant that had to be matched by community donors. Conditions of the grant were balanced budgets with contingencies; and use of contributed funds to eliminate debt, build cash reserves, and, if any funds were left, to build endowment.

Once the first two steps had taken place, NAS learned that the magic bullet of financial health was not endowment, but rather cash reserves, which are Step 3. If the organization did need to borrow for an operational problem, it needed to borrow from itself. NAS set a reserve benchmark of 25 percent of the operating budget (three months of operation). If reserves had to be used, the board was required to authorize a repayment plan for the organization. Reserves can be built over time by rolling unused contingency funds into reserves, designating unrestricted bequests to reserves, or raising funds from the community for this purpose.

After all of these steps had been implemented, the organization was on its way toward solid fiscal health.

The stabilization model was implemented in Baltimore, Seattle, Phoenix, and other communities through a series of challenge and technical assistance grants. NAS gained additional insights that further shaped its model.

The fiscal discipline to balance budgets, eliminate debt, and build cash reserves stifles creativity and risk taking, leading to a very dull organization. So a new Step 4 was inserted: a risk venture fund that organizations can use to create experimental programs to try new ideas without harming their operating budget discipline.

Now it is time for the next step, endowment. Yes, you should have it, but how much? Benchmarking indicates that if the other steps are in place an endowment that produces 20 percent of the operating budget would bring financial vitality to any organization.

Organizations have periodic needs for capital equipment and buildings, so a final Step 6 was added to ensure these expenses are considered. While developed to stabilize arts organizations, NAS concepts were used to assist other nonprofits and implementing them could be a big help in getting donors to consider gifts to organizations with less than stellar financials.

Exhibit 4.6 demonstrates how the stabilization model can be applied to a $10 million organization that just balances its operating budget in most years, has $100,000 in an endowment fund, $500,000 of accumulated debt, and $300,000 in equipment needs over the next five to eight years.

When you look at the ideal model, the $44.8 million of capital needs can take your breath away. That's why the three-year target column is important. Once you see the big picture, you need to figure out how much can be raised in the short term to begin the path to stabilization. For this organization, a campaign of $4 million was all that could be contemplated.

What common questions come up as you try to raise funds for a stabilization campaign? What are the pros and cons?

Does the 5 percent contingency need to be immediately implemented (Step 1)? No, of course not. For most organizations, creating the contingency in a single year would be too difficult. You may want to budget year one for a 1 percent contingency and grow the contingency by 1 percent a year until you hit the 5 percent target. You can always roll over unused contingency funds to the next year. For example, in year, one you budget a 1 percent contingency but only use half of that; roll the remaining half

EXHIBIT 4.6   STABILIZATION CAMPAIGN BUDGET MODEL

	Ideal	Three year Objective	Progress Toward Objectives
#1 — Balanced budget with 5% contingency	$500,000	$500,000	100%
#2 — Eliminate debt	$500,000	$500,000	100%
#3 — Reserve funds @ 25% of operations	$2,500,000	$1,000,000	40%
#4 — Risk venture fund	$1,000,000	$200,000	20%
#5 — Current endowment	$100,000		
Additional endowment needed	$39,900,000	$1,500,000	4%
#6 — Buildings & capital equipment	$300,000	$300,000	100%
TOTAL	$44,800,000	$4,000,000	

percent over to the next year so you start with a base of a half percent. In year two, start with the half percent left over from year one and add 1.5 percent to reach the target of 2 percent. You can use this part of the stabilization model as a case-building tool to increase annual fund giving, particularly from current and past board members who understand how operating budgets can fluctuate and will be more apt to help make donations to build the contingency fund.

Is debt repayment fundraising (Step 2) difficult? Yes, it is in isolation. However, we have found that showing donors the comprehensive stabilization plan gives them faith in the future and a greater willingness to erase any accumulated deficits. The six-step model also provides donors with a shopping list. They may not want to give to debt retirement but appreciate the fact you are doing it thus making them more willing to make a donation to your building campaign.

Won't donors frown on you having cash reserves (Step 3)? And, can you have too much money in your cash reserves? In researching the answers to these questions, we have found that most viable organizations strive for cash reserves of three to six months. The three-month target for stabilization is somewhat conservative. The National Council of Foundations studied the issue of cash reserves several years ago and concluded that cash reserves up to 100% of your operating budget are not excessive. The council did come down hard on a few organizations, one with 500 percent of its operating budget in a reserve fund, and suggested they spend down the excess reserves for new initiatives, which they did. You actually may have more cash reserves on hand right now than you think. Before starting any endowment campaign you should audit the current endowment you have on hand. How much of it is board-designated endowment (temporarily restricted or quasi-endowment) and how much is donor-designated endowment (permanently restricted or true endowment)? For donor-designated endowments, who were the donors, and when were the gifts made?

We worked with one organization that wanted an endowment campaign and found $2 million of endowment already on hand. One million dollars was board-designated endowment and the organization was unsure of the origin of the rest. After digging through a bank-like vault in the building, which contained all of the board minutes and financial records for the last 75 years, we checked for endowment gifts and could not find any for the last 25 years. We then started with board minutes in the 1920s and identified one board member who was soliciting endowment gifts and making board resolutions to thank donors for their gifts to the endowment fund. He personally raised the $1 million of designated endowment by 1935, when he passed away. Until this campaign in 1995, nobody on the board had any interest in endowment fundraising. It was a great story. We were able to capture the names of all of the endowment donors and put them in our gift recognition club for endowment and estate gifts and let their descendents know of these prior acts of generosity. Our other recommendation to this client was to reclassify the $1 million of board-designated endowment to cash reserves, as the board had been criticized for raiding the endowment fund a few years earlier to pay for a construction project overrun. We had to explain to donors that the board was really using cash reserves—not donor-designated endowment funds.

Audit all of your endowment funds to sort them out by board-designated and donor-designated sources of funding. If you have significant board-designated endowment, shift enough to reach the 25 percent reserve fund threshold to demonstrate your fiscal prudence to donors. (You can still invest these funds with your endowment funds and can pass a board resolution making access to these reserve funds difficult.) You want to make sure future boards and administrative managers understand they should borrow from the reserve fund (with interest, if you want) rather than going to a bank.

In Exhibit 4.6, the sample organization decided that the risk venture fund (Step 4) was not a high priority; therefore it would be only partially funded. If donors got excited about this area and wanted to overfund the three-year objective, that would be okay.

Even though the organization's planning work started out seeking endowment funds, using the financial stabilization model, it became clear that the endowment target for this round of funding would be only $1.5 million (Step 5). However, in showing the ideal model, the organization was planting the seed in the minds of donors that the real endowment need was $40 million. This messaging is critically important to share with donors who could provide endowment support in their estate plans. As one donor reflected upon learning of the enormous endowment need:

> I had no idea they required an endowment that large. They are in my estate but I need to go back and give them more. They won't get it for 15 years, hopefully longer, but I could do a lot more for them now that I understand what they really need to secure their future.

What a classic case statement reaction—the donor got it; the light bulb came on. The stabilization financial model enabled the donor to discover and connect with the needs of this organization that he had supported for decades. The facts of the case and the national benchmarking sold him on the need to make a larger estate gift for endowment.

Because not all donors will support endowment (remember, most foundations have guidelines against it and most corporations want more immediate impact), always include some non-endowment components in any endowment or financial stabilization campaign (Step 6). If you need a new building, this number could be $5 million. In Exhibit 4.6, the organization's needs were modest, but not zero. Given most campaigns take 3 to 7 years to complete and have pledge periods of 3 to 5 years, organizations should look at their special equipment needs for 7 to 10 years in the future as they assemble their capital equipment and building needs budgets.

The Role of Planned Estate Gifts for Endowment Cases   Even though you want to raise endowment funds and want to "sell" endowment, instituting a basic planned-estate-gifts marketing program can help you to build your endowment fund through undesignated bequests over time.

As you have seen from the previous sections of this chapter, endowment is a complicated concept. For donors who have served on numerous nonprofit boards, especially if some of these boards have been in higher education, many of the endowment concepts will be familiar so your endowment selling proposition is easier. For other organizations, however, all of this endowment information may be new and somewhat numbing in its complexity. You end up spending a great deal of time explaining a relatively unexciting concept to many people who want to see their gifts make an impact now (while the perpetuity thing does interest some people, others want to see their gifts make a difference in their lifetimes).

For people with long affiliations with your organization, leaving 5 percent, 10 percent, or even half of their estates to your charitable cause is a reasonable topic for discussion. While not selling endowment during estate-gift discussions, you can explain to people that by board policy all unrestricted bequests will go into the endowment fund (or as one organization's board decided, 50 percent was designated for endowment and the other 50 percent to the building maintenance fund to help preserve its historic buildings). Your marketing emphasis is finding historic members of your legacy society and asking new people to join it.

A survey reported in *The Chronicle of Philanthropy* found that:

> Bequests present another avenue for fundraising growth among wealthy donors; only forty-one percent of survey respondents had arranged for a charitable gift in their will. Patrick M. Rooney, director of research at Indiana University's Center for Philanthropy, was surprised at the low number. "You would think that a majority of these households, or even a super-majority, would have charitable bequests in their wills . . . ."[4] [Reprinted with permission of *The Chronicle of Philanthropy*, http://philanthropy.com.]

The Case for Comprehensive Campaigns

When you read about the megacampaigns run by major universities (such as Stanford's upcoming $4 billion effort), you wonder how they can raise such astounding amounts of money. While it may be a huge number, universities take a comprehensive approach to their campaigns. They include everything raised during the campaign.

Components of a comprehensive campaign include annual fund donations, special projects (usually a variety), building projects (usually multiple ones), endowments, and planned estate gifts. These large campaigns last 5 to 7 years (although some stretch up to 10 years in length).

The advantage of comprehensive campaigns is your ability to make the triple ask: (1) renewal of annual fund support, (2) a five-year pledge to buildings or endowments, and (3) a planned estate gift.

To make the case for the comprehensive campaign, you need to take all of the prior aspects of this chapter, the case for annual fund, buildings, and estate gifts, and combine them into one large story for the good of your institution. Such comprehensive casework is also helped by a good strategic plan and a clear vision of the organization's future (see Exhibit 4.7).

In Chapter 5, The Win-Win Ask, the gift table and its role in asking for gifts will be discussed. One reason to use the comprehensive campaign model is that lead gifts in campaigns typically are in the 10 to 15 percent range of the total campaign goal. For our sample organization's $22 million comprehensive campaign, a gift in the $4 million to $6 million range would be considered a bold, yet reasonable ask by a lead gift donor. This compares with only presenting the $5 million new building target where an appropriate gift would be $500,000 to $1 million. Some corporate donors will benchmark their giving at 1 percent of the campaign goal. By showing the full scale of the comprehensive philanthropic needs of the organization, you are making the case for a larger contribution to the campaign.

Case Statement Formats

When I started fundraising, we had only typewriters and carbon copies. Putting pictures and graphs into a case statement came only with formal production of a four-color brochure, which involved graphic designers, a large printing press, and a significant budget. Times have changed dramatically for case production technology in a quarter of a century. You can still do the old-fashioned 10- to 20-page narrative case statement with lots of gray pages filled with type and detailed information. However, just as technologies have changed so have our donors. The time and willingness of donors to read those 15 pages have dramatically diminished. Most donors are busy and want a document they can scan quickly. If they want more information, they will ask you to get it for them, or you can attach it to the case executive summary or outline, or you can post it on a prospective-donor-only web site.

EXHIBIT 4.7   COMPREHENSIVE CAMPAIGN MODEL

Annual Fund	We need to continue increasing our number of donors and build our operating support from $500,000 a year to $750,000 a year during the campaign.	$3 million (over five years)
	The following list of projects are needed to help our departments succeed:	$2 million (to fund six different projects in four departments)
Buildings	New building A for $5 million will help us achieve our mission by . . . plus the $2 million renovation of Building B will accomplish . . .	$7 million (for two buildings)
Endowment & Estate Gifts	$10 million is needed in cash pledges and estate gifts to endow three professorships and ten student scholarships to enable us to . . .	$10 million
Campaign Total		$22 million comprehensive campaign goal

- "I know I have the time to read the case document, I just don't have the patience anymore."
- "Our company advertises all of the time on TV and radio. We have given up on 60-second and 30-second ads; you can just barely keep peoples' attention with 15 second spots."

Always remember in writing and presenting your case that your goal is to achieve understanding and comprehension by your target audience of donors. It is not about winning design awards or fancy writing, but gaining understanding leading to a big gift decision.

As you develop the case, it serves as your copy platform throughout the campaign for a series of materials that need to be stable and inclusive for at least two to three years during the cultivation and solicitation phase of your campaign. Stability takes hard work and is good reason to go through the case-refinement process described later in this chapter.

Components of the Case Statement Copy Platform

1. A 20-slide PowerPoint outline with graphics for small-group presentations that can be printed into a presentation guide for solicitation calls.
2. A one-page executive summary.
3. A seven-minute presentation on DVD.
4. A 12-page color brochure.
5. Question-and-answer document containing frequently asked questions.
6. A 30-second elevator speech.
7. Web site links to full information on all aspects of the campaign projects (dozens of pages of narrative, architectural renderings, budgets, etc.)
8. Structural foundation proposals with every detail about the case (e.g., select the toughest, most demanding foundation that you will be approaching in the next year or two, follow their guidelines, and write everything you know for the 20- to 30-page proposal they may request—for building campaigns the Kresge Foundation is a candidate).

Presentation Guide   Depending on your writing style, you may want to write the long, detailed narrative case statement and then go from that format to an outline for the presentation guide, or you can prepare the presentation guide outline and then write the narrative later. The choice is a personal, stylistic one. Either way works fine.

Why a presentation guide? Over time, we have found that giving donors the 12-page, four-color, campaign brochure on a call did not work well. They would skim through it and not listen to my presentation of the important elements of the case. You could not tell where they were in their review of the materials. This led to the realization that the long brochure or long narrative case is a wonderful leave-behind piece but not an appropriate asking tool. It is more effective to develop a presentation guide using a bulleted outline style. In the olden days, you wrote the outline on a typewriter and then inserted each sheet of paper in nonglare sheet protectors in a three-ring notebook and you were ready to go. These same outline papers could be put on transparencies and used on overhead projectors for small-group presentations. Then, word processing made outline creation easier and improved its appearance. PowerPoint took the presentation to the next level in terms of consistency and the ability to include pictures, charts, and graphs. You can show the presentation on your laptop to one or two people, project the images on an LCD projector to a small group, or print off the pages for use in the old-fashioned, three-ring notebook (which is still the best tool for one-on-one presentations and on an asking call).

The presentation guide allows you to manage the flow of case information from you to your audience of potential donors. You can stay on the heritage page of your organization to focus on that topic and to answer any questions the donor may have. You can linger on the photos of people your organization has helped in the community. You can show building plans, summary budgets, gift tables, and anything else you need to tell your story.

One of the important characteristics of the presentation guide is its intentional incompleteness. It is meant only for presentations by a fundraiser and/or fundraising volunteer. While a donor can review the highlights of the case outline, it comes to life through a face-to-face meeting.

As a former magazine editor, I never forget the saying "a picture is worth a thousand words." Finding images for every page of the case statement is critically important to getting the emotional impact of the case to come alive for donors.

Why only 12 to 20 slides? Venture-capital presentations are structured with 12 slides with the goal of presenting the basic business concepts in 15 minutes. In presenting your case to donors, that should be your goal as well. As you engage donors with the case, they should begin asking questions and reflecting on your organization. Ideally, your 20-minute presentation expands into a 60-minute interactive discussion with this additional time donor driven. If you have too much information, too many slides and data, you will overpresent and not have time to listen and respond to questions. Always remember that adults learn by questioning and discussing, not passive listening.

Getting your case to this level of brevity is very hard work. For samples of case outlines, check out our web site at www.WinningGifts.INFO.

THE PROCESS OF CASE REFINEMENT

One person needs to be the owner of the case statement—the writer, the editor, the final arbiter of advice from the many people who will want to help make the case better. While a committee and many voices can help make the case stronger, you cannot write by committee or edit by committee. One person needs to own the case from start to finish. From many years of experience, we would strongly recommend this person be a professional fundraiser rather than a professional writer or someone from your marketing department. You can hire a copy editor or writer to jazz up the language and to make the writing snap and pop, but the basic writing and editing needs to be done with the major-gift donors in mind (see Chapter 2, Donor Values).

The title of this section is "process" of case refinement. Too often, people think of the case statement only as a product. And yes, you need to develop the initial draft of the case statement to have a product to test with others. But the process of case refinement, accomplished by sharing it with others within your organization and then by auditioning the case through focus group meetings and leadership briefings with donors and potential donors, is important in building ownership of the case and its messages of organizational importance and financial need. As soon as you start the auditioning process involving donors, you are in subtle, no-ask, fundraising mode. You should hurry to get to this phase of the case development process, but you do not have to rush to complete it until your case has stabilized. The more people you involve in your auditions, the more people you are cultivating for a gift in response to the case.

Share Internally

Depending on how long you have been at your organization, you may be able to write your case statement in isolation without input from your colleagues on staff. I have never been anywhere that long (or I'm not that smart), so I have developed a technique of interviewing the senior managers of my organization (or my client's organization) to help learn about the organization from their viewpoint. By keeping an open mind and an open ear, one can learn marvelous things about an organization that will make your case stronger, more memorable, and stickier. You get concrete stories and details from program managers that help you to defend the case when donors ask probing questions so they can better understand why you need to raise money.

Once you have completed your information-gathering interviews, write your case draft and then circulate it among your colleagues so they can fact-check information gathered from your interviews with them. This review builds internal ownership of the case and helps the senior management team better understand the fundraising process. In sharing the case with them, you will need to explain why you are writing the case and how it will be used by donors as they consider investments in your organization.

I had been on the job only 30 days as the director of corporate and foundation fundraising for Field Museum of Natural History in Chicago (yes, again, but it was early in my career and I had a lot to learn in those days), when the museum president got a call from a newly formed major foundation in Chicago. The foundation needed to meet its 5 percent rule for the Internal Revenue Service and give grants to reputable nonprofits, but it was still hiring program staff. Foundation officials were calling major charitable organizations in the city asking them to submit grant proposals of $100,000 to $250,000 in the next month with grant awards promised quickly to meet their IRS deadline. They did not need specific projects but rather the story of the organization and why it was worthy of operating support that year and in the future. I was called into the president's office with my vice president for development and told to get busy. A healthy grant could lay the cornerstone for years and years of support from this new foundation. I was in panic. I didn't know anything yet. So I asked for a list of the senior management team and sent out a memo asking for quick interviews to prepare for writing this grant proposal. Because of the substantial size of the prospective grant, and the president's interest in seeing it happen, I had instant access.

As I talked to the managers, they suggested which of their direct reports I should talk to—the vice president for research told me about five key curators (research faculty) who would provide me with good information; the vice president for exhibitions sent me to the exhibit preparation manager, the outreach coordinator for traveling exhibits, and so on. After a week, I had 15 interviews completed and piles of yellow notepads filled.

I started writing. Once the grant proposal was drafted I circulated a copy to every interviewee and got back corrections, clarifications, additions, and suggestions for additional interviews. Once completed, the grant was submitted and the museum got its operating grant. One of the fun by-products of this work was a call from someone in the human resources department who asked permission to use the grant (with a few edits to take out the funding request) as a new employee orientation manual. Nobody had ever written a comprehensive description of the museum that could be shared in 20 pages with new hires. This orientation version of the grant proposal also became useful for volunteer and new trustee orientation meetings.

In addition to engaging your colleagues and fellow employees with the fundraising process through case development you are helping build them into a cohesive marketing force for your fundraising program. Many donors, when asked for a stretch gift, will embark on kindhearted, but serious and thorough due diligence. They want to make sure their gift is a good investment and will find ways of cross-referencing and checking your case statement assertions with other donors, board members, and staff members (at all levels of the organization). If the case reactions from everyone internally and externally are consistent, the donor is more apt to make a great gift.

Marie Ann was asked for a $500,000 gift to our campaign. She had been used to making $100,000 gifts to a variety of organizations but had never been asked for a gift of this magnitude before. She was close to the organization and gave to it regularly but was not involved as a board member. She was pleasantly nonplussed by the level of our gift request and said she would need to think about it. I was part of the calling team and told her to let me know what further information I could provide her with so she could make an informed decision. I did get one phone call and then nothing for weeks. I heard from my staff connections that she was calling around asking questions. Then, one day I got the big call. She said she would make the gift and was proud to do so. She told me she had made 23 phone calls to staff, volunteers, board members, and other donors to the campaign to check on how we were doing. She said:

> I can't believe this organization has gotten its act together so well. They're well organized and know what they're doing. I'm pleased to make this gift. And, while you offered me the five-year pledge period I understand

that the section of the building that you are asking me to remodel needs to get done immediately, so I will send you a check in the next 90 days.

I can still hear her delighted voice telling me about her winning-gift decision.

Audition Externally

Once your internal staff has signed off on your case statement, it is time to start testing it with outside audiences. Just as musicals and plays heading to Broadway will audition out of town in Atlanta or Atlantic City to see how the production plays with live audiences, you want to preview your case with donor audiences. Let them know you are experimenting with the case and want constructive feedback. Based on their formal and informal reactions you want to recast the show, sharpen the tunes, drop some numbers, and add new scenes to make the production sparkle.

Start your auditioning by using the development committee of your board or the entire board. Board members know you very well from their attendance at meetings, and they need to understand the importance of the case as you want some (if not all) of them involved with your fundraising program. Their knowledge and acceptance of the case is critically important.

In presenting your case to small groups, use good presentation techniques to ensure your fundraising story is heard and noticed by your audience. Education theory tells us that some people are listeners and other readers. Reach out to both types of information gatherers in public meetings by using a visual outline of your key points. This helps to keep you organized as a presenter but, more important, burns in messages visually as the listener is absorbing your message aurally.

In their book, *Listen Up*, Larry Barker and Kittie Watson provide good advice for making effective presentations. They identify four levels of communication: perceiving, interpreting, evaluating, and responding. They offer advice for each of these levels to improve speaker interaction and reduce communication errors:

1. Perceiving—speak a little more loudly than normal, remove distractions, and move closer to the listener.

2. Interpreting—use relevant and specific examples, ask the listener to summarize, repeat major themes, and summarize your presentation.

3. Evaluating—reinforce critical points with energy verbally and visually, help listeners understand what's in it for them, emphasize the importance of the message by using hard data (statistics, factual evidence, expert testimony).

4. Responding—explain positive and negative consequences of different listener responses, ask listeners to identify actions they are going to take, send a written reminder.[5]

Many of these ideas you may use already or have seen public speakers employ at training sessions. Being an active speaker is important. Your energy and commitment can make all of the difference in the world. If you are passionate about your case for support, it will come across. Use some of the ideas here to engage your listeners so they are not sitting passively but actively interacting. For example, use a feedback form during the meeting to get people to summarize the important points they heard. Or have them share with a partner what they have learned and write out an action plan based on the information in the case.

When I was a vice president of a university going through this case-building process, I had the crazy idea of sending the near-final case draft out to every board member (30 people) with a request for editing by the end of the week. My staff almost killed me and thought I was crazy. I suspected, and was correct, that not everyone would respond so quickly. It was very interesting to see who did respond and took the extra time to thoroughly review the case. We were surprised that a couple of our major prospects on the board took the time and made some excellent comments. It was also intriguing to see who engaged through this written review process versus who spoke up at the verbal review meetings.

Throughout your auditioning process you want to empower dissent. You want constructive criticism that will make the case stronger. You want your board members to play one of their most important roles for your organization—representing the community. What questions would their friends ask? Their spouse/partner or business associates? What questions do they have before making a major gift to your campaign? By the way, this is a great time to tell the board members again that they will be the first asked to give. Others want to know that the board has participated in the campaign and that members have made stretch gifts to the best of their ability. It is always interesting to note that after this discussion of board participation in giving—total participation and early participation—board members ask much tougher questions about the case for support.

For the board audition plus the participative leadership briefing focus meetings discussed in Chapter 3, Listen, record feedback on a one-page (front and back) feedback response form to capture individual information from each board member, and eventually, each focus group participant. Case-related feedback forms could include the following questions:

1. What three things did you learn about ABC Organization at today's presentation?

2. What items need more explanation?

3. What questions do you have about the case statement?

4. Given the three elements of the case (a) _____, (b) _____, and (c) _____, please state which one is most important to you. Explain why.

5. What objections do you think your friends might make when they are asked to give to this campaign?

6. What other advice do you have for us?

☐ Yes, I'm willing to work on the campaign in some way.

Name (please print): _____

As a reminder, have them fill out this form first individually using 5 to 10 minutes of meeting time. Then have them pick partners and explain their answers to each other. Then the facilitator should ask each set of partners to report out to the main group. Collect these comments on flipchart sheets.

Just having a live audience will improve your presentation of the case. To let your presenters practice their presentations, hold a minimum of four auditions with various groups of donors. Have the same person present the case so this person (or team) can go up the learning curve of hearing questions and objections from participants, reading feedback forms, and reflecting on ways to make the case more memorable. Because each case presentation is the same, you can present three times a day, every week, until you have covered your constituency sufficiently. You want to complete your sessions within two to three months so you can move on to the next stage of case preparation—one-on-one interviews.

Processing the Complex Case   Donors in the community can take summary statements from your comprehensive case and trust that you have done your homework and due diligence in preparing it. Your board of directors should not be so trusting, nor you so complacent as to assume you can skip a thorough grounding in all elements of the case by your board, senior management, and professional staff (faculty, physicians, musicians, etc.).

But, how can you make this processing fun and thorough at the same time? Go into retreat mode (or *summit* mode, as we like to call it today). Ask for a one-day or, better yet, two-day off-site summit meeting to provide your leadership and management team processing time around the case for support. A summit will enable you to reflect on your organization's mission, vision, strategic plan, and how they all inform the philanthropic fundraising case for support.

After presenting the summary 20-minute case statement, distribute your leadership team (with spouses if possible) into breakout groups to hear a 30-minute in-depth presentation of each element of the case. You can rotate through the five to seven case elements in a day or a day and a half, capturing information on feedback forms and flipcharts. Each case element can have two presenters so one can be telling the story and the other listening and observing.

Here is a sample of a hospital's complex case for support broken into a retreat format:

Day 1

9 A.M. Overview of mission, vision, and strategic plan

Discussion

10 A.M. Case statement presentation

10:30 A.M. Breakout groups

Heart and Vascular Institute

Maternity/NICU

12 Noon Lunch

1 P.M. Breakout groups

Cancer

Orthopedics

2:30 Break

3:00 Financial Vitality through Endowment

Facilities and Equipment Upgrades

5:00 Break

6:30 Dinner and social time

Day 2

8:30 A.M. Breakfast

9:00 What did you learn yesterday?

General reflections

9:30 Breakout

Our People

10:00 Reports from breakout group presenters—What did your group learn?

Discussion by all participants

Lunch

1:00 P.M. Complete feedback forms

Our plan of action

If you have enough fundraising staff, assign one person to be the flipchart recorder and listener for each breakout discussion presentation. The breakout discussions can be co-presented by the administrative program leader and the professional leader. In our example, the Heart and Vascular presentation might be made by the product line administrator for heart services along with the physician medical director for heart services at the hospital.

After presenting their topic four to six times in two days and listening to questions from board members and their spouses, the topic leaders will start to understand the type of people-friendly language needed to sell their case. Worksheets from each person for their two days will also provide feedback on questions they had but did not raise during the discussions. The worksheets should also seek to identify project champions for each for your breakout sessions.

This type of two-day case summit is particularly effective when you have a high-net-worth board. You can get a year of cultivation work done in one weekend if you do this correctly.

One client we worked with did a similar type of weekend retreat with its entire top donor prospect pool. See what you can come up with to deepen your donors' engagement, feedback, and ownership of your cause as they interact with your case statement.

Importance of the One-on-one Interview   As powerful as group experiences are, nothing is better than the face-to-face, one-on-one interview to get case reactions from your most important donors and community opinion leaders. Fundraising consultants have used the philanthropic market research study (feasibility study or planning study) process for decades to help donors to engage with the case for support. These confidential interviews with people hired to listen rather than to sell help organizations gain a clear understanding of how well the case is being accepted and understood.

Does that mean you need to hire a consultant every time you want to test your case for support? As a consultant I would love to say yes, but unfortunately this is not brain surgery. Anyone good at listening can do this type of interviewing. Review the concepts in Chapter 3, Listen, for ideas about tuning in to a specific donor. Take good notes and remember your job is to listen, not sell.

Note: One reason consultants are hired for this type of listening is their total objectivity. They are not there to sell the case but rather to listen to case reactions. In addition, consultants have developed highly structured interviewing processes that enable them to interview 50 to 100 donors within four to eight weeks (of course, they have no operational duties so them can devote as much as time as needed to get the interviews done quickly).

One-on-one interviews are a combination of relationship building, subtle selling (as you encourage the interviewee to read the case), and listening for case questions, objections, and passions. In addition, these personal interviews allow follow-up probing and the chance for the donor to ask basic questions they might be shy about asking in a larger group (we find board interviews particularly interesting as many board members do not want to look dumb in front of their colleagues so they nod their head at board meetings without understanding what is being said).

No matter who does the interviewing, write up good notes, and publish a brief findings report on what was learned during the process. After reviewing the findings from the interviews, rewrite your case statement again using language and perceptions from the interviews as your guide.

Lock in Your Case

After gathering all of the information from leadership briefing focus group meetings and one-on-one interviews, it is time to lock in the case, to solidify it for use over the next two to three years. By now you should have a sense of the stable, simple themes that resonate with your donors. Your ultimate goal, of course, is the 30-second elevator speech that you can develop and then train everyone else on the fundraising team to put their own spin on to convince people to make gifts to your organization.

Make a Movie   To help solidify your case, make a movie. Produce a seven-minute DVD that uses candid interviews of your organization's volunteer leaders, donors, and CEO to make your case. Ask them to reflect on the importance of your organization, its vision of the future, and the need for contributed funds.

Just as a picture is worth a thousand words, a movie is worth a thousand brochures. The movie is usually better than any site visit you can organize for donors (if possible, conduct a site visit tour and then show the DVD at the conclusion of your tour). While site visits are powerful, your organization may not always be active with the full range of people who benefit from your services. Not all of your best volunteers can be there and not everyone remembers all of their best lines during the visit.

The movie is also highly transportable. How do you take your hospital campus, your food bank, or your college to donors 5 or 500 miles away? How do you capture the attention of the busy corporate executive who will give you only 20 minutes in her office? through the magic of motion pictures.

In the late 1980s, I was sent by my Los Angeles–based consulting firm to serve as resident counsel to work with Oregon Public Broadcasting in Portland, Oregon (resident counsel is when the consultant goes on site, full-time with a client for the duration of the campaign). When it came time to make the campaign video, my client told me I would work with one of its in-house staff members, Matt Miner. Matt did the station's on-air promotions and would be more expert in producing an eight-minute video than any outsider our firm could hire (and far less expensive, of course). Matt not only trained me for that particular video production that led to a successful campaign that went over goal, but he has teamed up with me to produce 15 other campaign movies that have helped to raise hundreds of millions of dollars. For samples of case movies that Matt and his team have helped create, check out our web site at www.WinningGifts .INFO.

What are the elements of a winning-gifts movie? Before scheduling any camera shooting, create an outline of the story you are trying to tell. Have your PowerPoint case outline completed so you can strategize on who the best people are to bring it to life. Who is your target audience? Given the limits of the short amount of time (six to eight minutes), you have to think simply. What are the three things you want the donor to remember from this movie?

1. This is a well-run organization doing good works in the community as attested to by influential community donors.
2. The organization has a problem and has identified a solution that requires financial investments.
3. I should consider a gift to this cause.

Select five people to be interviewed in the movie. One can be the staff leader of the organization. The rest should be board members and donors who believe in the cause, who are highly respected by other donors, who have given to the campaign, and who are passionate and articulate. The interviewer should be off camera and edited out of the production. Ask leading questions to get your subjects responding to the interviewer rather than worrying about how they look on camera. Keep things relaxed and look back to study interview notes to see who was passionate and had elements of the case ready to tell others. After two to three days of shooting interviews and "B roll" (background action shots of the organization making a difference in the community; B roll plays as a silent visual while your interviewees talk about your organization), review the many hours of recorded material to find the 15- to 30-second sound bites you can compile to make the case for the organization's campaign. It's a lot of work, but so exciting to see the case come together through everyone else's storytelling.

Moviemaking is the final step in locking in the case. Once the movie is done, you can grab digital images in the movie electronically for inclusion in pocket brochures and the coffeetable brochure.

Make It Stick   Now that you have your case statement in mind, how do you make it memorable and sticky?

In response to the excitement about *The Tipping Point* (see Part II, Seek Winning Gifts for Your Organization), Chip Heath and Dan Heath recently published a sequel focused just on the memorable, sticky message—*Made to Stick.*

They present ways of refining your messaging using their Six Principles of Sticky Ideas:

Principle 1: Simplicity

Principle 2: Unexpectedness

Principle 3: Concreteness

Principle 4: Credibility

Principle 5: Emotions

Principle 6: Stories

This book is a paradigm shifter that initially makes your brain numb (at least, it did mine). Many of their ideas, including several for nonprofit settings, help to clarify the importance of using as many of the sticky idea principles as you can.

The whole idea of simplicity is getting your message down to a core idea, a lead concept that gets to the heart of the matter. As mentioned in the previous section, creating a DVD helps to get to this core idea through the production process. They caution about the "Curse of Knowledge"—the idea that insiders tend to know too much and give out too much detail. Using your volunteers and the techniques of interviewing and focus groups will help to let others force you to simplify your message.

Unexpectedness is a way to capture listeners' attention quickly. A good story will do this as will several of the techniques mentioned in *Made to Stick.*

Concreteness has been explored earlier in making your case. Don't just tell the theory of endowment, but give concrete examples of the impact of a $50,000 scholarship.

Credibility was discussed by Robert Cialdini in *Ethical Influence* (see Part II) and, in fact, Cialdini is referenced in *Made to Stick.* The authors site the use of limited statistics to give the speaker credibility and discuss how to make statistics user friendly rather than overwhelming.

Emotions are important in all fundraising. You need the passionate volunteer, the compelling program leader, the DVD, and grateful constituents to bring heart to your message.

We've already discussed the critical importance of a story for every page of your case outline. Stories make your case concrete and personal.

Made to Stick is another must-read.[6]

WAYS TO ACHIEVE TOP-OF-MIND UNDERSTANDING OF YOUR CASE

The goal of all of your case writing, testing, and production is to help move your organization to a higher level of awareness with your potential donors. You are developing a tool kit to soften the ground for a philanthropic gift request. The more top-of-mind awareness you can get with donors, the less time will be spent on the ask meeting explaining what your organization is about and why it is worthy of support.

One of the benefits of the philanthropic market research study one-on-one interviews is getting donors to reflect on where your organization is in their philanthropic worldview. Are you their top charitable priority, top one-third charity, bottom third, or not even on the radar screen? This is the reality check for your organization. People may tell you that they had not even thought of the organization until the interview process. That is sobering but that is the reality for that particular donor. The good news is you are starting to interact with the donor and bring your organization to the donor's attention. Hopefully, your board members indicated that your organization is their top or top one-third charity (if not, you are recruiting and retaining the wrong board members).

Understanding study interviewee perceptions of your organization is critical to determining what marketing will be needed for your fundraising to be successful. It may be a blow to your ego or the ego of the board, but, if the market research study shows you are the best-kept secret in town, then you need to do more top-of-mind marketing than fundraising in the near future. This is another winning-gifts approach—delay asking for the gift when you know the donor is still trying to understand the value of your organization. Unless you have an emergency that demands immediate funding, be patient and allow the donor time to integrate your organization into his worldview of important charities.

This is why higher education has such a leg up on other fundraising endeavors. While the donors may have graduated 30 years earlier and be totally out of touch with the campus and academic life today, it does not generally take too long to catch them up to date, given their one-time familiarity with the campus. Recapturing memories is always easier than making them.

Realize for the older donor that is what you are trying to do: Recreate impactful, striking, meaningful memories that are powerful enough to crowd out or at least join all of the donor's other memories and experiences with other nonprofit organizations.

Resurrecting Good Memories

Of course, colleges have a big advantage in attracting potential donors given their ever-growing pool of alumni, many of whom have fond memories of their years on campus. But, as some college fundraisers will tell you, not all college experiences were positive. For some donors, telling someone from the college about their painful collegiate experiences helps to diffuse the problem and allow some of their fonder memories to surface. You need to listen to the painful stories and try to get the donor to reflect on what were the most pleasant college memories—football games, dorm life, a class that helped early career efforts, or whatever. Some people met their spouse in college; others picked up a hobby or enjoyed a poetry class. Help be the donor's guide to rebuilding nostalgic memories of the good old days (or at least a few of the old days that were good).

But what are the rest of us to do? For one Boy Scouts of America campaign, we asked former scouts to take a field trip back to summer camp to see what young boys of today were up to. We helped them "smell the campfire" and see young scouts in action to help rebuild memories of their own scouting days. We asked them to tell us about their most memorable scouting experience, and heard from one prominent corporate president about how he had just missed earning the rank of Eagle Scout because he could not do the 10-mile nature hike. Another major donor said he almost killed his troopmates when he felled a tree in the wrong direction (he ended up as a senior executive of a major lumber company). As those memories came alive, we asked them to reflect on the importance of scouting values in their lives and the lives of their children.

If you are working on behalf of a library, ask about times the donor may have used a library. When fundraising on behalf of a community college, ask the donor if he ever had a family member attend or hired an employee who woke up to the value of education at age 25 or 30 and turned her life around by attending a community college.

As you can see, many times we don't know if a donor has a memory related to our cause and we need to ask that question first. If the answer is yes or sort of, we can pursue one path. If the answer is no, then read on.

Creating Memories

Most nonprofits won't be able to tap into a memory the donor already has, so the organization needs to create new memories through concrete experiences. Create cultivation events, site visits, and program presentations that build new, lasting memories. This is where your case movie is so important—it creates memories. Your goal is to make elements of your organization clear, memorable, and understandable to donors.

Here are some examples. A university held a dinner party at its downtown social club asking professors to teach a 20-minute class at the dinner table before the meal was served. Their students were the donors at each table. Professors brought textbooks they authored, laser beams flashed through waterglasses and complex, exotic materials used to manufacture computer chips passed around—the classes were so popular we got groans from donors when the bell rang to tell people dinner was about to be served. We had to extend the experience another 10 minutes because everyone was having so much fun.

A hospital in mid-construction was opened to the community for a "dusty shoe" open house. Volunteers were stationed throughout the partially completed hospital to explain to their friends and neighbors how the surgery suites would work, why there were so many pipes and ducts in the ceiling spaces, and how the gaslines and firewalls worked in the patient rooms. A tour map and painted fountain in the dust of the unpaved parking lot showed the location of the "founders' fountain" of donor names that would help honor contributors to the project. Instead of the expected 500 guests, more than 1,500 people came to the event, sending staff scurrying to the grocery story to replenish refreshments.

A symphony orchestra invited prospective campaign donors to working rehearsals followed by a box lunch on stage with the conductor and several musicians from the orchestra. Donors got to wander the hall to sit in various seats to listen to the rehearsal. During lunch on stage they were able to find their subscription ticket seat from the viewpoint of the orchestra members and visit with musicians, who were wearing bluejeans instead of tuxedos. As one donor said after the rehearsal lunch:

> I learned more today in two hours at this event that I have sitting in my seat listening to the orchestra for 20 years. This was a lot of fun. And, those musicians are real people. They work hard and deserve our support.

Let your imagination go. Find something organic about your organization and work with volunteers to plan memorable events to create top-of-mind awareness of your organization with potential donors.

Creating memorable cultivation events is a great way for your fundraising volunteers who are connectors, but not askers, to help your organization. In addition to creating and shaping the event, they should help you develop the invitation list, sign the invitation letter (and include small personal notes whenever possible), and make follow-up phone calls to three to five of their friends to ensure good attendance at the event.

A quick word of advice: Once you have recruited a group of people to come to your event through a mailing and follow-up phone calls, do not assume they will remember to come. Start calling two days before your event to remind them of the upcoming occasion and stress its importance.

Importance of Mementos

Do you really understand the importance of giving donors a coffee mug, a keychain, or a window sticker? It really isn't about donor premiums or transactional fundraising; but rather a way of providing a memory jog to your donors. Giving them a coffee mug with your logo, name, and mission statement helps remind them of your organization and its impact on society every time they have that morning cup of tea or coffee.

That sticker in the window of their car helps them advertise their pride in supporting your organization. The memento conjures up the old memories or new memories of what your organization does. The keychain helps to keep your organization top-of-mind over time.

Newsletters, Letters, and E-mail Communications

You should be communicating to donors about recognition and stewardship. Please see Chapter 6, After Winning the Gift, for information on these techniques. Right now, though, we want to focus our communications on softening the ground so that we can raise money.

The major function of fundraising newsletters, letters of request, e-mail blasts, and electronic newsletters is case building. You want short, compelling, heartfelt stories with pictures of the people your organization benefits. Use every communication to inspire giving. Use some of Cialdini's influence principles such as testimonials and authority to confirm that yours is a worthwhile organization in which to invest.

Frequency is far more important than length. The ideal print newsletter is one page front and back (oversize paper is fine). For electronic newsletters, select three to five items only and provide links for more information if readers want it. Please do not use long newsletters. Even four pages is too long. Do whatever you can to be in the initial pile of quick-read-and-toss mail rather than the deadly to-be-read-later group.

Strive for getting your organization to be top-of-mind with your donors. Use quick impressions, dramatic snippits, and teasers. Think how your local television station promotes future broadcasts, or how newspapers run quick reviews of movies to entice you to see them. That's the job of your newsletters—to entice, to invite, to intrigue your donors and potential donors.

Mass and Target Marketing

Almost all of the techniques discussed so far are target market oriented. You have a list of 100, 500, 1,000, or even 5,000 donors and prospective donors and you mail to them requests for gifts, invitations to cultivation events, newsletters, donor recognition and so forth. You have targeted the marketplace.

One of your goals is to get your fundraising program to "tip"—to capture the imagination of your community—using techniques from *The Tipping Point.* Using the law of the few (mavens, connectors, and salespeople) along with a sticky message (your case statement) and the power of context (cultivation meetings, site visits, and participative focus group meetings) you can start to become top-of-mind with your philanthropic community:

> . . . philanthropic consumers believe that among the most effective ways for a nonprofit to reach them is through word of mouth (76 percent). . . . Trust in an organization (82 percent) and measurable

community impact (81 percent) are keys to decision makers when determining what causes to support.[7]

What is the role of mass marketing for philanthropic fundraising? Small. Why? Because most nonprofit advertising budgets are quite limited, you can-not expect the same type of public relations and advertising campaign as you would in a corporate setting. It is very expensive to purchase enough consistent advertising space to really penetrate the mass marketplace sufficiently to motivate donor giving. And, if only 20 percent of the people give 80 percent of the money—the *80/20 rule* derived from Pareto's Principle—then why expend 80 percent of your marketing budget on people who won't give you much, if any, money?

You will find times when strategic mass marketing is a good investment. This must be considered if your organization is young or poorly understood in the philanthropic marketplace. First, you should start with an aggressive PR campaign. Frequent, well-written press releases focused on timely news will pay off over time. I have watched some clients who were masters at PR and here are some lessons I've learned. First, have real news to report. Why would the newspaper be interested in your story? What's the human angle versus the institutional story? Human interest is always more exciting than organizational information. For the environmental group that has a massive volunteer beach-trash pickup day each year, share the statistics about how much trash and how many volunteers; but better still, find a volunteer with a great personal story to tell—an 80-year-old on a walker with a great smile who has 10 years of volunteer service picking up trash on the beach. Send pictures. Build personal relationships with reporters and feature reports at your local media outlets. Call them to see if they got the press release and would like a follow-up interview with your star volunteer or your executive director. Work the phones. Make the news.

Another technique is to use the unique credentials of your executive director, faculty, program staff, or physicians to serve as expert commentators on local and national news. One of my college's professors was the world's expert on elephant pheromones as they relate to reproductive issues. When our local zoo's elephant got pregnant, the college marketing office called local reporters to tell them about the professor's role in helping with the elephant's pregnancy and explain how her research was helping zoos throughout the world.

When you do make the news, make sure to leverage this visibility with your donors. Many times when you get a story covered in the local newspaper your donors miss the story. They are busy people and may be out of town, too busy to read the paper that day, or they regularly scan three to five newspapers and so miss articles. I learned a powerful lesson with one of my clients, Oregon Public Broadcasting (OPB). They were always in the news, and yet, when we talked to major donors, their perception was the opposite—how come Oregon Public Broadcasting never gets any press coverage? In probing further we found out these donors' travel and other reading obligations caused them to miss the few articles that were published. We decided to repackage all of the good press clippings into a bimonthly target mailing to our donors—*OPB in the News*. A year after starting this program, our donors thought we were always in the newspaper. The target marketing effort of the reprints helped bring this statewide public broadcasting station, which needed a new studio, top-of-mind for our donors. Every organization should consider this target marketing repackaging of mass-media technique. Note: You can do this with video clips from the local evening television station. Just request a videotape copy of the story (you have to do it within one day or they may erase the tape) and assemble several different stories on a VHS tape or DVD. Send them to your donors, and it will look like you are on TV all of the time.

While press releases can get you some newspaper coverage, you cannot control what they will pick up and when. Ask for an advertising budget and then figure out ways to stretch it. During a meeting with a newspaper publisher on behalf a hospital client, we discovered that he was interested in the hospital and would be willing to double the buying power of any ad budget the hospital used in his newspaper. He could not give space away for free but he could vastly increase the impact of our ad budget through an in-kind donation.

For capital campaigns, we recommend to clients that they remain in a quiet, nonpublic phase for quite some time. They can get all the news stories they want about the organization and its mission but not the campaign. Why a quiet phase to a campaign? Campaigns are conducted sequentially—first the very large, pacesetting gifts, then major gifts, and finally the general public campaign. The pacesetting and major gifts effort is where 80 to 90 percent of the gifts are secured. Target marketing and face-to-face cultivation and solicitation visits are the key to success at this stage. It is not a secret campaign, but rather a quiet one that is marketed by word of mouth and cultivation events rather than newspaper articles. You want to talk with each of the lead and major donors in your campaign personally as an "insider" before they read about it as an "outsider." The quiet phase can last up to 80 or 90 percent of your campaign (one campaign reached 108 percent of its goal before the campaign was announced to the public).

When you want to take your campaign public, consider asking your local paper to work with you on a full-page insert spread. The paper can sell advertising around the outside of the spread and provide you with a four-color, two-page layout to tell your story in pictures and copy. This is a very effective and free technique (although we learned the hard way with one client to provide the newspaper with our major donor list so that they weren't selling ads to these same donors without acknowledging their previous gift—a letter to major donors telling them about the newspaper insert will help as well).

Free billboards (or highly leveraged ones) can also help get your organization some buzz in the community. Don't be afraid to go to the vendors listed on your local billboards to ask for a donation. Many times, if you give them visible recognition they are glad to help, especially when they are in between major corporate account contracts. Ask them for one to three months of space as long as you, the nonprofit, pay for the signage and installation of the message. Sometimes they will donate this, too, but your key ask is the space.

One major art museum did a brilliant job of buying newspaper inserts in the local edition of the *New York Times*. It reinforced what I had heard from a donor, that to reach the donors don't use the local newspaper but rather buy ads in regional editions of the *New York Times* and/or the *Wall Street Journal*. They are the newspapers that high-end donors read regularly.

Do You Always Need to Make Your Case?

The simple answer is—no. But, wait; we just spent a whole chapter on the importance of making the case for your organization and its need for funding, and now I'm telling you that you can cheat and not make the case. You're confused?

You should always make the case for yourself, your volunteers, and your donors, as that will guarantee a winning-gifts strategy and ensure you will delight your donors. But, you can use certain diversionary tactics when your case is weak or if it is not resonating with your donors. For example, many times the annual fund case statement will be inherently weak. We are asking people to pay for utilities, janitors, accounting, fundraising, and lots of dull stuff that happens day to day in an organization to keep it moving forward. That's why a strong annual fund gift club can be a wonderful case diversionary tactic. Of course, you are making the basic case for your organization's impact on society, but the use of all of the gift club members' donations is budget-relieving, general operating support. You are telling people these donations are undesignated funds for the general well-being of your organization. Most people are fine with this, because the annual fund gift club offers the benefit of having donor names listed with other enlightened people in the community who want to help your organization. And while $1,000 seemed like a lot when you joined the gift club, after a couple of years you renew your gift out of habit and the good feelings generated by the periodic newsletters, events you go to, and information your receive through a variety of channels. So the case for why funds are needed is not as important.

Challenge grants are another great case diversionary tactic. They work in every type of fundraising setting but are particularly effective in endowment campaigns or other settings where the case is inspiring to only a segment of your donors. All of a sudden the campaign isn't so much about raising a million dollars of new endowment as it is earning the $2 million building challenge grant that can be earned only by raising $1 million of new endowment money to help run the newly renovated building. Nobody wants to lose that lead, challenge gift of $2 million, so everyone pitches in to raise matching funds. The case for how the funds will be used is not hidden; it's just not the main feature for the fundraising effort. Meeting the challenge is job number one. The case has shifted from endowment to meeting a challenge.

To raise money most effectively, you need four key elements for success (see Exhibit 4.8):

1. A great case statement
2. A pool of potential donors with lots of money
3. An eager and hardworking group of volunteers willing to open doors and ask for the gift
4. Readiness of the organization to staff fundraising

Key Success Factors for
Campaigns

Case for Support

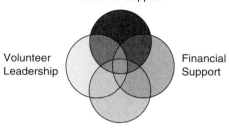

Volunteer
Leadership

Financial
Support

Organizational Readiness

EXHIBIT 4.8   KEY ELEMENTS OF FUNDRAISING SUCCESS

An eager volunteer leader and team of volunteer workers can overcome almost any shortcoming in the three other fundraising success factors. In working on your case, if you find that you are struggling with certain elements of it, find some volunteers to help you build the case and/or overcome its inherent weakness.

People give to people. Many an annual fund effort has been won by the relentless volunteer who calls on everyone she knows asking for a gift for "her" cause. In interviewing people during philanthropic market studies, we will ask: Why did you start giving to this organization? Nearly half the time the response is:

> Because Mary asked me to. Mary was so enthusiastic about her cause I couldn't tell her no, and after I got to know the organization I agreed with her and just kept on giving.

If your case is weak, enlist the law of the few and find some mavens, some champions, to help tell your story and achieve your fundraising objective. As the professional fundraiser, it will then be your task to follow up with donors who gave to "Mary" to make them delighted enough with their investment in your organization that they will repeat their gifts in the future. Build your case after the gift is made.

Using a combination of these techniques can make any campaign winnable. If you can get all four elements of fundraising success in alignment, every campaign effort can be assured of success. Yes, you will still need some luck.

A compelling, memorable case statement helps to bring out the hidden talents of volunteers. They become inspired by the case and go to unbelievable levels of fundraising dedication.

APPLY WHAT YOU'VE LEARNED

Here are some action items you can try to help apply principles presented in this chapter:

1. *Organizational listening to build your case.* Conduct background, case-building interviews with all members of the senior management team, with program leaders, and with board members. What themes were repeated in the different interviews? What general impressions did you come away with? What impressed you that you want to replicate in your case statement for all of your donors?

   Write up the case for a project, the annual fund, or whatever you need to help your fundraising this month.

2. *Refine your case.* Take an existing case document and test it with your development committee or select a small group of well-known-to-you donors. Don't write a new case, but take your annual fund brochure, your most recent direct-mail letter, or your annual report and hold a feedback session now. What did you learn that could help you raise more money immediately?

3. *Top-of-mind exercise.* For your next board meeting ,use this generative exercise to stimulate philanthropic discussions among board members.

   Ask each board member to answer the following questions on a piece of paper and then share the answers with a fellow board member.

   • What charitable organization did you give the most money to in the last calendar year? (It's okay if it was not our organization; being truthful is more important than being politically correct.) You don't have to share the amount with your partner, but tell your discussion partner why this charity was so important to you and why your gift was important to the organization.

- Did you donate to an organization in the last calendar year but now cannot remember why you gave to it? (It's okay to say our organization was the one.) Do you think you will keep giving to this organization?
- What did you give to our organization in this last calendar year? (You do not need to share this figure with your partner.) Where are we in your philanthropic priorities? What would it take to move us up a notch or two? If we are the highest, be prepared to tell the group why this is your most important cause.

After writing down their thoughts, hold 10 to 15-minute, one-on-one partner discussions between board members, then ask for volunteers to share what they learned from their partners. Capture the main ideas on a flipchart at the board meeting and have another staff member take notes during the report-out session. Collect the papers they filled out after asking them to put their names on them.

NOTES

1. Spencer Johnson and Larry Wilson, *The One Minute Sales Person* (New York: William Morrow, HarperCollins Publishers, 1984), 26.
2. Matt Oechsli, *The Art of Selling to the Affluent* (New York: John Wiley & Sons, 2005), 44–45.
3. Ann E. Kaplan, *2005 Voluntary Support of Education* (Council for Aid to Education 2006), 17, 25.
4. Nicole Lewis, "Half of Affluent Americans Say Tax Policy Doesn't Affect Their Giving," *The Chronicle of Philanthropy,* November 9, 2006, 14.
5. Larry Barker, Ph.D. and Kittie Watson, Ph.D., *Listen Up* (New York: St. Martin's Griffin, 2000), 157–165.
6. Chip Heath and Dan Heath, *Made to Stick* (New York: Random House, 2007), 14–21.
7. "Donors Expect Engagement and Communication," *Advancing Philanthropy,* March/April 2007, 13 (from a survey by Cone Inc., www.coneinc.com).

CHAPTER 5

The Win-Win Ask

Barry told me about the great respect he had for his late father, Nelson. Our calling team met with Barry and presented him with a short proposal letter to name the new life sciences building in memory of his father for $1,250,000. Barry said he would have to think it over. Nothing happened for weeks. Then, at our board meeting, Barry announced he would make the gift. He was so pleased to honor his father in this way. He thanked us for the thoughtful proposal.

One of the first rules of philanthropic fundraising is that to get gifts you need to ask for them. The trick is how to do it with style and with the goal of delighting your donors as they make significant gifts to your organization.

In this chapter we'll discuss:

1. The ideal asking team to define the best partners in making a winning-gifts request

2. The best ways of preparing the ask to help maximize your chances of success

3. Making the ask and closing the deal

As you begin to read this chapter, take a moment to think through the concepts we have already discussed (or for those of you who skipped ahead

EXHIBIT 5.1   **THE PAUL STORY**

I was the new vice president for development at my university. Fundraising had never been done before in an organized way (the school was only 20 years old). We needed to establish philanthropic traditions. In discussing this issue with board members we came up with the idea of creating The Paul _____ Award. Paul, who had passed away before I started, was one of the founders of our university. He was also a co-founder of one of the major high-tech firms in town. In addition to serving on the founding board of directors, Paul had left our organization and several others in town large bequests. His gift became the basis of our endowment fund.

At the first annual Paul Award ceremony we honored his widow with the award and asked that she and several of Paul's closest associates speak to his values. One of the speakers, Jim, was the retired general counsel (attorney) for Paul and his partner's high-tech firm.

Jim told a great Paul story at the awards event. He respected Paul and was with him doing legal work frequently when various senior managers of the company would come in to make requests for project funding, new personnel, new research initiatives, or new product lines. Jim said that over and over again Paul would rather brusquely say "no." After session after session of no's, Jim finally asked Paul why he told everybody no. Paul said:

"I tell everyone 'no' the first time; that gets rid of 90% of all of the frivolous requests. If they're serious and they really care, they will be back. They will have done more homework and do a better job of presenting their ideas. We'll still have a lively discussion but many of these projects will get the nod to go ahead."

The lesson for fundraisers? No usually means "not yet." It may mean you haven't made your case or, if you're dealing with a Paul, it will always take at least two requests to get to "yes."

---

to get to the ask chapter right away, take a few minutes to skim through the previous chapters). In Part I, A Winning Gift for Your Donor, we read about Stephen Covey's concept of win-win or no deal as applied to fundraising. This concept is so important to the whole premise of making a thoughtful gift request. Always remember, it is their money—they don't owe you a gift but rather you owe them a thoughtful proposal of why their gift will make an impact on society and how it will be a win for the donor. Covey's comments on the importance of "no" are well illustrated by the story in Exhibit 5.1.

As you get ready to ask, it's a great time to review *The Six I's of Philanthropic Fundraising*. Have you done all the steps that you can? Is the donor well cultivated? As involved with your organization as possible? Have you listened to the donor? Does he have a deep understanding of your organization? If you've covered all of the *Six I's* except for "invest," then it is time to ask.

Remember principles of Chapter 1, People Centered Fundraising, and review the general principles of donor values and motivations from Chapter 2, Donor Values. Which of the *Seven Faces of Philanthropy* does your donor exhibit? Using techniques from Chapter 3, Listen, what have you learned on your discovery calls with this donor? How will this information help shape your ask?

Using concepts from Chapter 4, Make Your Case, make sure you have told your story and engaged your donor in a discussion of case issues. How do you know the donor has heard you? Has she rearticulated the case to you? To others? Has he made a public testimonial that confirms he understands the impact of your organization and how a gift will help your organization benefit society?

Now that you've reviewed your work with the donor, it is time to make the win-win ask. Let's start with the best asking team you can assemble.

The Ideal Ask Team

How *do* you make the ideal ask? What is the most powerful team you can assemble to win the greatest gift? How do you maximize a gift?

Over the years, it has become apparent that the most powerful ask is one financial peer challenging a fellow financial peer to match a gift. "I gave a million dollars and here is why. I know you have as much money as I do, maybe more, so I want you to match my gift." This "power ask" works just as well at the $1,000 level as at the $5,000,000 level. Some volunteers can pull this off with great style and élan.

The ideal fundraising call is made by three people: 1) the volunteer who can open the door, serve as a role model donor, and preferably make the gift request; 2) the executive director who can share the vision for the organization; and 3) the philanthropic fundraising professional who prepares the ask team, is the designated listener on the call, and is prepared to ask if need be.

Of course, there can be exceptions to this ideal team. You may have a president who is so close to the donor that you don't need a volunteer. But we have found over time the most powerful gift request is peer to peer.

We wish that every volunteer would be a fearless and tenacious asker. However, those people tend to be the exception. Thus, in the ideal ask team of a volunteer, the nonprofit leader, and the professional philanthropic fundraiser, each has a unique and specific role to play. But, why three people?

In talking with volunteers who should be great at peer-to-peer asking but were not, it turns out that many of them were so busy that they understood only the big picture of the case but not the details. They knew their friends would ask tough questions and they also knew they were not prepared to answer. So, they did nothing. Having the president or a program manager for the special project for which you are seeking funding on the call solves this problem. She is now the answer person. The volunteer can ask the nonprofit executive to supply answers to tough questions, and to handle questions about the details of the organization during the ask meeting. It takes a huge burden off of the volunteer to have the executive director, the college president, or the hospital CEO on the call to share the vision and the potential impact of the gift, and to relate how donor dollars will be stretched through good management.

So why three people, why the fundraiser? While you may be aware of some wonderful askers, usually the combined calling experience of volunteers and the nonprofit leader in making large gift requests is quite limited. The fundraising professional may have been on 100, 500, or even 1,000 gift-request calls. Through years of experience, the fundraiser begins to hear "gifting noises"—indications of gift support that the other two ask meeting participants might miss (many times, they are more focused on presenting their story than listening to the donor and the implications of what is being said).

It also turns out that no matter the extent of their training and pre-ask coaching, many volunteers will freeze when it comes time to ask. Make sure your volunteers understand that even though they will have signed the gift-request letter and should plan to make the ask, if for any reason they don't feel comfortable during the ask meeting, they should signal you, the philanthropic fundraiser, and you will initiate the gift request. Once you pop the question, the job of the volunteer is to reinforce the ask through follow-up discussion and reiteration of why the volunteer made her own significant gift. Everyone needs to be clear that the prospective donor understands this is a gift-request meeting and that you can't disappoint the donor by not asking. Unless something drastic happens at the beginning of the meeting, you will make the ask.

Remember, the professional fundraiser's job is to be the observer, the listener, the prompter of lines for the volunteer who has forgotten the great

EXHIBIT 5.2   **THE IDEAL ASK TEAM**

Fundraising Volunteer
  Open the door, present outside credibility, ideally make the ask.
President (Executive Director)
  Share vision of the organization, express how gift funding will improve the community.
Professional Philanthropic Fundraiser
  Actively listen, orchestrate presentation, make the ask if need be.

---

testimonial speech, or the president who usually describes a glowing vision for the future. The fundraiser's job is also to create pauses in the presentation from time to time to allow the person being asked for the gift to react to the discussion so far. What questions does he have? What values around philanthropy does she hold?

Exhibit 5.2 describes the perfect ask team of three people: the fundraising volunteer, the executive director (president), and the philanthropic fundraiser.

Do you need three people on every call? No, but three people is the ideal. Naturally, there will be times when the professional fundraiser has a good enough relationship with the donor that a volunteer isn't really needed to close the gift. Of course, you can go ahead and ask yourself or with your president. However, if you intend to grow your volunteer force of fundraisers, always try to bring a volunteer with you on an ask call as the volunteer will learn from the process and be more ready to tackle prospective donors that only that volunteer can lead to the team. If you leave them out of the well-prepared calls you are ready to close, they will be discouraged and not trained when it comes time for some of the tough cases they will have to deal with.

For long-term executive directors with close personal relationships with their major donors, a solo ask frequently can be made. And while this is very efficient, it likewise short-circuits the learning curve of other people on the fundraising team. When the executive director runs out of personal contacts, then what happens? In addition, because the president is alone it will be difficult to present and observe donor reactions carefully at the same time. It helps to have a highly trained professional listener on the call (the professional fundraiser).

Is three too many people on a call? Usually not; most donors are pretty strong people and many feel honored by the attention of a well-rehearsed calling team. Certainly use your judgment. If Mary, who is 85 and quiet, would feel invaded by three people visiting her home, then reduce the size of the calling team.

Let's explore further the issue of why not just send out the president on the call. While many private university presidents do an excellent job of asking for spectacular gifts and have polished their skills over the years, they are still not the number-one choice as gift requestor. No ask is more powerful than the person who has given $100,000 dollars asking his lifelong business associate and friend for a significant gift of the same size. These two probably know much more about each other's net worth than they will ever admit to your staffs additional discussions will take place at the golf course, at the social club, or at dinner with spouses. Many executive directors and presidents who think their job is to ask but who are afraid to because of lack of training and experience will be relieved to know they are not expected to be the primary askers. Reinforce to the CEO that his job is to describe the vision of the organization and how the donor's gift will make a difference in meeting the organization's mission. The president should show leadership, vision, and management skills to help reassure the donor that the organization is capable of handling this significant gift. Let the volunteer or the professional fundraiser make the ask. Please do not simply pick a big name on your board to make the ask. Make sure the volunteer fundraiser is active, deeply committed, and has already made a gift to the campaign. The power of the volunteer ask is telling the story of his own gift decision-making process and announcing the size of his pacesetting gift. As one foundation executive director said:

> I would rather talk to the highly committed, no-name board member who is passionate and knowledgeable about the organization than the big-name board member who is superficially involved. I love listening to committed board members.

The other reason to bring a volunteer on the call is to add external validation of your organization's value to the community. The president and fundraiser are paid by the organization to say good things about it. The volunteer can walk away at any time. It is the volunteer's lifelong stature in the community, personal reputation, and commitment to community causes that give her statements such weight with peers.

Just as you will customize the ask to each donor, customize the ideal ask team. Who knows the prospective donor the best? Who has leverage professionally? Who is a financial peer? The more thoughtfully you

EXHIBIT 5.3   "MUST" HAVES & "NICE-TO" HAVES OF IDEAL
ASK TEAM MEMBERS

	Fundraising Volunteer	President (Executive Director)	Philanthropic Fundraising Professional
Maven	Nice to have	**Must have**	Nice to have
Connector	**Must have**	Nice to have	Nice to have, **must have over time**
Salespeople	Nice to have	Nice to have	**Must have**

put together the calling team, the more honored and delighted the donor will be.

The ideal ask team describes what you would love to have on every call. Can you get by with less? Sure. Exhibit 5.3 shows the required and optional attributes of your calling team.

Of course, this chart is simplistic. In Part II, Seek Winning Gifts for Your Organization, we discussed how *The Tipping Point* helps you to see the various roles your volunteers can play in the fundraising game. While we would love every volunteer to have in-depth knowledge of the organization and the fundraising projects (maven), and while we would love for them all to be terrific askers (salespeople), the norm is for them to be connectors. In fact, experience shows that 80 percent of all board members are connectors, 10 percent are champions, and 10 percent are salespeople. The rare volunteer who knows the case in depth, can connect, and also sell is probably 1 in 100 (well . . . maybe 1 in 50).

Lewis B. Cullman, a prominent New York philanthropist, published a pamphlet to encourage volunteers and staff members on how to make effective million-dollar-gift requests: *How to Succeed in Fundraising by Really Trying*. In a *Chronicle of Philanthropy* story:

> He says he suspects that people who cannot pull off a final deal are not sufficiently convinced or confident about the charitable cause. "There are a lot of people who can make a good sales pitch and talk about the institution, but seem unable to get a signed document." Mr. Cullman says he has sometimes won a big gift by citing donations from a charity's own staff members to a fund-raising drive. Those gifts, he says, are "a great weapon."[1]

Lewis Cullman currently serves on 10 nonprofit boards. He and his wife, Dorothy, have donated more than $250 million to such charitable causes as the New York Botanical Garden, the Neurosciences Institute of San Diego, and the Museum of Modern Art in New York City. More information about Cullen's brochure can be found at www.lewis.cullman.com.

Over time, long-term university presidents and other nonprofit executives will become connectors and will have highly personal relationships with their donors. And, of course, it would be great for every staff leader to be a great gift closer. But, that is not their first job—their first task is to be the maven and champion for projects and for the vision of the institution and its impact on society.

Too often, philanthropy professionals (development officers, major gift officers) are hired as connectors when their real job is to be salespeople. It would be wonderful if every hard-charging, close-the-deal (nicely of course) fundraiser was also a maven and a connector. And, with experience, a good fundraiser will start to find projects within the organization that resonate personally that they can champion. And over time, the fundraiser will build a network of relationships that can be more far reaching than any volunteer's (as they do it full-time). But, if the fundraiser cannot gracefully present gift opportunities and negotiate winning gifts, the individual is in the wrong business. Fundraisers need to understand they are salespeople first. Remember the old movie, *They Shoot Horses, Don't They?* The remake is, *They Shoot Fundraisers, Don't They?* The half-life of a new fundraiser is 18 months—if you don't raise money and meet the financial needs of your organization, it will fire you (and it should; the fundraiser is a salesperson who is measured by clear financial objectives).

PREPARING FOR THE ASK

You want to be prepared going into the ask meeting. The more prepared you are, the more confident you will be and the more ready to deal with the various directions in which the meeting might go. Write a strategy memo outlining how you see the ask meeting unfolding. Who are the ideal ask team members? What is each person's role? Review your contact reports from the discovery calls and cultivation visits with this donor. What do you know about this donor's values and motivations around giving? What is the donor's giving history to your organization? What is the donor's volunteer history? What questions do you expect the donor to ask? What possible objections might the donor raise? What project should be presented? How much should you ask for? Why will this project and this gift amount be a winning gift for the donor and the donor's family? What impact will the gift have on your organization? Is there anything you can do between now and the ask meeting to deepen the donor's knowledge of your organization or strengthen his relationship with your nonprofit?

As you start to answer these questions, begin envisioning the call. In your mind's eye, see yourself at the meeting. What smalltalk would work to start the meeting? Is this person a football fan or does she go to the opera? Has he been on a trip lately? Your contact reports from discovery calls will be invaluable. You want to demonstrate that you listened at previous meetings, thus laying the groundwork for listening well during the ask meeting.

Sometimes as you write the strategy memo, and rewrite it, and rewrite it . . . new ideas take form. You realize that some background documents that would be helpful on the call are not ready, or you have the building plans but they need to be updated by the architect because of planning meeting changes from last week.

Envision the meeting place. The best spot is the president's office or the executive director's conference room—a place of special honor and significance that gives weight and formality to the ask meeting. As you begin concerted fundraising efforts, decide on a standard calling space. Many executive directors will have a small four- to five-person conference table as part of their office. Use a white linen tablecloth, simple dishes, and serve an appetizing but not overly fancy lunch. (Remember *The Millionaire Next Door*, where most self-made millionaires consider themselves tightwads? They expect you to be frugal, too.) You can set up easels with diagrams of buildings or projects and a television monitor can be ready to show your DVD so your impact is clear. The first call will take you days to prepare for. But after three or four asks, you will get yourself and your organization's support teams into a pattern and getting ready for calls becomes easy.

A special note: Avoid restaurants for ask meetings. You want a quiet, confidential setting. Some of your best donors may be hard of hearing and hearing aids do not work well in a noisy dining room. One of the worst calls in my career was in a restaurant where the volunteer finally got up the courage to ask for a $100,000 gift only to have the donor ask, "What? What did you say? You want me to give what?" This was said at the top of his lungs, thus getting the attention of diners 15 feet away. I guess that's how you learn in this business; the hard way. If you're in a business club, use a private meeting room rather than the general dining room (while it will be quiet, most private clubs prohibit papers and materials on the table in the general dining room).

The Written Proposal

Always, always (please) write out a simple one- to two-page letter of request ahead of every major solicitation meeting. This letter will usually be left with the donor at the end of the ask meeting to provide a record of your gift request. Writing the letter helps you think through the gift request—the case for your organization, the problem that philanthropy is trying to solve in helping people in the community, the size of the gift request, terms and ways of giving (pledge period of up to five years, the annual fund, combined cash and estate gift)—and close the letter with commemorative naming opportunities for donor recognition if that would be of interest to the donor.

After your first draft of the proposal, go back and read all of your contact reports with this donor. Does your request reflect what this person has told you over time? Based on your earlier meetings, what questions do you expect the donor will ask you and how could you put your answers in the proposal proactively? What attachments should go with the proposal so the donor has enough information for further research and reflection (and to share with family members and professional advisors)?

Now, rewrite your proposal. Then, let it sit for a few days (ideally over a weekend) and then edit it again. Keep your style simple, direct, and inspirational. The impact of the gift on helping your organization meet its mission of serving the community must be clear.

If you are part of the calling team, you want the written proposal with you, signed by your lead volunteer and/or the nonprofit head of staff or program leader who will be on the call. Sometimes only your president will go or the president and the volunteer. They will need your written proposal, too.

Will you always present this proposal at the ask meeting? Not 100 percent of the time; sometimes when you begin the ask meeting things change and you realize the ask may be too high, too low, or for the wrong project, or the timing is poor—just leave the proposal letter in your pocket. But, usually you will use it as a closing device so the donor can reflect over time on the gift request.

Having been on hundreds of gift solicitations, I have observed donors as they are being asked for significant gifts. Many thoughts start moving through the donor's mind, not only the immediate reaction to your request, but questions such as: What will my spouse think? What will my kids say? How will my accountant and attorney react? How is my cash flow? How much can I afford to give? How much visibility do I want? Need? Regret getting through a previous big gift? How will I protect myself from other requests? How do I to respond to my friend who made the ask?

If you watch the donor's eyes, you can sometimes see when he has left the room and is literally lost in thought. The written proposal provides the security of having your request well stated for future rereading and sharing with others who may influence the decision. Do not expect the prospective donor to remember all of your case points. Use the written proposal, attachments, your campaign movie, and brochure as touchpoints for the donor's due diligence and future consideration.

How Much Should We Ask For?   Once the written proposal has stabilized through four to six drafts and reviews by other members of your calling team, the last big question is, how much to ask for? Many times the answer is clear as you have a sense of the donor's gift pattern to other organizations in the community. In doing simple research you may find the donor giving $50,000 gifts at several different organizations. A $100,000 request would not be out of line. Sometimes, though, you may have data that indicates only potential of at least $25,000. You may not know if the donor's gift was $25,000 or $250,000. So be careful not to read too much into these lists.

A good rule of thumb for a capital gift request to a highly engaged donor is 10 percent of the donor's net worth. Somebody making a gift of that amount is truly making a lead gift and announcing your organization as a life priority. Some donors may respond by giving you half of the gift request in cash over five years and the balance in their estate—that's okay.

As you get a sense for where a donor might make a gift, look one level higher on your gift table and ask for that gift as a sight raiser. If you think the person can make a $250,000 gift, ask for $500,000. Always stress the five-year pledge period, as some of the gift patterning you are seeing in the community could be one-year gifts, so the patterning is actually low compared to what the donor could do over five years. You can stress the need for immediate funds to encourage a donor who is able to write you a

$500,000 check to do so. But be careful, keep pledge payments flexible. Most donors realize you need the money soon (because you made your case so eloquently) and they will advance their pledge payments as fast as their other family, business, and community commitments will allow. Even the wealthiest people have cash-flow challenges.

In another of Robert Cialdini's books, *Influence: The Psychology of Persuasion*, he notes:

> Because the rule for reciprocation governs the compromise process, it is possible to use an initial concession as part of a highly effective . . . rejection-then-retreat technique. . . . One way to increase your chances would be first to make a larger request of me, one that I will most likely turn down. Then, after I have refused, you would make the smaller request that you were really interested in all along. Provided that you have structured your requests skillfully, I should view your second request as a concession to me and should feel inclined to respond with a concession of my own, the only one I would have immediately open to me— compliance with your second request.[2]

You can ask men more boldly than women (see Chapter 2, Donor Values). Men will be flattered by a high ask and may, in fact, be insulted by too low an ask. It's an ego thing.

Women, on the other hand, are more relationship driven. They don't want to disappoint you, so be careful your gift request is not too aggressive. For women it may be better to indicate a range of gifts and share your caution in suggesting a gift amount (you still need to get a number on the table as donors like guidance on what you are expecting them to do). Sharing what other women have given to the project and why is also helpful. The lesson— be more cautious with women donors to preserve your relationship.

Thayer Willis, a woman who comes from a wealthy family and who is a licensed social worker, comments in her book, *Navigating the Dark Side of Wealth: A Life Guide for Inheritors*:

> People who possess material wealth usually battle with a sense of selfishness over it. Before making material or cash gifts, an inevitable thought process ensues that the gift will not diminish one's wealth to the point of psychological pain. "Giving till it hurts," in the jargon of charity fund-raisers, is not something the wealthy do willingly.[3]
>
> In the course of making these financial choices, sooner or later the subject of philanthropy will occur to you. Your first thoughts about giving

EXHIBIT 5.4	HOW DO WE KNOW WHEN IT'S THE RIGHT TIME TO ASK?

1) You are hearing "gifting" noises.
2) When you run out of cultivation tasks, you know the donor well—the time to ask feels right.
3) When the donor asks you about the gift he has been thinking about.
4) Your volunteer in charge of the account tells you *"Now is the time."*
5) A challenge grant deadline is approaching.
6) When your boss or the campaign chair forces the issue—let's be real, this happens.

away some of your wealth may come in response from a charitable organization. . . . As you become inspired, you may enter a period of self-examination as to whether philanthropy represents a moral obligation, an opportunity for personal growth, or both.[4]

Knowing Willis and her thoughtfulness and the many counseling sessions she has held with members of wealthy families, it is fascinating to get this insight into next generations of wealth. There is some insecurity associated with giving inherited money away versus money you have earned yourself. Willis goes on to talk about the importance for most inheritors of never invading capital or the principal of their wealth.

So be careful about how you ask and think through the timing of your ask (see Exhibit 5.4).

Claude Rosenberg Jr., retired head of RCM Capital Management, managed $26 billion of investments for high-wealth individuals and high-wealth institutions. In 1994, he published a book, *Wealthy and Wise: How You and America Can Get the Most Out of Your Giving,* in which he notes:

What I found was that, on average, most people have been giving far less than they could. My research resulted in a startling conclusion: the charitable donations of the IRS's top income group averaged less than ten percent of what they could safely afford![5]

. . . this top bracket group's donations do not reflect the conservative estimate that they own over seven times the asset for each dollar of reported income than do lower income tax bracket earners. . . . Instead of contributing approximately 40 times what the lower-income earners give, they could afford to contribute 450 times as much.[6]

Rosenberg's book is a good resource for people who are grappling with their philosophy and attitudes toward philanthropy. He takes Andrew

Carnegie's philosophy and uses modern investment research techniques and his own philanthropic attitudes to challenge high-asset individuals to give more generously.

In 1998, he formed New Tithing Group, a charity in San Francisco to conduct research around wealthy donors:

> . . . in the case of charity, it is important to think of your efforts as *providing opportunity*. Providing those who are less fortunate a chance is the philosophy to follow—a chance to feel productive, to earn a living, to attain happiness from the opportunity to live in a positive environment.
>   . . . Another reason for thinking optimistically about the rewards of philanthropy is spiritual in nature. The tenets of practically all major religions encourage benevolence. Buddha, Muhammad, Maimonides, Jesus Christ, and others teach us the wisdom, importance, and yes, joys of sharing. And do not neglect the personal psychological lifts that can be produced through philanthropy, not the least of which is self-esteem.[7]

In *Selling to the Affluent*, Dr. Thomas J. Stanley talks about watching for signs of personal euphoria in timing a request. For people in sales, financial management, and other types of high-end services, find out when yearly bonuses are awarded. For the business owner, look for moments of liquidity such as a public stock offering, a corporate merger or buyout, announcement of retirement from chief executive officer to chairman, and so on.[8]

Recruiting and Preparing the Ask Team

We talked earlier about the theory and general attributes of the ideal ask team; now we need to bring reality to the team for each specific donor. We need to get the ask team in place and trained. Hopefully, over time you have identified the lead volunteer for each of your leadership gift and major gift prospects. Some will be obvious matches, while others can be mysterious for a long time.

The strategy memo and written proposal usually help to clarify your thinking on who is the best person to deliver the key message points. Ideally, you are recruiting a financial peer who has already given a leadership gift to your annual fund drive or campaign. A long-term personal relationship between the volunteer and the donor is ideal. Other times, you may need to rely on a volunteer who knows the prospective donor somewhat but not closely. The volunteer's passion for the project makes him the best person to make the ask. In addition to seeking a financial peer (both the volunteer and the donor are worth $25 million to $50 million, for example), you want a volunteer who has given at the request level or higher for this call. If your prospective donor is capable of making a $100,000 gift over the five-year pledge period, then you want a volunteer who has made a gift of that amount or more. It is very difficult for volunteers to "ask up"—to request a $100,000 gift when they have given $10,000. I have seen only one volunteer in my entire career pull this off. Bill was a fearless asker and long-time leader of the campaign's organization. He had a reasonable net worth (probably $5 million to $10 million, or so). But he could ask anybody. He used this challenge to others when asking for a big gift:

> Here is what I have given, and I want you to give more than that because as a percentage of our net worths, my gift was more sacrificial. I know you can make this bigger gift if you want to—and I want you to consider doing just that.

Bill was a bold and highly successful as a fundraiser volunteer. He is one of the top five fundraising volunteers and campaign chairs I have ever worked with.

Once you have a volunteer in mind you need to recruit him. This is where having the ideal ask team concept description helps. Once the individual sees that it is a team effort and that each of you has a role to play, most volunteers become more comfortable. The assurance that the professional fundraiser is always willing to ask for the gift if the volunteer becomes uncomfortable during the meeting is critically important. Some volunteers are up front and will tell you they will not ask for the gift. They are glad to be in the room, willing to give a strong testimonial including explaining why they made the gift they did, but they will not ask. Sign them up. Your team will do just fine.

The idea that all board members become great fundraising askers the minute they join your board is absolute bunk. Most are not good at asking and they know it. So when they tell you they don't like to ask for money, believe them and respect their good judgment. They still need to go on the call and witness the ask, sign the written proposal, and share their passion for the project.

Once recruited, gather the ask team for a strategy meeting to verbally review the strategy memo and to visually review the written request. Does the proposal make sense from the volunteer's point of view? Is the ask amount correct? If you have selected the right volunteer with a lifelong relationship and who is a financial peer, the volunteer will have more knowledge about the donor's gift potential than he will ever share with you. The volunteer's reaction to the amount of the suggested ask is critically important. He may raise your sights and suggest a bolder request because of information only he has. He won't tell you why, but listen very carefully to any ask adjustments he recommends. As you have this discussion, make sure to reinforce capacity versus tendency. Just because the donor has never made a million-dollar gift before does not mean we should not ask for it now. We know the donor is worth $100 million and should start being philanthropic, and we hope this is the cause that closes the individual's first seven-figure investment in the community.

At the rehearsal meeting talk about roles of each member of the ask team. Who will start the meeting? What stories will each person tell about their passion and vision for the organization? Who will turn the meeting to the ask? Who will make the ask?

Also ask your volunteer to anticipate tough questions the donor may ask during the call. What is the best way to answer these questions given the personality of the prospective donor? The more your volunteer helps in dealing with questions, the better off you will be.

Earlier in this chapter we referenced Claude Rosenberg and his mission of challenging wealthy donors to be more generous. In a recent *San Francisco Chronicle* article, he indicated he has been asked at least 500 times for charitable donations. Here are questions he asks during a request meeting:

Key Questions to Ask a Nonprofit Organization before Investing

1. What is your organization's mission?
2. Please describe how your annual goals have been achieved and at what annual costs.
3. On a scale of 1 to 5, how do you rate your efficiency at achieving your annual goals and results?
4. Please name other nonprofits with similar missions in your geographical area.
5. How do you differ from them, and how do your results compare with theirs?

6. Have you ever considered a merger or serious collaboration with any like entities? If not, why not?

7. How much turnover of your organization's personnel have you experienced in the last two years? Has there been any turnover at the top of your management team?
If so, who has left, and why? Who has replaced those departures?

8. What turnover has occurred in your board of directors over the past two years?

9. Roughly how much in annual donations did your organization receive in the latest full year, and what are realistic expectations for this year?

10. In the last full year, approximately what percentage of donations came from:

    a. Individuals and family foundations?
    b. Public foundations?
    c. Corporate foundations?
    d. Government agencies?

11. What percentage of donation dollars came from your directors?

12. Most for-profit organizations have restructured themselves in recent years to become more efficient and productive. How, if at all, have you implemented some version of this approach?

13. To what degree have you assigned day-to-day management responsibilities to one or more specific individuals? Do you rely on your board to run the show daily?

14. Does your organization hire fundraising solicitation companies? If so, what percentage do you receive of the donations that they produce?[9]

Not every person you approach for a gift has been asked 500 times and will be this tough with their questions. But be prepared for the toughest donor, and it will give you confidence on all of your other gift requests.

The Pregnant Pause Walk your team through the importance of not stepping on the "pregnant pause"—the need for absolute silence once the gift request is made: "Joe, would you consider making a five-year pledge of $25,000 to our project?"

Be quiet . . . let there be silence . . . stop presenting . . . stop convincing . . . shift hard to listening mode.

Earlier in this chapter we talked about the many thoughts that go through a donor's mind when a gift request has been made. The pregnant pause issue is not a power game: The first person who speaks loses. But rather, the donor is really not in the room any more—let her reflect upon your request. When the donor reengages and returns to the room, she will start asking questions, raising objections, or tell you about family or work situations that will impact her gift decision. The donor is lost in thought—so shut up and be ready to listen for reactions, questions, objections.

If the members of your ask team are experienced, these comments will resonate with them as they have seen them before in other ask settings or have experienced them when asked themselves. If the ask team is new at this, it will take some restatement and role playing during your ask strategy meeting. If nothing else, tell them to look at you as the professional fundraiser for guidance. The first person to talk, except for the donor, should be the professional fundraiser (which will help everybody else to wait on you—and you've got to wait, too).

Final Preparation Steps

In the preparation meeting, ask your volunteer to reflect on what questions the donor may ask. What objections might they have? Ask your president to respond to these issues during the rehearsal. Ask the volunteer if he buys the answer. If not, what clarifying information is needed?

Once everyone feels ready for the ask meeting, determine who will set the appointment. Ideally, it should be your volunteer, but make sure she is comfortable doing so. If you detect any hesitation, offer to set up the meeting yourself. Think carefully about where to hold the ask meeting (remember, no noisy restaurants). Keep the room small and cozy to create a feeling of intimacy and energy in the room, even if you have only four or five people in it. You want the setting relaxed but somewhat formal for this important occasion—the big ask.

To eat or not to eat . . . that is the question. If possible, break bread over a big gift request. The sociability around eating together makes the ask go better. It can be any meal, it doesn't matter.

After the preparation meeting, go back to your office and update your strategy memo and make final edits on the written proposal. Get the final draft back to the other members of the ask team so they feel prepared. Take the captured questions and objections from the rehearsal meeting along with the answers and write them up—add to what you heard and get this information back to your teammates.

All of this preparation is a lot of work but as Thomas Jefferson said: "The harder I work and the more prepared I am, the luckier I get."

MAKE THE ASK

Everything is ready to go. You are as prepared as you can be with draft 5 or 10 of the strategy memo and the written proposal. The rehearsal meeting went well. The appointment is set.

Call everyone on the ask team and the prospective donor the day before to confirm the meeting time and location. Suggest the ask team arrive 30 minutes before the scheduled appointment to review the strategy one more time, reread the written proposal, and rehearse their roles. This pre-meeting preparation time is particularly important for the busy volunteer who may have done 100 things since your planning meeting. A quick review and your volunteer will be fine, but if you expect total recollection without this rehearsal, you could be in for trouble.

The first part of the ask meeting is easy. You all talk about weather, sports, vacations, kids, grandkids—the usual smalltalk of life.

But warning; As the professional fundraiser and process monitor, do not let the smalltalk go on too long. Ten to 15 minutes is fine; 20 minutes and your team could be heading for trouble. I have learned the hard way that the chitchat gets extended if everyone is avoiding the ask. Of course, ask avoidance at this point is ironic because the donor knows he is there to be asked and is politely waiting for the ask. So get to the ask. But how?

Asking Tools

Over the years, we have found that playing the campaign movie is the best way to transition elegantly to the ask. As the fundraising listener, observe and monitor the opening of the meeting chitchat and as you sense a dying down or at the 15-minute mark gently move into the conversation suggesting: "Let's watch our campaign DVD, I think you will find it interesting." A good movie of seven minutes will provide testimonials from respected community leaders, show your organization in action serving the community, and set up the gift request nicely. A good production does not close a gift but rather helps inspire a gift. Even if you are on-site for your ask meeting, and even if you have done a pre-ask meeting tour of your organization (which is a great tactic, by the way), the best way to show the full range of your activities is a DVD movie. Now that you have the prospect's attention, use your campaign presentation book (in the olden days of my early career, a typed outline of the case, and now a printed PowerPoint of the case in nonglare sheet protectors in a three-ring presentation notebook) to walk your prospect through your case for support, the project, and the gift request. Four-color printed campaign materials are useful as a take-home memento of the call, but are not useful for making the ask (I know, as I have the scar tissue of failure to prove it). The narrative nature of a typical brochure means people are reading rather than listening. A good presentation guide, on the other hand, is just a series of key-word bullet points with pictures on the page so that the focus is on you and the energy behind your words. The outline style works well as it encourages the donor to ask questions and seek clarifications because not everything is on the page. This presentation outline style also works well as you can customize each donor's presentation. For the long-time board member, you can take out the beginning sections of the case outline that talk about your heritage and basic mission. You can get to the project quickly. With donors who have been giving for 5 or 10 years but not at the major gift level, you cannot assume they know anything, so you need to cover all of the bases in your case statement. Customize the presentation book for each of your fundraising calls.

As you are presenting the case, make sure to observe the donor to see if he is listening. Go back to what you learned in Chapter 3 of this book and think about the situation from the donor's perspective. Is she taking notes? Is he nodding his head? Encourage questions. Do you sense the donor is listening actively? Empathically? Slow down and don't worry so much about rushing through your presentation as engaging the donor in an active dialogue around the case. What does the donor think about this page? Does she understand your mission better? What questions does he have? Will others in the community understand your story?

One of the last pages of your case should be your gift table. The gift table shows the range of gifts needed for your campaign to succeed (see a sample in

# of Gifts Required	Size of Gifts	
1	$1,500,000	
1	$1,000,000	56
3	$500,000	Lead Gifts
6	$250,000	of $25,000
10	$100,000	or more
15	$50,000	
20	$25,000	
50	$15,000	Donor
75	$10,000	wall
100	$5,000	
Many up to $5,000	$250,000	
Total	$10,000,000	

EXHIBIT 5.5   **TABLE OF GIFTS NEEDED**

Exhibit 5.5). While mentioning the five-year pledge period (hold up your hand with your palm facing the prospect with all five fingers spread to emphasize visually the five-year pledge period), point to the gift area you are about to suggest to the donor to foreshadow the ask that is about to come. Establish the importance of the key gifts needed to give the campaign momentum and to help it succeed.

As you can see in the sample gift table for $10 million, 56 key gifts of $25,000 or more account for 80 percent of the campaign goal. Secure those gifts and the campaign is well on its way to success. Use a description of the major gift club level at $25,000 or more for this campaign and show a list of the people who are already at this level. It will comfort the donor to know he is joining a group of enlightened community leaders in giving to your cause.

Note the importance of six- and seven-figure gifts in reaching the goal. Walking a potential donor through a list of possible commemorative naming opportunities will help him to think about a larger gift.

As you use the gift table as a discussion tool, the donor begins to wonder what level of gift you will be requesting. The table helps orient the donor on the scale of gifts needed.

For the first 5 or 10 gifts, you will need this first, theoretical gift table. Once you have some lead gifts in place you can move to the next version of the table, seen in Exhibit 5.6, Table of Gifts Needed and Achieved. Showing gifts already pledged helps give the campaign credibility. The pace has been

	# of Gifts Required	Size of Gifts	# of Gifts to Date	$ Given to Date	% of Goal
	1	$5,000,000			
	2	$2,500,000			
133 key gifts of $25,000 or more	5	$1,000,000	1	$1,200,000	24%
	10	$500,000			
	15	$250,000	2	$500,000	13%
	20	$100,000	5	$525,000	26%
	30	$50,000	1	$70,000	5%
	50	$25,000	2	$55,000	4%
	250	$10,000	5	$60,000	2%
	1,000	$5,000	15	$75,000	2%
	Friends of the Foundation $1,000 yearly gifts	$3,000,000	102	$135,000	5%
	Total	$39,000,000		$2,620,000	7%

EXHIBIT 5.6   TABLE OF GIFTS NEEDED & ACHIEVED

set by these early gifts (be ready to talk about the gifts at the top of the table by naming names, or if anonymous, describing the motivation of the donor making these lead gifts). Remember Cialdini's principles of ethical influence by showing the participation of similar others. Showing gifts in place helps a lot.

If you are asking for one of the first gifts, talk about the need for someone to set the pace, to establish a pattern of giving. Here's a great story in that regard. We were starting out on a $4 million campaign that to me looked very doable but to the organization's leaders and volunteers seemed daunting. From our study interviews, I sensed that Joyce might be ready to make an early lead gift. She was so passionate about the organization and its impact on her life that she teared-up and got emotional every time she and I talked about it. We sat down with the ask team, mentioned our campaign chair's $250,000 lead gift, and asked her to match it. She made the gift and we celebrated with her. Eighteen months later when we announced we had surpassed the goal, she looked at me and smiled, knowing she had helped set the pace for a successful campaign. The rest of the story—even though we were over goal, new needs had emerged and Joyce made a second quarter-million-dollar gift to help cap off the campaign. Being an early investor made Joyce feel like a winner.

In Chapter 3, Listen, we reviewed many sources for listening tips. One of them, *Listening: The Forgotten Skill*, spends a few pages discussing "guidelines for talkers."

1. Know what you want to say—have the objective of your message and your information clear in your mind. It is difficult for the listener to understand information clearly if the talker conveys it in fuzzy terms (make your case).

2. Know as much about the listener as possible—as you interact over time you will learn to read the other person's nonverbal cues.

3. Gain favorable attention—vary your vocal inflection and speed to hold the listener's attention.

4. Secure understanding—simple, specific terms are less likely to be misunderstood. Present ideas one at a time or in small bits.

5. Aid retention—associate new ideas with those already familiar to the listener. Periodically summarize. Ask the listeners to restate what they have heard.

6. Encourage feedback—solicit questions from the listeners to test their understanding of what you have said. Ask for ideas and suggestions.[10]

Popping the Question

The gift table is a good transition to making the ask. Big requests for anything in life are nerve racking—from asking for your first date, to proposals of marriage, to getting a raise or promotion. They're all big asks and so is this fundraising ask, whether it be for a capital campaign or for the annual fund.

Train your volunteers to use the gift table as the asking device—point to a gift level and ask the donor to consider a gift of $100,000. I had one campaign that was highly successful where the campaign chair never asked for a gift amount in dollars. He just pointed to a level on the gift table and said: "This is where I would like you to consider giving."

Remember, it is a gift consideration, not a demand. You say, "I hope you would consider a gift of $_____ over the five-year pledge period." (See Exhibit 5.7 for the rationale of why you should offer up to five years for the donor to pay off the pledge.)

A reminder: Talking about your own gift decision and amount, followed by "I hope you will match my gift," works well.

EXHIBIT 5.7   WHY OFFER A FIVE-YEAR PLEDGE PERIOD?

To set up a winning–gifts proposition for your donors, offer five-year pledges. While you would love for them to write a check for the entire amount, even the wealthiest people have cash flow issues because of their investments and liquidity, other charitable pledges, and the number of tax deductions they can take in any one year. Many nonprofit executives ask: *"Why not push for a three-year pledge?"*

In talking with donors they have said that being aware of the urgent cash needs of the organization is good. If they can advance their pledge, they will, but if we want it in writing it needs to be over five years. One donor offered a $15 million gift but wanted a 10-year pledge period. Verbally, he indicated a desire to complete the pledge in seven years but didn't want that in writing. Another donor said: *"I can give $100,000 a year. Do you want three years of it or five?"* I think we told him five.

Every person will develop his own asking style based upon his role: volunteer, executive director, or fundraiser. Use role playing during your rehearsal to see what works best for each person.

It is extremely important to remember it is the donor's money we are talking about. The donor does not owe it to us; he's not "down for a gift" or expected to do anything except to hear our story of the case and consider making a significant investment in our organization and in our community. Request a gift consideration; then be quiet . . . respect the pregnant pause.

Remember to use the written proposal to reinforce your verbal request. This allows the donor to reread the ask amount, the project description, and the commemorative naming opportunities. Also remember that the power ask is volunteer to prospective donor with the philanthropic fundraiser serving as backup to step in if needed to make sure a clear and distinct ask is made.

As the donor starts talking, take notes like mad. Everybody should be in full listening mode. If you have asked for a stretch gift commitment, your chances of closing the gift at the ask meeting are small. If you have challenged the prospective donor's thinking, the donor will need time to think about it. So as he speaks capture his immediate reactions, thoughts, questions, objections, and next steps. Draw out his feelings toward your organization, the project, and your gift request. And do it in that order. Stop presenting and start listening.

The Role of Challenge Gifts   Hopefully by now you are getting the sense that asking for the gift is not that hard. But, how do you make the ask easier?

We mentioned earlier in this book that Benjamin Franklin created the first challenge grant in America by making a conditional gift to create a Boston hospital. He put up half the amount needed as a challenge to the community to match and earn his gift.

Challenge gifts are just as important today. It's wonderful to go into an ask meeting and announce that you are halfway to earning a million-dollar challenge gift from donor X or foundation Y. "If you would consider a gift toward this challenge you will help bring this money to our organization." The donor you are asking is doubling the impact of his money. Asking for a match to earn a challenge grant helps to sweeten the deal. One of the reasons you are asking is to help meet the challenge. It gives you the excuse of asking and motivates volunteers to make the ask in order to earn the challenge gift.

Another great ask is to go to a lead gift donor to create a challenge situation. Nothing is more important than the first challenge gift of a campaign.

> We are seeking $5 million for our new building and need a lead gift of $500,000 to give the campaign credibility and to set the pace. To encourage your giving we want to issue your gift as a challenge to the community. We have to raise another $500,000 to earn your gift.

This type of challenge request is very powerful for entrepreneurial types, who like to see their gift leveraged by stimulating and motivating others to give.

One campaign I was involved with ran seven different challenge gift programs at different times and for different target audiences. We had a challenge from the board chair that could only be matched by other board members. We had a million-dollar challenge from a foundation to build our annual fund of new and increased gifts of $1,000 for three successive years (the last year was hard). Another mid-campaign challenge was for endowment only. One foundation wanted us to go out-of-state for foundation support and gave us $300,000 that had to be matched 3-to-1 from outside foundations over the next three years. Some of these challenges were extremely difficult (in fact, the last one required a one-year extension and many airplane rides across the county) to meet. I regularly cursed the idiot who wrote all of these challenges (oh, wait, that was me).

One organization was off to a great start with its campaign. Then it slowed. By chance, two major foundations announced major grants but only as top-off challenges. Between the two grants $1 million could be earned, but they were both top-off challenge grants. To get from the $4 million the campaign was at to the $7 million goal required $2 million of gap-matching gifts—the final $1 million was already pledged through these top-off challenge grants. It motivated everyone to get us to the end. They did not want to give that $1million of challenge money back to the donors.

The deadline of the challenge grant is a tool fundraisers have been using for years. It's real, imposed by a donor, and gives the gift request urgency— we need a decision to meet our deadline. Robert Cialdini references deadlines as an effective influence tool. They play off the scarcity principle. Use deadlines to help motivate your fundraising volunteers, your donors, and yourself.[11]

The bottom line—challenge grants really work. They motivate donors, volunteers, and staff to ask for gifts.

The Triple Ask   Usually, when you make a gift request you are focused on one project—would you consider a gift of $500,000 for our building project. But, in most organizations you will be talking to donors of record; people who are already giving to you. Based on the importance of your annual fund you need to make sure the donor understands that the capital gift request is over and above his annual operating gift. For most hospitals without an annual fund need, this is not important. I grew up fundraising for the arts where the annual fund was 35 to 50 percent of the operating budget. If people got excited about the capital campaign and directed all of their money there, operations were in big trouble because annual support would go down. People would not get paid their regular salaries (the symphony musicians, and more importantly, me). So in arts campaigning, the "over and above your annual support" language needs to come before the ask, during the ask, and after the ask. There can be no confusion with the donor. To help make this clear, we suggest adding a line to your gentle letter of intent confirming the concept of ongoing annual support first and the capital gift commitment second.

So, what is the triple ask?

#1—The first ask is annual fund recommitment.

#2—The second ask is the capital project five-year cash pledge.

#3—The third ask is consideration of a planned estate gift.

Use a three-part, gentle letter of intent so that the triple ask is clearly laid out graphically (See Appendix E). Typically, when the donor is ready to close his capital gift, you will bring out the form, confirm the annual gift, document the capital gift, and ask his consideration of an estate gift. Ideally, you have set up this question by discussing the importance of endowment in your case statement and mentioning the role that planned estate gifts can make.

While you should use the triple ask, don't be surprised when you don't get the triple close. Usually the first ask, annual fund renewal, is confirmed quickly on the letter of intent. The second ask, the multiyear capital pledge, has been verbally committed, so it is usually not too difficult to get this aspect of the letter of intent signed. When you get to the third ask, the planned estate gift, you will get a variety of responses from: "No, an estate gift is not possible," to "I would consider making one; let's talk about it later," to, "Yes, you're already in my estate; let me sign the form."

The triple ask format for the gentle letter of intent helps to get discussions of planned estate giving under way with your donors.

What's Different about Corporate Requests?   The hardest part of corporate fundraising is getting the meeting with the decision maker. If the right leverage is brought to bear at the meeting (a volunteer who does business with the company you are asking), and if you can show what other companies are doing, you have a good chance of getting a gift when you ask. But, you have to get the meeting.

It helps to do your homework by creating a donor profile showing this company's many years of support of your organization. Do some basic research in the community to find out what other organizations the company gives to regularly. Is there a pattern of capital gift support that will help you to establish a request amount? Several companies have a 1 percent-of-the-building total amount guideline. Others will not give to campaigns but will give to support equipment purchases. Some will commit to a multiyear pledge; others will not. Do your homework as best you can before the meeting. If you are not sure, just ask the executive you are meeting with. Let that person be your guide within the company. Usually corporate giving guidelines are very clear so that corporate officers and directors do not inadvertently make mistakes that will generate bad publicity for the company.

If the company has a corporate giving officer, meet with this person first or ask your corporate contact at the donor company if that person should join the ask meeting. Sometimes the executive will ask the giving officer to join you as he will have to go through the giving officer to secure a gift for your organization.

Your mission at the ask meeting is to get agreement that your organization fits the company's guidelines and is worthy of gift support. Your next job is to negotiate a request amount that your internal champion is willing to support (only rarely does one executive have total discretion on giving; your proposal must usually go before a giving council or the management team of the company for review and consensus approval). Once you get the green light for a gift at a specific gift level, ask what type of paperwork the company needs. Some will ask for a one-page letter of request. Others may have forms. Follow their guidelines so you can help expedite your gift decision internally.

Be sure to get the company executives to think through how they would like their gift recognized. Tying gift levels to various forms of recognition can be a great way to motivate a company to make a larger gift. For example, for a $25,000 gift, the company name will appear on your donor wall, be listed in your newsletter, and be included in the final donor thank-you advertisement in the newspaper along with other donors at that level. For a $100,000 gift, the company would get all that plus the main reception desk at your hospital would be named after it so that all of your 50,000 patients and their families each year would be aware of the company's generosity. One of the most popular corporate naming areas is the elevator lobby. Sound strange? It did to me, too, until a corporate executive asked me to think through how many people push the elevator button and stand around waiting for the elevator to come. They have plenty of time to read the corporate donor plaque. It is a high-traffic area with a built-in pause so that plenty of eyeballs see the company's name. If you can get the company thinking about combining its philanthropy and marketing budgets, it may be able to give you a larger gift.

If you can get a corporate executive to think big-gift thoughts for your organization, help protect the company against other big requests in this new gift realm by emphasizing what is unique about your organization (this also helps individual donors). The uniqueness helps set up at least a low barrier for the company so it is not deluged with new requests when its gift to your organization is publicly announced.

How Do Foundation Requests Work?   Foundations exist to give money away, so asking them is easy. As a matter of fact, foundations appear so easy to ask that all of your volunteers will want to spend all of their energy in seeking this 12 percent portion of philanthropy. Just remind them that individuals give 80 percent of the money.

Getting a meeting with foundations can be either very easy or impossible. Foundations tend to have their own culture around meeting potential recipients—some encourage it, others will talk only by phone, and a few will meet with you only once a proposal is officially submitted. It is not unusual to find some foundations that never meet with grant applicants. Do your homework to see what each of your target foundations is willing to do.

Of course, you always want a meeting. Bringing in your ideal ask team to see a foundation program officer and/or trustee is a great way of putting real people to your proposal. Yes, you will still need to submit a detailed proposal, but now the foundation officer has a face and the memory of a meeting to go with that stack of paper.

Since you know the foundation gives money away and since the level of its giving is public, the purpose of your meeting is to let the foundation know a request is coming, to test the amount to be requested, to see if a challenge aspect to your proposal is important, and to determine if the project you will be submitting is of interest to the foundation. Always bring three conceptual ideas to the meeting in the priority you want them funded. Most foundations have guidelines that you must follow, but once you do that they are careful not to twist your priorities to meet their needs. They want you to present your most compelling programmatic need. Finally, you want to determine if named recognition is beneficial to them (sometimes it is, but usually foundations try to avoid recognition as a motivation for making a grant).

A great source of information about how family foundations deal with funding requests can be found at the National Center for Family Philanthropy (www.ncfp.org). This organization conducts research projects and issues publications of case histories of family foundations and their approach to giving:

> Through TPC (The Philanthropic Collaborative), our family funding collaborations are a structured, more formalized way for us to put these values into practical projects of limited time duration. With a family as large as ours, now numbering over 200, we needed a mechanism that

would help us engage other family members without constant solicitations by each other for every cause and issue of importance to any one of us.

By using TPC's collaboration format, we, as family members, are provided with a structure to seek partners and like-minded people to work together on any given topic; the format also assures us that the topic has been thoroughly researched and that there will be staff to provide support services with the necessary follow-through, facilitation, and access to the best professional expertise needed available.[12]

The National Center for Family Philanthropy web site provides a clearinghouse of financial advisors for wealthy families as well as case histories about philanthropic impact.

If You Get an "I Need to Think About It"   The most likely response you will get to a big stretch request is this one: "I need some time to think and to discuss it with family and advisors." That's fine. Reflect on the time you need to take to think through major financial decisions such as purchasing a car or buying a house. Try to imagine the amount of work needed before someone would invest a million dollars in a business venture. Most smart, savvy people do not like to make snap decisions, especially when the decision involves large sums of money.

Once the donor has told you he needs time to think before making a gift decision, use the rest of the ask meeting to draw out questions and determine what additional information the donor may need to make an informed decision.

Give the donor a takeaway kit of organizational information, a campaign presentation book, a copy of your DVD, and, of course, the written proposal. As you present this information, ask what else the donor might like to see to make an informed decision.

One caution: Do not, I repeat, *do not* send a pledge form home with the donor. You are wasting paper and unwittingly inviting a lower gift. You want the donor to know a personal meeting will be the next step. Of course, if the donor insists on a pledge form and then repeats the request, you cannot be rude; you must honor the request. But, have zero expectations it will be returned to you.

Before ending the meeting, negotiate an appropriate time to schedule a follow-up meeting. Rather than asking when, suggest a time that you feel is right. "Is it okay to call you in two weeks to see when we can set up another meeting with the three of us?" Or, "It sounds like you need some time and have a trip scheduled; is it okay to call you in six weeks?" I would keep the follow-up time frame in weeks rather than months. Going longer than two months is not a good idea. Even if the donor is not ready to make a decision, you still want to check in to see how the donor is feeling about the gift request, what additional questions have come up, and what steps the donor thinks you should take next as a philanthropy team (the ask team and the donor).

If You Get a "No"   Many times a no is really a "not yet." Listen respectfully to the donor's reasons for saying no. Usually a flat "no" is a surprise if you have done your homework and a series of cultivation interactions over the past year or two. It is important to find out why you got this type of response.

Sometimes you will hear about health issues with the donor or a close family member. Or, you will learn about others' calls on their money: children in college or graduate school, a mother in a nursing home, another major campaign pledge, or a recent business investment that has reduced the donor's liquidity.

If the donor tells you the reason in detail, and sometimes more detail than you would ever imagine, then you have an authentic "no."

> One of our children has a severe, chronic emotional problem. Insurance doesn't cover treatment, so all of our extra dollars are going for care. We can't even think of giving money away when we have this issue facing us the rest of our lives.

Respect the decision and ask if you can call again in a year or two to see if the situation has changed. (Be sure this is an appropriate question; sometimes you need to exit gracefully because of the donor's pain around a personal situation.)

Sometimes the donor will be very open about the timing for follow-up. "You know I have three years of college tuition left with our youngest daughter, so get back to me in a few years when that is done and let's talk again. I'm interested but please understand I'm giving all of my extra dollars to XYZ University tuition payments."

If you get stonewalled, a "no" without good explanation, you have probably misjudged the interest of the donor in your organization. Somehow you missed signals and did not listen well during the cultivation process. Most people who will tell you "no" without explanation probably wished you had not asked them at all. They cannot figure out why you think they are a good prospective donor. All of us will run into a few of these, but if you are seeing a regular pattern of stonewall no's, slow down your asking and do more discovery interviews and cultivation events. You are probably rushing to ask for the sake of asking rather than waiting for the donor relationship to be mature enough for a significant investment. My wife bakes wonderful cinnamon rolls, the world's best (that's why I'm so skinny, *hah*). But no matter how hungry I am, the rolls still need to rise twice and bake the right amount of time. Taking them out after five minutes because I'm impatient just means I get gooey, icky warm dough. They need time to grow and warm up before they are fully cooked, delicious cinnamon rolls.

If You Get a "Yes"   Of course "yes" is what we want. We want to be a winner and get the gift. So the donor says yes to your entire gift amount. Celebrate. Shake her hand and congratulate her on being an enlightened donor on behalf of your organization. Take out your gentle letter of intent, fill it in with the donor and ask her to sign it to make the gift official (if you do not have it in writing, it is not a gift commitment. Verbal promises are great, but if the donor gets hit by a truck on the way out of the meeting you have nothing). Use the concept of "letter of intent" rather than pledge form as some communities have been stung by organizations suing donors over pledges. The letter of intent is a morally binding, not a legally binding, commitment to make a gift to your organization. You can put in optional language that will make the gift commitment binding on the donor's estate. (I had one donor ask that I put this in his letter of intent and he suggested we do it for all donors so his $3.5 million gift would be made even if he passed away.) A note on pledges: The Federal Accounting Standards Board, The official accounting governance body, passed a ruling a few years ago giving a special definition to the word *pledge*. The definition can cause problems on your financial statements as well as those of your corporate donors. The gentle letter of intent is much easier to deal with (by the way, I added "gentle" just to make donors smile . . . and they do).

Sometimes your "yes" response will come at the initial ask meeting. Have your letter of intent ready to go. Many times the yes comes at the follow-up meeting after the donor has had time to think and talk with family. Because you asked for one level higher than you thought the donor would be willing to go, never be disappointed in the eventual decision. It's the donor's money and you do not know all of the calls upon the donor's resources by family members, business investments, and other charities the donor is supporting. Have the donor sign the letter of intent, celebrate, and move on.

As you close the gift, discuss gift recognition. Part of the sample letter of intent you can find in Appendix E has a section on gift recognition. Ask the donor to think through various options around recognition and what it means to both the donor and your fundraising effort:

1. A "role model" donor—the gift is widely publicized in the community to help stimulate other donations, the donor's name appears on the donor wall, and commemorative gift recognition can be awarded (see Chapter 6, After Winning the Gift).

2. "Somewhat visible"—the donor's name is listed publicly at the appropriate gift club level and in printed materials as a donor of record but the specific gift amount is kept private (for example, for a small hospital in Montana donors asked that the donor wall recognition stop at $25,000 as the $100,000 donors did not want their neighbors to know they were that wealthy).

3. "Basically anonymous"—you can tell people privately about the donor's contribution if this knowledge will help stimulate a gift from someone else. But you agree that there will not be any printed listings anywhere.

4. "Totally anonymous"—only the fundraising staff knows you have made a gift (I had one couple who were so secretive that they would not even allow the clerical staff or business manager to know of their gift. They asked that only I, as the outside consultant, know of the gift. I had to put them in touch with an attorney 100 miles away whom I knew to work with them to shelter their gift and privacy.

When you are done with the closing ceremonies of signing the gentle letter of intent, celebrate (dance to the music). This is a wonderful moment for you and for your donor. You've achieved a winning gift for both your organization and the donor. If you have done your job right, you have delighted the donor in the gift-making process.

What if the donor gives you far less than expected? Thank the donor. Try to probe as to why they cannot respond with a gift closer to your request—but be careful. This may be a test, only a test. Donors will sometimes give you an initial low gift to test your response or to see how you use the gift. Be sure to assume it is a test that you need to pass gracefully. Do not bad-mouth the donor to your board for the low response (believe it or not, this has happened as several donors have painfully explained). If you know the donor has more gift capacity than this gift decision indicates, be patient. Keep cultivating the donor and come back later in your campaign for a top-off gift or an investment in a different project. Wait a few years; keep listening for the project that will delight the donor. Be patient.

Thank the Donor

See Chapter 6, After Winning the Gift, for a full description of donor thank-you policies and advice on donor recognition and stewardship. Our immediate concern in this chapter is closing the loop once the donor announces a gift decision: what to do when you get a "yes."

Many times the donor will call the professional fundraiser to announce the gift decision. Make sure this information gets back to the ask team members instantly. Go into communications and thank-you mode. Stop; do not do anything but immediately call your fellow team members so they can celebrate with you. It's easy to get distracted at moments like this and to go to your colleagues in the office to celebrate. Make your two phone calls first. Do not use e-mail unless you absolutely have to. Pick up the phone to call your teammates and make it personal. You can fill in the details of the gift and relay the donor's enthusiasm, words, and delight in making the gift. Request that your fellow team members call the donor as soon as possible to say thank you for the gift decision.

Next, go to your fellow fundraisers and celebrate and write a personal, detailed, and heartfelt thank-you note to the donor. Finally, go to Chapter 6, After Winning the Gift for more detailed information on donor thank-you's, recognition, and stewardship.

DETECT AND CONQUER ASKING OBSTACLES

Let's go back a step. What stops a successful ask? You would think that once we have defined the ideal ask team and delineated the roles, everything should be set for a successful ask. But, unfortunately you will find barriers to the ask. Some of these barriers are so high that the ideal volunteer is unwilling to join the solicitation team. Or, the volunteer will agree initially to help with the ask only to drag his feet by putting off the ask meeting and avoiding follow through on assignments. Or the seemingly successful philanthropic fundraiser all of a sudden is not effective for your cause. What's going on?

An excellent book by George Dudley and Shannon Goodson, *Earning What You're Worth: the Psychology of Sales Call Reluctance*,[13] helps suggest some reasons for these challenges. The concepts in this book are a revelation that helps make sense of our fundraising world. Why are some volunteers and staff successful yet others, while well intentioned, never get the job done, or freeze in the midst of an ask meeting? What is going on and why?

Dudley and Goodson are psychologists who were hired by the insurance industry to research why some insurance agents did so well while others failed or only achieved moderate success. What training could they provide to help mediocre salespeople develop into stars? And, how could they make sure they were not inadvertently setting up barriers for their sales teams?

Dudley and Goodson identified a number of call-reluctance factors in their research. Here is a list of asking challenges to fundraising. Some are adapted directly from Dudley and Goodson; others are unique to philanthropic fundraising. What would you add?

As philanthropic fundraisers it is important to have our eyes and ears open to detect these barriers and to use various techniques to solve the issue—or realize the volunteer or staff member may not overcome the barrier and may need reassignment.

#1 Don't Understand Impact of the Gift

Here's a true story: Jerry, one of the board members on a client's annual fund committee, was worried about his lack of action. He said:

> You know normally I'm a confident person. I can't schedule these fundraising calls because I don't understand this organization's operating budget and why we're out fundraising all of the time. What difference will these gifts make?

Obviously this organization had not made its case to Jerry. He gave money out of habit, which was okay, but he couldn't tell the story of impact and need to others in order to enlist their financial support. Your organization's mission and need for funding must be understood by volunteers and potential donors.

Prominent people in a community are highly visible. Once they start giving to charity and it becomes apparent they have money to donate, everybody will start asking them for a gift. The donor starts asking himself tough questions about why this group needs support more than the one he is supporting. The donor will ask the person soliciting a gift these same penetrating questions. The volunteers field these questions, sometimes with staff present, and many times when staff is not available to provide answers (golf games, church, dinners, and business meetings).

Empower your volunteers to ask tough questions in your fundraising meetings so these issues get out on the table. Don't let there be parking lot discussions among your volunteers where they ask each other, "how come?"

Make sure the impact of the gift and the need for money are crystal clear.

#2 Outrageous Goal

Nobody plans to be a fundraising failure. But, if your organization establishes too lofty a financial goal, people will freeze up and unknowingly refuse to work toward it. Dudley and Goodson's call reluctance research and practical fundraising experiences confirm this painful and too-frequent problem. If your organization has regularly been raising $1 million a year in its annual fund, and management comes to the fundraising office to announce that this year's goal is $2 million because of a big gap in the operations budget, it can be devastating. How in the world can you make that kind of leap? It's like when you're hiking and you get to a small creek running across the trail. It's too big to step over, but it looks like with a running start you may clear the 3 foot gap and get across. That's very different from looking at the 10 foot raging river that blocks the trail further ahead—the hike ends there or you can go further upstream where there is less water and a challenge to find an easier path that you know you can achieve.

Fundraisers and enlightened nonprofit executives have tried to maintain staff and volunteer motivation around campaign goals by asking consultants to reality test the goal through a feasibility study—how attainable is the goal? A philanthropic market research study (feasibility study or planning study) helps determine how strong the case for support is but more importantly what the potential for financial support appears to be. The consultant will come back to the organization recommending a realistic, yet stretch campaign goal.

A fundraising goal needs to appear achievable both in aggregate—with hard work we can raise the $20 million needed—and through breaking the goal into smaller sections and dividing the labor. Set up a leadership gifts division with a goal of $10.5 million, a major gifts division seeking $5 million, a corporate committee looking for $3 million, a staff committee targeting $500,000, and a public phase committee going after $1 million. Now we have five team captains, and each has his own objectives and set of volunteers. The $20 million seems more possible because of the presence of a realistic plan of smaller, achievable objectives and work teams.

Nonprofits should be thanked for consistently testing their capital campaign objectives through feasibility studies. More work could be done in setting realistic, achievable objectives for the annual fund. Looking back at a five-year average helps (take out any bequest income during those years as this is hard money to replicate). Think through typical renewal benchmarks in annual giving—first-year donors average a 50 percent renewal rate, multiple-year donors 80 percent. Just because you raised $500,000 last year does not mean raising the same amount this year will be easy. People die, move away, and have other priorities in their personal and professional lives that make just repeating last year's number hard work. If your organization wants more than a modest 3 to 5 percent increase in your annual fund, you need to hire additional staff and/or consider conducting a full-scale development audit and annual fund reengineering effort.

Keep yourself and your volunteers confident of success through realistic goal setting.

#3 Lack of Information

The lack of information factor was listed in Dudley and Goodson's call reluctance research. It makes sense that anybody in sales needs to be trained on the organization's product offerings and benefits.

In philanthropic fundraising the need for good information is critical. Certainly not all, but most donors are wealthy because they work hard, are

240 CHAPTER 5 THE WIN-WIN ASK

perceptive, see the big picture, and watch for details. And while they can be nice, they can also be impersonally tough—all of these attributes help people to make money and get rich enough to give it away to benefit the community. This type of donor expects the fundraising team to have good information at the tips of its fingers.

The good news? In building a strong case for support you need to gather lots of information and put it in some sort of order so that you can present it to others. If somebody else in your organization does the case-building information gathering, find ways to dig deep enough in the organization so that you are comfortable that you can explain the impact of your nonprofit on society. Take your chief financial officer or business manager out to lunch and ask her to explain your latest audit. Read three of the most recent, longest grant proposals submitted by your organization (these usually contain a wealth of information).

Anticipate questions donors will ask and prepare simple answers. Develop a written Q&A or FAQ document to capture your answers (Questions & Answers or a more high-tech Frequently Asked Questions). Share this document with colleagues and volunteers to see what additional questions they would add and to help test your answers.

All of this may seem obvious. And, for capital campaigns, gathering information to build the case is standard operating procedure. But, think about your annual fund. How clear is it why these funds are needed? Do you have a one-page budget summary of your operating budget? Are there project sponsorship ideas for line items in your budget? To get the annual fund donor who has been giving $1,000 a year for the past five years to jump up to the $5,000 level will take case building and lots of information.

If you were going to your dad to ask him to give $10,000 to your project, what questions would he ask, besides "Are you crazy?"

Now that you have the information, find ways to transfer your knowledge to your volunteers. Every fundraising meeting should start with a mission-focused testimonial. If you're a hospital, bring doctors to each meeting to talk about their specialties and the latest advances in medicine from their viewpoint. If you're a university, ask faculty members and students to share the importance of the university to them and society. If you're a YWCA, ask a woman who is a graduate of your transitional housing program to share how it impacted her life. Ask the chief financial officer to come in for a five-minute training session on your organization's financials. Use a variety of information-delivery channels to get your messages across—written documents, annual reports, grants, guest speakers, and so forth.

It's fun to see volunteers share tidbits of knowledge they have gained at your fundraising meetings, at a cultivation party, or on a fundraising call. They're proud of the information they know about you and more confident and willing to ask for gifts. You can conquer the "lack of information" asking obstacle.

#4 Focus Diffusion

Focus diffusion becomes a problem when you give a normally effective person too much to do at once or send the person in too many directions at one time. They loose focus because of too much to think about at once. This ask reluctance problem can be solved through good management practices.

Focus diffusion can strike fundraising volunteers when they take on too many people to call at once. Limit their calling assignments to the best three to five names that they know. They may indicate a willingness to call on 15 or 20 people, and that is fine over time. If you give them too many names at once, it confuses them. The work looks too hard. Keep laser-tight focus on the top three names where they have the most impact—longest-term relationships, net worth comparable, the person may owe them a favor, and so on. Keep the volunteer focused on a manageable number of tasks.

For fundraising staff focus diffusion is a huge problem. Most nonprofit fundraisers have too many projects in their portfolios and too many prospects to deal with at once. Each fundraiser should have only three to five institutional tasks (ideally just three so he can focus for success). In *The Tipping Point*, Gladwell mentions the number of 150 relationships for people. Having 125 to 150 names on your list is fine, but you need to set a clear priority so you don't get an attack of confusion, of focus diffusion. Who are your top-10 prospects right now, and what can you do with them this week? Who are the next best 25 and what can you do with them this month? Who are the future 65 to 100 who can be cultivated at quarterly events and through your newsletter and e-mail communications?

Another focus diffusion issue for both volunteers and staff is the complexity of the case statement. Large institutions must create multi-dimensional case elements to meet the variety of needs within a large hospital or university. To keep the marketing and sales job easier and to maintain a concerted focus, case elements need to keep to the rule of three by three—three major themes with each theme having three subpoints. Ideally, each volunteer and staff member will become a champion on one specific issue with general knowledge of the big picture. Testing these three memorable themes requires working with your volunteer committees, presenting to focus groups, and interviewing donors through study and discovery call interviews.

#5 No Transaction

One would think that high-powered, corporate salespeople who agree to serve as solicitors for your nonprofit would be highly successful fundraisers. They know how to get ready by learning the case (the product), they know how to qualify prospects, they're not telephobic—and yet, they can fail miserably. Because selling products was their full-time job and the lack of success was so surprising, failure analysis debriefings became important. What was holding them back from nonprofit fundraising success? They were puzzled, too.

One volunteer told me: "I sell multimillion-dollar computer systems all over the world and I can't figure out how to do this nonprofit fundraising thing. What is wrong with me?" The major-gifts chair for another organization complained: "I'm used to selling tractors and high-end farm equipment to ranchers all the time. For our historical society building campaign I want them to give me $25,000, but I'm not giving them a tractor. This is a lot harder than I thought."

This lack of a transaction issue is a big one with volunteers trained in corporate sales. They are used to touting the benefits of the product they are selling and making the sales transaction—the computer system for $1,000,000, the tractor for $25,000. In nonprofit fundraising we are asking them to ask for the $25,000 and give nothing concrete in return.

So, how do you solve this? First, realize that your organization has already given value to the community and the donors. Talk about the intangible benefits the nonprofit has been providing society for 50 or 100 years. The symphony orchestra celebrating its centennial anniversary has performed thousands of concerts. The donations we are seeking for the endowment campaign are just a way of paying back the orchestra and its musicians for its many decades of service. Or for the college that has been giving away hundreds of thousands of dollars of unfunded scholarships each year helping countless numbers of students, it's time for donors to help the college through funding these scholarships.

Use Cialdini's ethical influence principle of reciprocation and remind people of the many favors the nonprofit has been performing over time. The hospital deserves gift support because of the free charity care they have provided over the years to help families in medical need.

Make the intangible tangible, make the nonprofit's services apparent to the donor and the volunteer—make your case.

#6 Can't Say the Number

Not being able to ask a donor for a specific gift amount, to say a number during the ask meeting, happens more than you think. The ask may be well rehearsed, everything is set, and yet the volunteer can't say the number (it seems to get caught in his throat somewhere). As mentioned in the ideal ask team section earlier in this chapter, the professional fundraiser should always be ready to jump in to cover the ask if the volunteer flinches for any reason. And while that is fine, the ideal person to make the ask is still the volunteer. One partial solution to the "can't say the number" problem is using an annual fund or campaign gift table. The gift table is the most powerful asking tool that you have. It is much easier for a volunteer to point to a level on the gift table so that the actual dollar number doesn't have to be mentioned.

Another subtle way to make the ask is to request consideration of a six-figure gift rather than asking for $100,000. Or, mention that you gave $50,000 and you hope your friend will match your gift.

One volunteer was eager to run our new $1,000 annual fund gifts club. He helped edit the language and come up with club benefits, and was eager to sign invitation letters to cultivation events. He would get up at events to promote the gift club and did a wonderful job. But in my three years of watching him build membership in the club from zero to 300 he never once said the word "$1,000." He would wave the brochure, ask people to look at the current membership list, have them take out the pledge form and say: "I hope you join me in being a member of the club so we can raise money to benefit this great cause." His passion for the organization and the respect with which he was held in the community enabled him to be a great success even though he couldn't say the number.

#7 One Leg at a Time

The premise of this classic ask-reluctance barrier is that many of us are afraid of people of higher social and/or economic status. We sometimes forget they still put their pants on one leg at a time.

In philanthropic fundraising, we intuitively conquered this problem by stressing "peer solicitation." A donor who has given $5,000 can ask for gifts at that level. You can ask for a gift the size you have personally given and you can ask for a gift less than what you have given. But rare is the volunteer who can ask higher than they have given.

In reflecting on my more than a quarter-century of fundraising experiences I can think of only two volunteers who broke this rule and could ask anybody for any amount of money. With only two people out of thousands I would say this is a valid barrier.

Stress to your volunteers that they really don't have the right to ask someone else for a gift until they have made their own. They need to be ready to tell their gift-decision story during the ask. Hopefully, their contribution will be seen as a stretch gift that will raise the sights and inspire a gift of equal value.

Even when a donor has given a million dollars and is getting ready to ask another donor for a million, too, the difference in their net worths can give pause. As one of my volunteers, A, who had made a $6 million gift and was a fearless asker, said: "Boy, I've got to think through asking George. He's got real money." I don't know how much money A had, but it was somewhere in the $50 million to $100 million range and for A not even close to George's net worth of a billion dollars.

In the *Art of Selling to the Affluent*, Matt Oechsli cites Dudley and Goodson's research on call reluctance and notes that social self-consciousness harms salespeople about 35 percent of the time and has been documented in more than 73 industries. Oechsli devotes an entire chapter to this issue as he feels it is a major reason that salespeople fail at selling to the affluent.[14]

#8 Don't Want to Ask My Friends

In the philanthropic fundraising world the ideal prospects to call on are your friends. Nonprofit fundraising has to overcome this issue as the best ask is friend to friend.

In *The Art of Selling to the Affluent* research showed that the strongest influence on a purchase decision was word-of-mouth information from friends.

> Rather than mass mailings, national advertising campaigns, or simply cold calling, you concentrate on the power of networking and word-of-mouth-influence to achieve your prospecting goals. . . . The opinions and suggestions of immediate family and trusted friends are the strongest influencers when affluent buyers begin their search for the products and services they need and want.[15]

So why do some volunteers say they can ask anybody for an annual fund gift except their friends? It doesn't make sense . . . or does it? Put yourself in your volunteers' shoes for a moment. They have asked you to call on Jon, a friend of yours for more than 20 years. You go way back and are both business associates and good friends who golf and go out with your wives to dinner. Even though you know Jon could give $25,000 to the campaign, you are reluctant to ask him for it. You like the cause but do they really need the money enough to jeopardize your long-term friendship with Jon? Is it worth risking a friendship for a nonprofit staff fundraiser whom you have met only a couple of times? Is the college president solid? Does she have her act together? Jon's a friend but can be tough in business meetings. What questions is he going to ask me?

One of the true readiness tests for each of your volunteers is to request that they select their closest friend with the most gift potential and start asking. Empower your volunteer's questions, objections, and reasons for being reluctant to make the call. Because this is the volunteer's best friend she probably knows what reactions she will get during the ask meeting. You should role play to determine how to deal with each of these issues and discuss what a comfortable yet stretch gift request would be for the friend. What other gifts has the individual made in the community? Are there any special family circumstances that suggest we lower our gift request? If the friend really got excited about the campaign project, how much could she give over a three- to five-year pledge period?

It may take several meetings to build the relationship between you, the professional philanthropic fundraiser, and the volunteer so that the volunteer will trust this long-term relationship. You need to build mutual trust and understanding. You need to make clear to this volunteer your customer focus, work ethic, and commitment to making the volunteer look like and be a winner.

I had a wonderful example of this. We were off to a great start to our fundraising and had used many traditional techniques to generate names of potential donors for our cause. After a year of successfully cultivating gifts and receiving some wonderful donations and many stories of delighted donors related at our campaign volunteer fundraising meetings, all of a sudden we started to get new names recommended to us. The floodgate opened for new prospective donors. After the end of one particularly productive brain-storming session on new people to approach, I asked one of my volunteers what was going on. Everybody had been so friendly the year before but I was starting to feel like they had been holding names back and now for some reason it was okay to give up their friends' names. My volunteer said:

> Sure, what did you expect? You were new to us and this organization hadn't been fundraising before. While we liked you and the president, we really didn't know how you would treat our friends. We didn't know if you would break their arms for a gift, or if you would guide them along nicely. Now that we see how you work we can trust you with our closest friends who have the real money.

You'll need to earn the trust of your volunteers so they can share their most important relationships with you. Go slow at the beginning. Be patient. Once they see you are on the path of the win-win ask, that you want donors delighted because they made winning gifts, new doors will open for you.

#9 Can't Ask My Family

Unlike #8, Don't Want to Ask My Friends, family-ask reluctance is hard to conquer. Every family can experience complicated dynamics that make an intergenerational ask tricky. If you add the complications of wealth and the challenges that large sums of money can bring to rich families, you can begin to see why a volunteer might have ask reluctance.

The first place to start solving the family ask challenge is with your case. If your volunteer feels the case isn't strong enough to stand the scrutiny of Mom and Dad, then you can do work immediately to clarify the story. Have your family guide reflect on possible case questions or objections based upon the volunteer's usual family meetings and discussions.

If your case is compelling but the family dynamic prevents a direct ask, family member to family member, seek the permission of your family insider to serve as the official asker. Get your family champion to provide background information on family giving histories to other organizations. Many family members want to play a more subtle role of being ready to advise a family member positively once an official ask has been made by the nonprofit organization. It is critically important that you have a family member guide to assist you with finding the appropriate project and request level for your request. Your family guide can be a good resource in helping define which outside-the-family volunteer would have the biggest impact at the ask meeting.

While many family challenges can come about as a son or daughter anticipates asking Mom or Dad for a gift from the family foundation, this generational tension can flip. In one family, Dad was in his late 70s. He wanted to transfer decision making to his children but realized he was almost too powerful in their eyes. In asking for a gift from his family foundation he offered to be the guide in the background, but he wanted a formal presentation made to his children so they could be the family leaders with the gift. He wanted to empower the next generation to develop its own decision-making style. He would offer advice but would not ask his children even though he loved the nonprofit and had been involved with it for many years.

#10 Telephobia

While seeing a few instances of telephobia in my career, I never really understood how pervasive telephone avoidance at work was for salespeople until learning about it in Dudley and Goodson's book on ask reluctance.

One can see where a fear of the telephone could be a barrier to asking. If you can't use the phone to set up the ask meeting, you're in real trouble.

It is fascinating to interact with some normally gregarious people who are telephobic. I had one client who was supposed to set up interviews for our philanthropic market research study. When I arrived in town after a full day of travel I found that no interviews had been set up. He hung his head and admitted that he was so new to fundraising he just couldn't envision making the calls. This normally talk-your-ear-off person simply did not like to use the telephone. It's just not his style to talk on the phone. He's more of a face-to-face communicator as he seems to intuitively know it is a more effective way to interact.

By the way, remember this rule: Unless you absolutely have to, do not ask for gifts on the telephone; ask face-to-face. Remember our listening research that showed that 55 percent of all communications are nonverbal (Chapter 3, Listen). It is easy to reject a request by phone because you don't have to look at the requestor in the eye and deal with the nonverbal emotional reactions.

So get over your telephobia and set up the ask meeting. You do not want to close a gift by phone, anyway. Write out your script before making appointments for gift-request meetings. Rehearse the call in your office with the door closed. Stand up for the call to give yourself more energy. Smile. Have all of your materials handy. Use a telephone headset so your hands are free to be expressive. Eventually you will become fearless on the phone.

What do you do for a telephobic volunteer? In one campaign I found out that Doug, who was a fearless face-to-face fundraiser, wasn't setting up his next round of fundraising appointments. He had suddenly and mysteriously stopped fundraising. We went out to lunch to catch up on life, the campaign, and to see how to get him back on the campaign trail. Doug finally admitted he was not comfortable on the phone. He did not know why, he just froze every time he was ready to pick up the phone to make the ask appointment. I thanked him for being candid and sharing his challenge and asked his permission to serve as his personal assistant. Could I call in his name as his personal appointment secretary? His friends might call him to confirm he wanted the appointment and that I really was calling for him. But, I would be glad to do his telephone work. He agreed; I made the calls for appointments; and my campaign chair was back in action. The campaign ended up way over goal.

#11 Image Rejection

Many people don't like to think of themselves as salespeople or solicitors, but in asking for money for your nonprofit organization you do need to be in marketing and sales mode. One of the fascinating comments from Dudley and Goodson is that the more a particular sales field rejects their sales image the more they will obfuscate their titles. Me? I'm proud to be a philanthropic fundraiser, and I am surprised by the number of odd titles that my colleagues use to hide what they do for a living from the world and themselves—development officers, advancement officers, or resource development are so vague that most donors don't understand what those jobs really entail.

In Stephan Schiffman's brief book, *The 25 Sales Habits of Highly Successful Salespeople*, he notes:

> Habit 24: Telling everyone you meet who you work for and what you sell.
>
> Why not make a point of broadcasting your profession to anyone and everyone—with pride? This is not the same as subjecting everyone you meet to a sales pitch! Simply pass along your name, profession, and company affiliation to every new person you meet.[16]

Staff fundraisers need to be proud of their job of selling their nonprofit so their volunteers can also be proud of their role in the gift-asking process.

I applaud the Association of Fundraising Professionals (AFP). That's who we are, professional fundraisers, and we should be proud of our work and role in society.

If you are a manager of fundraising staff, this is an important issue to discuss with your team. Rejection of the sales title may mean you have a staff member who is rejecting his image and who may have trouble orchestrating ask meetings.

Let volunteers know they are serving on the philanthropic fundraising committee, not the development committee. Set up a "Golden Glove" award for the most successful volunteer fundraiser of the year. When a volunteer completes a successful ask, have the person explain the techniques used to peers. Celebrate the volunteer's acumen as a great solicitor of charitable donations.

#12 Overpreparation

Constantly working to get prepared for the ask is an obstacle that relates more to professional fundraising staff than volunteers. Some staff, in trying to get ready to make fundraising calls, keep preparing and preparing rather than making calls and interacting with people. Even with all of the background information provided in this book and the steps of cultivation and preparation that are important for success, you must get fundraising staff out of the office to interact with donors. If in doubt, go out and meet donors to learn more about their values and their perceptions of your case statement. And, at a certain point, you must ask them for a gift. They know that is your job and will think it odd that you are always hanging out without asking them to fully engage in the organization by becoming a donor.

I grew up in the arts as a musician, conductor, orchestra administrator, and concert promoter. We had a saying: "Print the tickets and the show will get ready." For fundraising staffers who have the tendency to procrastinate and use the lack of preparation as an excuse for not asking, use the arts technique of printing the tickets:

> I know you're not quite ready to visit with Joe and Mary about their gift but why don't you set up a meeting with them for three weeks from now. That will give you plenty of time to get ready. With the meeting date set, you will be motivated. Necessity will really become the mother of good fundraising invention.

Buck Smith, the originator of the cultivation cycle and moves management process, talked about readiness in a talk to AFP a few years ago:

> Readiness is a subjective measurement of how developed the relationship is with a prospect and whether an individual is ready to consider making a "major" commitment and investment. Readiness to give is identified using five categories:
>
> A—ready to invest or reinvest.
>
> B—needs some cultivation.
>
> C—needs extensive cultivation.
>
> D—has marginal interest.
>
> U—undetermined.[17]

The only way to determine if a donor is an "A" or a "D" is to meet with them. Stop preparing—just do it.

#13 Disorganized

The art of fundraising has many critical elements—people skills, listening ability, empathy, and being able to tell good stories to make the case. Complementing the art of fundraising is the science of fundraising—tracking of fundraising moves, to-do lists, yearly reminders of giving, and the whole organizational side of fundraising.

Some of the best relationship people (the art of fundraising) can be the worst at the discipline of fundraising (the science of fundraising). It can really hurt your asking and closing abilities if you are disorganized. You can't just cultivate a donor forever. You need to keep track, on paper, of the relationship contacts and calendar, write up contact reports, and know when it is time to get to the ask. And then, once you have asked, you need to track the follow-up meeting negotiated in the ask to set up the closing discussion. It's not enough to just ask; you need to close.

Here's a true story heard during a study interview:

> You know this college was really odd about their fundraising. They did a good job of getting me interested. I went to a few of their events with my friends and was impressed by the president and the college's mission. They invited me on campus for a tour and asked me for $50,000. They had a nice presentation book and gave me a good personalized proposal. They did everything right. I told them I had to think it about because that's what I tell everyone when they ask. But that was six months ago and they have never called me back. I guess they don't really need the $50,000 I was intending to give them.

This story is a great reminder that fundraising isn't just about asking for gifts. You need to close them, too.

#14 Afraid to Talk about Death

If you only raise annual-fund dollars, you don't have to worry about this challenge. However, if you ever want to seek planned estate gifts from donors, you need to be ready to talk about death. That's when the gift comes. You need to be able to help your donors think through the ultimate disposition of their lifelong assets and the type of legacy they want to leave the world when they are gone.

The fact that the donors won't need the money after death is the reason you can have a good discussion about the ultimate disposition of their wealth. Lead with the concept that family comes first. Get the donor to think through the nonprofit charitable causes they have supported in their lifetime and what legacy they would like to leave each of them. Reread Chapter 2 to reflect on Andrew Carnegie's *Gospel of Wealth* and how the rich should deal with their money.

While younger people may struggle with thinking about death (we are immortal, aren't we), as you talk with donors nearing retirement or retired you will find that because of retirement planning they have had to deal with mortality tables, the payout rates for pensions, how soon to retire, what that means for Social Security benefits for the rest of their life, and the myriad other details that come with retirement. Most people by their 60s and 70s have gone through the death of a few colleagues, friends, family members, and parents.

I was in my early 30s when I did a planned estate-giving campaign in Sun City West, Arizona, for a nonprofit organization there. As I worked with one of my volunteers, Frank told me bluntly:

> Sonny, if you can't talk about death, you're in the wrong business. We know about death and, while not volunteering, are ready to accept it. We don't even buy green bananas here. So learn to understand death. It's not your donors who can't talk about death, it's you.

Of course, Frank was right. As I thought through issues of death and was able to say the "death" and "after you're dead" words, it became much easier to discuss planned estate gifts with donors.

Personalize These Obstacles

As we've covered the challenges and obstacles to asking for a philanthropic gift, I hope you have been taking notes and thinking about your own personal issues; the issues of your senior management team; board members; and your fundraising volunteers. Don't give up on any of them if they are call reluctant. Instead, use the material in this chapter to diagnose what their problem is and how you can either overcome their issue or avoid it by assigning them to another aspect of your fundraising program.

One final story for this chapter. We were seeking funds in Sun City West, Arizona, for the new hospital building. Planned estate gifts would count as the population was older and the hospital had taken out 30-year bonds for construction. Any gift that we could expect to receive during that time would count toward the campaign. Our calling team met with Albert seeking a $250,000 unitrust gift. He had already indicated he could do something substantial but that he needed a lifetime income for his wife and himself. He was all set to close the gift but said there was one small detail. Could I call him for a lunch meeting to discuss it? Sure, no problem. We met and Albert said his only condition on the gift was that I had to teach his wife Martha how to drive his Cadillac. She had a much smaller car and he was losing his eyesight so he wanted to sell her car and just drive his. The problem was if he tried to teach her to drive his big car they might kill each other as they both were volatile personalities and he just didn't have the patience to teach her. I agreed; how hard could that be? It turned out to be quite the challenge. While he was losing his eyesight she was losing her mind. Early Alzheimer's. We would get going and she would forget where she was in the small town of 6,000. It was really scary driving with her. We got her comfortable with the size of the car, parking at the grocery store and driving to the bank. I reported to Albert that she was fine driving the car but that she couldn't remember where she was going. He said that was okay. She would be the eyes and he would be the brains and as a team they would do just fine. He thanked me for my patience and signed his pledge form. Now, that's a win-win gift.

SUMMARIZING THE WIN-WIN ASK

As a final review, remember you want a winning gift for the donor and the organization. You want a contribution proposition that delights the donor because it matches her value system, makes a clear impact on the community, and helps your organization's mission to succeed.

Be thoughtful. Use the tools in all of the previous chapters to listen to the gifting noises that lead to a win-win ask and gift decision.

APPLY WHAT YOU'VE LEARNED

Here are three tasks for this chapter to help bring these concepts into focus:

1. *Strategy memo.* Take your top-three donors from this last year and write a strategy memo for each envisioning your next gift request. Go back to the strategy memo section of this chapter to make sure you included all the steps that you can. Review and rewrite your strategy once a week for at least three weeks in a row to see how your thinking matures.

2. *Personalized-proposal.* Now use each of these strategy memos and develop a one- to two-page personalized request proposal for each donor.

3. *Make a win-win ask.* Visit with the donor whose strategy memo and proposal you feel is the strongest. Find a volunteer to help you request the gift. Go through all of the steps in this chapter to prepare for the meeting and to ask for the gift. Then, just do it—ask for the order.

▓ NOTES

1. Holly Hall, "Closing the Deal: A Multimillionaire Creates a New Guide to Help Charity Trustees Ask Their Friends and Peers for Big Gifts," *The Chronicle of Philanthropy*, August 31, 2006, 29–30.

2. Robert B. Cialdini, Ph.D., *Influence: The Psychology of Persuasion* (New York: Collins, 1984, 1994, 2007), 38.

3. Thayer Cheatham Willis, *Navigating the Dark Side of Wealth: A Life Guide for Inheritors* (Portland, OR: New Concord Press, 2003), 167.

4. Ibid., 149.

5. Claude Rosenberg Jr., *Wealthy and Wise: How You and America Can Get the Most Out of Your Giving* (Boston: Little, Brown, 1994), 7.

6. Ibid., 15.

7. Ibid., 37.

8. Dr. Thomas J. Stanley, *Selling to the Affluent* (New York: McGraw Hill, 1991), 299–300, 329.

9. Craig Marine, "The Philanthropist Claude Rosenberg Epitomizes the New, Western Way of Giving, and He's Trying to Convince American Millionaires to Follow Suit," *San Francisco Chronicle*, Sunday, December 2, 2001.

10. Madelyn Burley-Allen, *Listening: The Forgotten Skill*, Second Edition (New York: John Wiley & Sons, 1995), 150–152.

11. Robert B. Cialdini, *Influence: Science and Practice*, Fourth Edition (Boston: Allyn and Bacon, 2001), 207–208.

12. Eileen Growald, excerpted from *Collaborative Grantmaking: Lessons Learned from the Rockefeller Family's Experiences* (National Center for Family Philanthropy, www.ncfp.org).

13. George W. Dudley and Shannon L. Goodson, *Earning What You're Worth? The Psychology of Sales Call Reluctance* (Dallas: Behavioral Sciences Research Press, 1992, 1999).

14. Matt Oechsli, *The Art of Selling to the Affluent* (New York: John Wiley & Sons, 2005), 55–75.

15. Ibid., 41, 108, 111, 112–113.

16. Stephan Schiffman, *The 25 Sales Habits of Highly Successful Salespeople* (Holbrook, MA: Bob Adams, 1994), 115–117, 129.

17. "From Business as Usual to Making a Difference: A Conversation with G.T. "Buck" Smith, AFP Oregon Chapter, February 13, 2004.

6

After Winning the Gift

You know, naming this building for me was more fun that I thought it would be. I realize I originally told you no but I'm glad you worked with my wife to talk me into it. This is something special. I appreciate the fact you let me think this through and let my wife and me have time to make a good decision.

In the previous chapter, The Win–Win Ask, we addressed the immediate actions following a positive gift decision. In this chapter we'll look at three important areas of operational importance to philanthropic fundraising offices:

1. Thank-you systems for your entire office

2. Donor recognition policies and best practices

3. Stewardship donor relations programs that will help to keep you connected to donors after their donation is completed

In the same way that asking best practices have developed over the years, fundraisers have created patterns of how best to thank donors, recognize them, and steward their gifts to help encourage further investments in your organization by them in the future. Thanking a donor for a gift has gone way past the simple thank-you note of a quarter-century ago. Initially, thank-you systems were defined by good manners (as taught by Mom) and by the

Internal Revenue Service (IRS). These are still two excellent standards of good behavior, of course.

Recognition is defined as negotiating with a donor the amount of public visibility the gift would normally receive, should receive, and that the donor wants it to receive.

Stewardship is the process of ongoing communications about how the gift is used (fiduciary stewardship) as well as the impact the gift has on the organization and society (philanthropic stewardship).

A Thank-You System

In the previous chapter we talked about the need to begin the thanking process as soon as donors formally announce their gift intentions. Ideally, this intention is documented in writing through the signing of the gentle letter of intent. A personal letter indicating the donor's gift intention works just as well as a letter of intent you have designed. So before the thank-you process gets into full swing, make sure your formal documentation from the donor is complete.

Once donors have made a gift decision, start celebrating with them personally. Many donors are low key and may not tell you directly that the gift request you made was 10 times more than they have ever given before, and their final gift decision is 5 times larger than ever before. This is personal information that may come out later, but usually not at this stage of your relationship. So celebrate.

It is important for the philanthropic fundraiser to be the chief cheerleader in gift celebration. Many times the president may have dreamed of a big gift where every penny requested was granted by the donor. The volunteer may have had equally high expectations. Both of these players may be pleased to have a gift decision completed yet slightly disappointed that the full gift request was not met. The professional fundraiser knows the gift offered is significant in the eyes of the donor. Shake the donor's hand and create a sense of enthusiasm in the announcement setting.

As soon as you get back to the office or end the phone call, start orchestrating the thank-you process. Because you have come to know this donor well through the cultivation and solicitation process, be thoughtful about the best way to thank this donor. Get your president or CEO excited about the gift and have the first phone call of congratulations and personal letter of thanks come from her. Take out a sheet of paper and handwrite heartfelt thanks about what this gift means to the community, to your organization and the people you serve, and to your fundraising program. Keep this note to one page and make it highly personal.

You also need an official thank-you record for your files and the donor's tax records. This should be typed and formally restate the gift purpose (restricted or unrestricted) and terms (outright, multiyear, mixture of cash and estate). This is the formal document that can be used by your successor if you get hit by a bus tomorrow and by the donor to give to his accountant or attorney to aid in the execution of the gift. Set a policy at your institution as to who will sign these formal letters—your president, executive director, or chief philanthropy officer.

Please note: If a check accompanies the gentle letter of intent you will need this official thank-you to mention the amount and date of the check, the sequence of the pledge payment if applicable (e.g., "Thank you for the first payment of $10,000 toward your five-year commitment of $50,000"), and standard wording that the IRS requires about the lack of any tangible benefits to the donor in return for the gift.

Set a standard for yourself and your office that the first personal thank-you note from the president or chief philanthropy officer will go out within the first working day after learning of the gift decision. This immediate response will buy you time to get other thank-you's completed. Please see the upcoming section on thresholds of thanks to refine this one-working-day thank-you policy.

Involve Your Asking Team

While this seems obvious, it is a lot of work to ghostwrite different types of thank-you notes from each of the ask team members. It takes discipline to set up the standard letters from these team members, customize each one after a gift is received, and get the letter produced on the appropriate letterhead (ask each volunteer to give you letterhead or permission to send documents to their administrative assistants for final letter production). Then you need to get the letters to each signer and make sure they complete the work by adding a personal handwritten note to the letter. Ideally, you would like the team members' administrative assistants to photocopy the signed letter and send you a copy as they mail it out. If the volunteers want the fundraising office to handle everything, then find a way to pick up the signed letter from their offices.

When the first million-dollar gift comes in, this work is easy. But as your campaign or annual fund program keeps moving forward, getting these thank-you letters completed by your office, signed by each person, and mailed out within one week (or sooner) will become a lot of work. Appoint someone in your office as the official thank-you czar to make sure discipline is maintained throughout the year and throughout your campaigns. Your organization can stand out by adhering to a highly systematic, professional thank-you process. None of this is hard, but it is hard work.

Remember to thank the request team for their time, effort, insights, and influence in helping secure the gift. Of course, they will be rewarded by success, but a personal call from you acknowledging their role in securing the gift will encourage them to make other calls for you and your organization. Also thank any of the staff in your organization that helped make the gift happen. The doctors who toured the donor through the cardiac surgery unit, the program officer who described how adoptions worked during the site visit, and the receptionist who welcomed the donor to your offices. Let this be a winning gift for them, too.

Others Can Participate in the Fun of Thanking Donors

For board members who are apprehensive about asking for money, a good way to start easing them into the fundraising process is to ask them to place thank-you calls. They are not supposed to ask for money, just thank the donors for their gifts. What could be more fun than that?

In your board fundraising report share the list of donors, top down alphabetically. Start with gifts of $10,000 or more, then $5,000, then $1,000, then up to $1,000. Display these names on a screen at the board meeting and ask for board members to indicate whom they know and would be willing to thank (this well help to identify connections for later). As you present the lists, have another staff member make careful notes on who is willing to call whom and any general comments that are made about the donors that might be useful later. This information flow can come quickly and from multiple sources, so be ready to capture comments fast.

Pass out a simple thank-you script to make it easy on your volunteers. The script should include a brief one-sentence reminder of the mission and impact of your organization on the community to reinforce to the donor why he gave.

When you send board members the confirmation list of thank-you calls they are to make, provide the best contact phone number that you have and a simple gift history—the amount of this gift, any restriction, and a note on whether this is a first-time gift or if this donor has contributed regularly or occasionally and for how many years.

Having a one-page customized script for each thank-you call with your organization's mission and impact language and a couple of questions to ask the donor will provide your volunteers with a worksheet to make notes from the phone call that they can send back to you (or that they can reference when you make your follow-up calls to make sure the work was done). Include a preaddressed stamped envelope so volunteers can send their completed forms back to you.

Use this thank-you call by your board member to gather some simple information about the donor. Sample questions might include:

1. I notice you have been giving since 1995; what got you started?
2. This is a wonderful gift; what motivates you to give to us each year?
3. I noticed that you designate your gift to scholarships. Why are they important to you?
4. I understand this is your first gift to our organization. What prompted you to make this gift?

Ask each of your volunteers to think of any additional questions they would feel comfortable asking. If they know the donor well, they can really go into depth on the questions.

Be sure your volunteers take notes and debrief them on what they heard for future reference.

Keep the focus of these phone calls on thanking the donor for the gift. Two to three minutes of simple questions are fine. But keep it short unless the donor wants to talk a lot. End the call by thanking the donor again. If you have a cultivation event scheduled in the near future, mention this at the end of the call (the script can set these up for your volunteers to reference).

Just as your ask-reluctant volunteers can help with thanking so can ask-reluctant staff members. Thank-you calls by faculty members, physicians, curators, or program managers can bring real delight to the donor and help your professionals better understand the motivations of donors. Ask for volunteers as you wander the halls of your organization. Ask them to start small and build (remember Cialdini) by making only two or three thank-you calls. Show them a sample script and offer to come to their offices for their first call or two to help them prepare and debrief after the call. Once they try it they will enjoy the positive reactions from the donors and will want to help again.

By marshaling your volunteers and staff you can expand your acknowledgment process to far deeper levels than you would ever be able to afford by paying staff.

Thresholds of the Thank-You System

If you are a small organization with a limited number of gifts coming in each week, you can afford to be generous and apply all of the ideas mentioned to every single gift that comes in the door whether it is $1 or $100,000. For programs just getting off the ground, that is what you should do. Your strategic advantage over the large fundraising shops with thousands of donors is your ability to personally thank each donor every time they make a gift.

As your program expands, reality begins to set in. You can do only so much. And, you need to set standards of accountability to make sure the largest gifts are acknowledged first and more personally. Otherwise, you will thank everyone poorly. Set up a triage system for dealing with significant gifts to your organization. Here is a sample system from an actual organization that had transitioned from a $1,000 annual fund program into a capital campaign. You can adapt these procedures to your organization by defining what constitutes a major gift for your organization and how much time you have to devote to this process. As you will see, the tier-one thank-you steps are highly involved and customized. You can afford to do a couple of these a week, but not many more than that.

Tier One—All Annual Gifts of $5,000 or More and All Capital Gifts of $25,000 or More

1. A personal, handwritten thank-you note will be sent out within one working day by the president or chief philanthropy officer.

2. Any volunteers or staff involved in the ask meeting will be notified of the gift within one working day (ideally much sooner) and a

personalized thank-you letter sent within two working days of the gift announcement (this means the fundraising office has the volunteers thank-you letter customized for this particular gift and ready to sign in the volunteer's office—you cannot control when the volunteer will be available to sign the letter). Follow-up with volunteer and/or staff to make sure the letter was sent out within one week of sending the letter draft to their attention.

3. A formal, typed thank-you form indicating gift size, use (unrestricted or restricted), term (outright or pledge length), and IRS statement confirming no benefits to the gift, signed by the chief philanthropy officer, and be sent out within three working days.

4. Volunteer chair of this division should send his own thank-you note if he was not involved in the ask. The thank-you letter should go out within five days.

   For example: Joe is chair of the annual fund committee this year. He was not in the gift request meeting nor does he know the donor, but as chair of the group of volunteers responsible for achieving the $2 million annual fund goal he thanks the donors for helping the organization achieve its mission and maintain financial stability through this annual fund donation. A similar thank-you letter would be sent by a capital campaign chair who was not involved in the gift request meeting. This step is important as you may find your volunteer chair does know this donor and will want to pick up the phone for a personal thank-you.

5. At the next board meeting and/or fundraising meeting (development committee, annual fund committee, capital campaign steering committee) list names of recent donors to secure volunteer thank-you callers. Get scripts and gift histories to volunteers within two working days. Follow up within two weeks to debrief thank-you phone callers.

Tier Two—All Annual Gifts of $1,000 or More and All Capital Gifts of $10,000 or More

1. A personal, handwritten thank-you note will be sent out within three working days by the president or chief philanthropy officer. (You may want to review the donor's name within your Identification and

Qualification (IQ) prospect listings to determine gift potential for this donor. If this $1,000 donor is a million-dollar prospect you may want to accelerate the thank-you process by moving this person up to tier one status.)

2. Any volunteers or staff involved in the ask meeting will be notified of the gift within five working days (sooner, if possible) and a personalized thank-you letter sent within five working days of the gift announcement (this means the fundraising office has the volunteer's thank-you letter customized for this particular gift and ready to sign in the volunteer's office—you cannot control when the volunteer will be available to sign the letter). Follow up with volunteer and/or staff to make sure the letter was sent out within two weeks of sending the letter draft to their attention.

3. A formal, typed thank-you form indicating gift size, use (unrestricted or restricted), term (outright or pledge length), and IRS statement confirming no benefits to the gift will be sent out within seven working days signed by the campaign director or annual fund director as appropriate.

4. Volunteer chair of this division should send his own thank-you note if he was not involved in the ask. This letter should be drafted for signature within 10 working days.

5. At the next board meeting and/or fundraising meeting (development committee, annual fund committee, capital campaign steering committee) list names of recent donors to secure volunteer thank-you callers. Get scripts and gift histories to volunteers within five working days. Follow up within four weeks to debrief thank-you phone callers.

Pay particular attention to tier-two gifts from high-level prospects. One way of checking the progress of your fundraising program is to evaluate the number of high-level "never" donor prospects that you convert to first-time donors through your annual fund gift requests.

Tier Three—All Annual Gifts up to $1,000 and All Capital Gifts up to $10,000   For your organization this may mean gifts up to $500 if you are a small shop or gifts up to $10,000 if you have a large, big-gifts fundraising program. For every size gift, it is important to have someone on staff do a quick prospect research analysis of the donor. At tier-three level, you are only doing basic thank-yous *unless* the donor comes out highly ranked in prospect research. If so, elevate the thanking status of that donor to tier two or even tier one (yes, this is the undemocratic, pragmatic part of philanthropic fundraising).

You need to base your tier-three basic thank-yous upon the numbers for your organization. If you have 1,000 people giving $100 to $999 and another 3,000 people giving $1 to $99, put in a four-tier system. Some organizations will just send a standardized postcard or a computer-signed, nonpersonalized letter to a tier-four donor if they have that many people to deal with. Of course, the ideal is higher personalization, but what is the cost of delivery based upon the revenue generated from this tier?

1. No personal handwritten notes for annual fund donors up to $1,000 unless a highly rated prospect. Capital gifts should still receive a handwritten note.

2. For capital gifts up to $10,000, any volunteers or staff involved in the ask meeting will be notified of the gift within five working days (sooner, if possible) and their personalized thank-you letters sent within five working days of the gift announcement (this means the fundraising office has the volunteer's thank-you letter customized to this particular gift and ready to sign in his office—you cannot control when the volunteer will be available to sign the letter). Follow up with volunteer and/or staff to make sure the letter was sent out within two weeks of sending the letter draft to their attention. For lower-end annual fund gifts generated from direct-marketing techniques (direct mail, e-mail, telethons) you can skip this step.

3. A formal, typed thank-you form indicating gift size, use (unrestricted or restricted), term (outright or pledge length), and IRS statement confirming no benefits to the gift will be sent out within 10 working days (ideally sooner) signed by campaign director or annual fund director as appropriate.

4. Volunteer chair of this division should send his own thank-you note if he was not involved in the ask. This letter should be drafted for signature within 10 working days.

5. At the next board meeting and/or fundraising meeting (development committee, annual fund committee, capital campaign steering committee) list names of recent donors to secure volunteer thank-you callers. Get

EXHIBIT 6.1   THANK YOU PROCEDURE CHART

	Tier One	Tier Two	Tier Three
1) Handwritten thank-you from CEO	1 day	3 day	For rated prospects
2) Volunteers and/or staff in the ask meeting thank-yous	2 days	5 days	5 days
3) Personalized letter of acknowledgment from fundraising office	3 days	7 days	10 days
4) Vounteer chair thank-you letter	5 days	10 days	10 days
5) Board or staff thank-you calls	2 weeks	4 weeks	4 weeks

scripts and gift histories to volunteers within five working days. Follow up within four weeks to debrief thank-you phone callers.

Exhibit 6.1 summarizes the three tiers of thanking described here. Remember, if you have a larger donor base you may need to expand to four or five tiers to help manage your system. You must seek a balance of appropriate thankfulness while leaving time for your staff to raise money.

Gifts of Stock and Other Appreciated Assets

Gifts of appreciated assets can usually be treated like cash in terms of thank-yous. The only distinction, and the reason for this section of the book, is a commonly made mistake in recording the gift amount of the stock being transferred. While it may seem logical to thank the donor for the amount of money the charity deposits in its bank account at the end of a stock transfer, that is not the real number that you need to tell the donor for tax purposes.

The donor of the stock gives up legal ownership of the asset on the day of transfer. The high and low average of the stock price *that* day is what determines the tax-deductible gift amount your thank-you letter should include. This is the number needed for the donor's tax records rather than the net amount after the stock is sold and the stockbroker's fee is deducted. Differences between the transfer date and the sale date can result from the stock increasing or decreasing in price. Usually, the difference between the two dollar amounts is usually quite small and will not make a big difference to the donor or the nonprofit organization (however, there can be dramatic exceptions).

A traumatic true story: One donor made a gift to the institution of $6,000,000. The gift was made in one lump-sum transfer of stock to the organization. The advice of the nonprofit's stockbroker was to spread out the sale of the stock so that its price would not be depressed by dumping all of the shares on the stock market at once. Unfortunately, during the six months the organization owned the stock and was in the process of selling it, the price of the stock drifted downward, resulting in eventual net proceeds of $5,100,000. The tax-deductible gift the donor made was $6 million, the value of the stock the day ownership was transferred from the donor to the nonprofit organization. The $6 million number is what the donor told his accountant for the tax deduction basis. The difference between the donated amount and the net after the sale was an investment loss by the organization. Luckily, upon learning of the asset shrinkage during the sale, the donor made good on his gift intention by donating an additional $900,000.

Valuing the gift the day of stock ownership makes even more sense when you think of a hypothetical increase in a stock's value after it is donated. Let's say Alice and Morrie donate stock worth $10,003.42 on December 26 to honor a pledge they had made to the annual fund earlier that year. By the time you are notified of the gift and are back in the office after the holidays it is January 3. You authorize the sale and, lucky you, the stock value has gone up and you realize $10,542 from the gift. How do you thank the donors? For tax purposes the thank-you letter needs to indicate that W shares of XYZ Corp. stock were transferred on December 26 with an average stock price per share that day of $Y resulting in a gift of $10,003.42. Those are the facts of the gift that Alice and Morrie need to give their accountant so they can receive the tax deduction for their gift. You may want to call them to tell the great news that, in fact, because of a market fluctuation your organization really gained $500 more. That would be a nice way to delight the donor. But, remember the gain is your organization's and is not part of the donor's tax-deductible gift.

Be sure to keep clear records on all stock gifts to note the date of ownership transfer and the average price that day, not the net price on the day the stock was sold by your organization (even though that is the amount deposited into your nonprofit's bank account). To maximize your organization's benefits from stock gifts, see if a stockbroker on your board will donate his commissions from stock donations back to your organization. If you don't have a stockbroker on your board, you may want to recruit one (as long as the individual loves your cause, of course). Be sure to go over these record-keeping issues with the stockbroker your nonprofit uses regularly so he can provide you with day-of-ownership-transfer share price information.

RECOGNITION OPPORTUNITIES

Recognizing donors helps thank the donor who made the gift and helps the organization raise money from other people (remember Robert Cialdini's ethical influence Principle #6—consensus—unleash people power by showing responses of many others, testimonials of others; see Part II, Seek Winning Gifts for Your Organization). Most of the recognition we offer donors is more of a win for the organization than a way to delight the donor.

The good news is that by displaying your donor lists frequently at events, in the annual report, and on donor walls you can build a sense of community around your organization so that people really do want to be seen on the lists. Now it is a winning proposition for the donor. To keep it a win for every donor, make sure and let them know they can remain anonymous if they wish. And, they need to be listed as they want to be. At one board meeting, we had a donor complain vocally that his wish that his wife's name be listed along with his in the donor honor roll had been ignored. He was not happy. The whole idea of recognition is to delight your donors. It takes a lot of work to do it right.

A good example: One symphony orchestra regularly thanked its donors after each gift and asked that donors review their names as listed in the thank-you letter to make sure they were correct for the program book listing for next season. One year, because of the need to subtly suggest donors consider increasing their giving to appear in the next-higher donor category in the program books, a proofsheet of names was sent out to all of the donors asking for final corrections in the context of the full list by gift category. Each name was highlighted individually in yellow on the enclosed proofsheet. Fully 30 percent of the donors sent back changes. They wanted Tom and Sally Jones versus Mr. and Mrs. Thomas Jones. Or they requested similar types of small adjustments to a basically correct list. The lesson—they were not reading the thank-you letter beyond the simple thanks and tax receipt information. In trying to combine thanking with recognition we confused the donors. The context of all of the names helped give them perspective on how others want to be listed. Keep recognition separate, highly personalized, and in context of other donors to your organization.

When asking donors for their permission to be included on donor lists and donor walls you will receive a variety of responses. Showing an existing list helps to show that others have granted permission. Some donors want to be highly visible; they want the ego satisfaction of being on the list and, for many, in the top donor category on the list. Others are ambivalent; it is okay with them whether they are included on the list or not. Hopefully over time, they will get some positive feedback from their friends so they feel good about being on the list. A few people are very reluctant to be on the list. It is not a win for them to be visible to other organizations. They know they will get asked for gifts to other causes (this happens a lot when a new donor makes the first big capital gift and inadvertently makes a splash in the community). You may want to provide this type of donor with some defense mechanisms when he is approached aggressively by other groups (to protect your organization so the donor will give more to you in the future, but more important, to insulate the donor from a lot of gift requests). Remind the donor of his feelings of mission commitment to your organization, the number of years he has served on the board, and the importance of the impact of this specific gift to his personal values. If other causes can meet this same criteria, the donor should invest just as much. If he gets an ask for a cause he doesn't care that much about, he doesn't have to make a gift.

The key message here is don't assume recognition is a win for the donor or a way to delight the donor. Determine donor values around recognition just as you determined their values around giving.

Power of Gift Clubs

Make the distinction between a level in a ladder of giving and an active gift club. A ladder of giving is just a series of donor levels at which donors can choose to contribute—"Please indicate your gift of ❏ $25 ❏ $50 ❏ $100 ❏ $250 ❏ $500 ❏ $1,000." You certainly want to give donors options. However, this is different from promoting the President's Club at $1,500— "Please join the 200 other members of the President's Club to provide scholarship funds for students; see our listing of members at the back of our brochure, and join us at our quarterly luncheon events on campus and our annual President's Club dinner in December."

In addition to recognition by listing members of your major gift club (which you do at the various levels in a ladder of giving), you stress the sense of community among the members of the club. Ideally you should assign one staff member to the gift club as its executive director. Design a specific logo for the club, stationery, and brand identity. This should echo your institutional brand but be distinctive enough that you are building this sense of community and identity as club members.

The important recognition for the gift club members comes from the ribbons on their name tags at all institutional events, their welcoming as new members at the club meetings, the feeling of fellowship with long-term members thanking new members and building new friendships. You build a sense of gratitude to gift club donors for their community leadership and philanthropic commitment to your organization. This type of recognition is far more powerful than a ladder-of-giving printed recognition.

Value of the Donor Wall

Many long-established nonprofit organizations have a donor wall, a wall of honor to recognize contributions over time. Donor walls take many forms—from simple listings to highly designed artistic elements of a building lobby to the latest high-tech multimedia, flat-panel virtual donor walls.

Donor wall systems have traditionally been used to honor contributors to a specific building. With multifaceted, comprehensive capital campaigns donor walls were expanded to include all donors to a campaign by giving level in a total recognition system.

Some organizations have developed this complete system of donor wall elements to recognize annual fund donors, capital donations, and planned estate giving. Hospitals, which have typically not had annual fundraising programs, use cumulative donor walls plus a listing for their legacy club members (for planned estate gifts).

A good donor wall system is the tangible, highly visible symbol of a winning-gifts fundraising program. The donors feel recognized through correct listings and the organization establishes role models for giving in the community that help stimulate additional gifts—everybody wins.

Some lessons learned over the years include the painstaking attention to detail that must be given to the spelling of names. One organization completed its building program and cast a bronze plaque commemorating all of the donors to the capital campaign. A donor came up afterwards to remark that her name had been misspelled. This $10,000 donor will forever see her name spelled incorrectly as it was too expensive to redo the $5,000 bronze plaque. You cannot spend too much time or energy in checking name spellings and the proper way to list names to delight your donors. Be ready for Joe Smith, who gave the gift, to want his plaque to read "Mr. and Mrs. Joe Smith," or "Mr. and Mrs. Joseph Smith," or "Joe and Mary Smith," or "The Smith Family," or "Frank and Agnes Smith" (to honor his parents). Work top down by donor category and sit down with each donor to review name-listing options. Once finalized, print the entire donor plaque by category so the contributors can see their names in the context of others (Gladwell's "the power of context").

When you are ready to unveil your new donor wall, make it a major cultivation event. Invite everyone listed on the wall to come to the official unveiling. This recognition event creates a spirit of gratitude to the donors that is special.

Commemorative Naming Opportunities

In addition to the donor wall (which may include The Founders Society of $50,000-or-higher donors to your organization and levels of giving at $25,000, $10,000, and for estate gifts) you want to offer donors the chance for special recognition by naming rooms in your buildings, specific locations on your grounds or your campus, or even your organization. The ability to commemorate a family name, a loved one, parents, or a mentor can be a powerful motive to make a great gift and can also make a donor feel recognized and appreciated by the organization.

At the beginning of a capital campaign take an inventory of your organization to see what has been named already. Sometimes you are surprised to see the number of plaques already in place that may be taken for granted, partially hidden from view, or have poor or missing signage. As you establish a naming system for the future, include the history of what has been named to date. This analysis of past naming for your organization helps to show the concept is not new to your organization.

If your organization is reluctant to begin naming rooms and buildings, look to peer organizations in your community and within your service sector. Find role models that have done naming successfully and tastefully. How have they used naming to honor donors as well as raise significant funds? Don't reinvent the wheel; look at role models for lessons. Talk to their staffs to see what has worked in the past and what they would do differently in the future.

As you develop the list of naming opportunities, start to think through the size of gift needed to name the area. One rule of thumb is to name buildings for at least 51 percent of the costs of construction. Some organizations have gotten into political hot water by naming a building for too little money. One group that built a facility through a public-private partnership took immense political heat in the local newspaper for giving naming rights away for $1 million for a $20 million project (three-quarters of which was funded through a tax bond).

Look at the square footage of space in particular rooms. What percentage of space is this of your entire project? Take that percentage of the fully loaded budget and you have a start on what naming rights could cost. Then take into account public perceptions of the space. An entry lobby, while relatively inexpensive to build, is highly attractive to donors as it is the first thing people see and is a high-traffic area. As mentioned earlier, one of the most sought after corporate naming areas is the elevator lobby. Why? The number of eyeballs of people waiting patiently for the elevator—they have the time to read the corporate sponsor's name.

For the same actual cost, the auditorium is naturally more exciting as a naming opportunity than the mechanical room. Some spaces are not namable. See the recognition list sample in Exhibit 6.2 for ideas that might work for your organization.

Once you have a preliminary list of rooms by price tag, share this with some of your fundraising colleagues to see what they think. After making some adjustments to the costs if needed, convene a commemorative naming volunteer committee. Recruit 10 to 20 people to attend two or three meetings to review all of your organization's recognition systems. Walk them through your gift clubs, donor walls, and commemorative giving opportunities. Do the gift levels for rooms make sense? If you involve people who have named rooms at other organizations, they will have a good feeling for your program.

One organization convened such a committee and after two meetings reviewing naming lists and rationales one of the committee members came up to the head of the organization to claim a $250,000 space that the donor highly valued. She wanted to acquire the naming rights immediately. This type of volunteer involvement makes your organization smarter and gently markets the commemorative naming opportunities to potential donors.

EXHIBIT 6.2   COMMEMORATIVE NAMING OPPORTUNITIES LIST

Rename the College	$500,000,000
Campus	$250,000,000
Campus Quadrangle	$100,000,000
Library	$75,000,000
Science Building	$50,000,000
Humanities Building	$25,000,000
Administration Building	$15,000,000
Playing Fields	$10,000,000
Endowed Faculty Loan Repayment Fund	$5,000,000
Auditorium	$5,000,000
Office of the President	$5,000,000
Office of the Provost	$2,500,000
Science Labs	$2,500,000
Deans	$2,000,000 each (4 available)
Senior Faculty Chair	$1,500,000
President's Council	$1,000,000 cumulative giving
President's Suite	$1,000,000
Library Reference Collection	$1,000,000
Faculty Recruitment Fund	$1,000,000
Library Checkout Counter	$1,000,000
Employee Education Fund	$1,000,000
Business Collection in the Library	$1,000,000
Science Collection	$1,000,000
Literature Collection	$1,000,000
English Department	$1,000,000
Faculty Recruitment Fund	$500,000
Boardroom	$250,000
Endowed Student Scholarship	$100,000
Faculty Lounge	$50,000 each (3 available)
Name Edowments	$50,000
Faculty Offices	$25,000

Once your commemorative naming list feels stabilized, ask that your campaign cabinet formally adopt the list and formally recommend it to the organization's nonprofit board for an official resolution of adoption. Ask the board for this resolution so that all gift levels are apparent to everyone before gifts are made and nobody is surprised when you come back to announce a room naming. For some organizations you may need to establish policies for what cannot be named or who is not allowed to name something. In one church campaign we discussed what on the sanctuary platform could be named (the pastor's lectern, chairs) and what could not be named (the communion table). Several national health organizations have had strict policies against tobacco or alcohol companies naming anything related to their organization. Think it through in advance. If your organization is tax supported in any way, get the appropriate governmental body to preapprove your naming list. If you are a public library, your list should be approved by the campaign committee, the library foundation board, and the county board of commissioners or city council (whichever group is in administrative charge of the library's budget).

One city-owned performing arts center got in hot water when a long-open naming opportunity for a performance space was selected by a Jewish family for $500,000. When the gift was announced to the city council some of the elected officials wanted to increase the naming level to $600,000 since the previous level had been set 10 years earlier. The family was incensed and felt the council's decision was anti-Semitic (which it was not, but it certainly showed poor judgment). The family pulled the gift after a nasty newspaper article brought the entire issue to the surface. The family finally gave their half-million-dollar gift to another, more thoughtful nonprofit organization.

Preapproval is critical to keeping recognition a winning-gifts strategy. You want to delight donors, not get them mad.

Many people may not be attracted to naming a room when you first present the idea to them. It sounds too egocentric for many donors. Remind them that an organization with a tradition of naming has a sense of heritage and community as you look at the rooms named by prominent people over time. Because nobody wants to be first, make sure to show your opportunities list with rooms already taken (list rooms and specific donors who have named them). Early naming is a way for your board and campaign committee to show their leadership. They need to give first and then be role models in the naming of rooms. If donors do not want the recognition personally, ask them to consider a family name, or memorialize both sets of donors' parents, or a favorite faculty member or doctor, or for women, their maiden names (as for some, who are the last of the line, a room naming is one way to keep the name alive).

Because corporations like visibility, they will be eager to take advantage of naming opportunities. In fact, the naming rights can be a major motivator for a corporation for making a gift. It should be part of the gift-request process.

While you want to mention naming opportunities to all donors in your formal letter of request, be careful. Walk a donor through the options and then listen carefully—does the donor get excited, yawn, or make a face? It's only a winning idea if the donor likes it. If he is ambivalent or opposed to the idea, retreat quickly and leave the room-naming discussion until after the gift is made.

Many foundations appreciate some type of naming visibility but only once grant decisions have been made. They want the grant-making process to stand on its merits and not to be swayed by recognition issues. Other foundations may be highly motivated by a naming opportunity. Talk to your foundation grant officer to see how important naming is to the trustees.

Work with your building architect's interior design team to come up with tasteful plaques that will serve as room signage as well as donor recognition devices. If you have an older building, you may want to engage an interior designer to create an overall image for your naming plaques. You want them clear, but not garish. You want the signs functional so the room naming is visible to all users (as opposed to the one plaque we saw that was located behind the door on the inside of the room where it had remained hidden since installation).

Once you have named your facilities, brand the buildings and rooms through usage so that your organization begins to appreciate the impact of philanthropy and so that donors see that naming is not just a plaque but institutional. For example, for our fall science lecture please go to Fronk Hall in the Cooley Science Building; please be a guest at our next board meeting, which will be held in the Karr Board Room; and when you come to our hospital please turn on Bochsler Drive.

In listening to donors one hears some amazing stories. One that relates to commemorative naming is a caution. Ralph is a donor I have known for 15 years. We see each other every couple of years on projects of mutual interest. This gives us a chance to catch up on Ralph's many philanthropic projects. One naming story sticks in my mind—Ralph had given $50,000 to name a small library room at a social-service agency in honor of his mother. She liked reading and how books can help people improve themselves. Ralph was flying his mother in from another city about six months after the nonprofit's new building had opened. He wanted to surprise his mother for her birthday by showing her the library named in her honor. He decided, just by chance, to stop by the nonprofit to look at the library to make sure everything was in order. To his dismay he found out that the construction costs went over budget and his mother's library had been converted to a large storage closet. He was somewhat understanding that the nonprofit had run out of money but he wished they had talked to him. One wonders how many people this clearly undelighted donor told about how his gift recognition was messed up.

Recognition Events

To provide donors with appropriate recognition use special events to create a sense of family and community. A gathering of the President's Club is a collective, community-building recognition event. Use subtle recognition to honor donors for their generosity. Simple convention ribbons attached to name tags work well. They can be color coded by donor club and multiple ribbons (either horizontal or vertical) can be used to recognize donors who give to the annual fund, a capital giving level, and your legacy society. Donors want to know who else is giving at their level and board members want to thank generous supporters. Welcome new members for the year and celebrate those reaching their 5-year anniversary of membership, 10-year anniversary, and so on.

For big-gift donors, a building naming event will be unique to them and should focus on their generosity and the impact their gift will make on the future of the organization. It also holds them up as a community role-model for philanthropy.

To keep your events people centered, enlist the help of volunteers to test your recognition ideas and to create the proper atmosphere for the type of recognition you wish to provide. In addition to your annual-giving club, you can hold recognition events around a building opening, annual scholarship awards, your heritage society for planned estate donors, to celebrate new members for the year, or for the completion of special-project funding. You want some diversity to your recognition, but be careful that every event is truly special. Start small and simple with your recognition program and let it build over time as your events become standardized and your staff is able to add more programs while keeping the same level of excellence. If it doesn't delight the donors, it's not a winning event.

Be sure to capture feedback from your volunteer committee and/or an evaluation form from event participants. You can bring distinction to your organization if your recognition events go over and above your donors' expectations.

For an example of the challenges in delighting donors, see Exhibit 6.3.

EXHIBIT 6.3   A RECOGNITION MEMENTO STORY

I was resident campaign counsel for Oregon Public Broadcasting (OPB) in the late 1980s. The campaign was going well. We created a $50,000 leadership gifts donor level for this $15 million campaign. We planned to recognize donors of this level on the donor wall and wanted to present them with some type of recognition memento at the building dedication event.

The volunteer committee was shown typical donor memento items—plaques, acrylic desk tombstones, clocks, etc. Nothing caught their fancy. Finally one of the volunteers called me up to invite me to join him on a visit to the local high-end jewelry store downtown. We met with his friend who owned the store to brainstorm about something special for OPB's donors. We got a tour of the jewelry store's expensive trinkets and finally decided on a three-inch cube of French crystal. We would engrave the public broadcasting station's logo and campaign theme on one face of the cube and present them in purple velvet drawstring bags. Very elegant. The cost—$200 a piece. My budget? $20. We explained the budget dilemma to the owner. He said no problem. He was going to Paris in the next few weeks and would be glad to talk to the supplier about a donation to the campaign.

He came back later that month with the donated crystal. His store donated the engraving and we got a spectacular campaign memento for free. We literally got *oohs* and *ahs* as we gave out the crystals at the dedication event. We delighted the donors.

Planned Estate Gifts

Planned estate gifts, while taking place sometime in the future and usually revocable, deserve recognition now. Even though you will not receive the proceeds from a bequest or IRA distribution until the donor dies, please, *please* recognize the donor's generosity now. Recognition is not expensive and it is so much more fun to thank someone who is alive. Some organizations are reluctant or refuse to recognize estate gift donations until the gift is officially in the bank. However, since the donor is dead at that point, the recognition tends to fall flat.

Getting an estate gift out of the blue is a great experience. Mary Jones leaves your organization $250,000 in her estate. Who was Mary? How did she know about you? You wish you could thank her. It's almost sad to get the largest donation of the year to your organization from a stranger you can never say thank-you to.

To indirectly thank the Marys of the world whom you never thanked, do all you can for donors who make future plans for your organization. And, if you do this right, you can help stimulate more planned estate gifts from other people in your donor community.

Create a heritage society or legacy society to honor all donors, dead and living, who have given you an estate gift. You can indicate deceased members by a special symbol "*" to show that you have received their gift. As long as a living donor indicated his estate commitment to you in writing, or better yet, shares with you the section of his will naming your organization in his estate, give him membership in your legacy society. Give him a ribbon for his name tag at special events and list all members of the legacy society in your annual report and on your donor wall.

One reason to count planned estate gifts in your donation totals and to provide recognition is to clarify and solidify these types of gifts. Sometimes the donor's intention may be only partially carried out through their well-intentioned but poorly designed bequest gift intentions. In recognizing the gift you can also learn more about it and help the donor to clarify his intentions with your charity, other nonprofits, and family members.

A classic story of a gift that may have been made poorly was described in an article on the front page of a local newspaper. It told the wonderful story of a lady leaving the local police department's horse patrol a $650,000 bequest. The picture with the story showed the police captain in charge of the patrol and quoted him as saying he had never met the lady and wasn't sure why they received the gift as they really didn't need the money. The article went on to say that the lady had also given her local parish church a $10,000 bequest. End of story . . . or was it? Reading between the lines, what might have happened is this lady, who loved her church, made a big bequest of $10,000 to it. She only had her house and a few funds in savings so that seemed like a big gift. She gave the residual of her estate to the horse patrol that had its station house near her home. She had no idea of the size of her estate nor the fact that by giving a fixed amount to one charity, probably her favorite one, and the residual to another beneficiary that her favorite charity (the church that really needed the money) would only get $10,000 and the secondary beneficiary, which didn't really need the money, would get the bulk of her estate. The lesson, meet with your donors to be sure that what they intend to do with their estate is what they have written up legally.

Go back in time to capture all past estate gift donors to show how the thoughtfulness of others has helped to make your organization the success it is today.

Some organizations object to giving recognition to bequest donors as these gifts can be revoked. It appears that donors are more apt to change their wills to disinherit family members than to disinherit charities. In recognizing the donor, you are cementing the relationship and strengthening the donative intent of the planned estate gift. Some people who have told a charity about a bequest intention will release funds later for a building project as they realize the charity will get the money anyway. Always remember the power of the screwdriver—if the planned estate gift does not come, you can always get a screwdriver out and remove the donor plaque.

Some of this angst over estate gift recognition is being alleviated by the irrevocable estate note.

Kaizen

This Japanese word for continuous quality improvement—*kaizen*—is critically important for donor recognition. (See Rafael Aguayo's book, *Dr. Deming: The American Who Taught the Japanese about Quality*, for more information about *kaizen*—especially how Toyota has implemented processes of involving everyone in the organization to make small enhancements every day.) If you don't do this, you will be surprised by your donors, who last year wanted to remain anonymous and this year, having watched others get recognition, decide that they, too, want to participate. Keep checking back with your best donors to see how the recognition you offer feels to them. Is the annual report listing accurate? How was the last President's Council dinner?

Your program will morph and change year to year as will your major donors. Keep in touch with them so you are constantly delighting them yet not going overboard so they feel donated funds are being wasted on recognition.

STEWARDSHIP

After you have thanked the donors and recognized their generosity as publicly as they would like, it is time to talk about their next gift, isn't it? Of course, as professional fundraisers we will. But, philanthropic fundraisers need to take one more important step—stewardship—informing the donors over time of the impact of their gifts.

The stewardship movement in fundraising became formalized in the early 1990s through a transition in higher education fundraising from informal communications with donors of record (particularly named endowment donors) to formal structured reporting to these high-end donors. As endowed chairs, scholarship funds, and named funds began to accumulate at colleges, staff members, usually somebody behind the scenes and not in the major-gifts solicitation arena, naturally wanted to communicate with donors to let them know how their scholarship fund students were doing or what the faculty member in their endowed chair was doing. These formal reporting sessions and documents were successful—donors loved the feedback and they enjoyed talking to people who had benefited from their gifts. They told their friends and they made additional gifts.

Everyone in fundraising has intuitively known the importance of gift accountability and stewardship. We all did some of it. But, as we did our job and developed a list of 50 to 100 donors that needed high-touch, personalized stewardship reports, a new job description was created—the director of stewardship or donor relations.

While widely accepted in higher education, all organizations should consider formalizing their operations to make donors feel good about their investments so they both encourage others to contribute and consider additional gifts in the future. If nothing else, it's also good manners.

Stewardship can be thought of in a variety of ways: follow-up reports, evaluations, meeting the student who received your scholarship, examining the new piece of hospital equipment purchased by your gift, and annual reports.

To develop a true culture of philanthropy within your nonprofit organization, stewardship needs to flourish. It's not enough to accept the donor's money. To keep the gift a winning proposition for the donor we need to show the contribution made a difference for our organization and for society. For small-gift donors this can be a challenge. Even for $1,000 donors to the Friends of the ABC Organization this is difficult. Usually these undesignated annual gifts go toward meeting the operating budget of the organization.

You can set up a spirit and philosophy of stewardship by mentioning the project to be funded in your gift request. The direct-mail letter can mention the importance of the music needed for this year's symphony performances—did you know we spend $75,000 a year renting orchestra music, another $15,000 purchasing music for our permanent library, and $50,000 for a full-time music librarian who keeps track of all of the music, gets it ready for performances by renting it or buying it, marking the bowings indicated by the concertmaster, assembling the music folder before a set of rehearsals, and then undoing this after the concert is over? This may not seem like an important task, but the musicians have to play off clearly marked copies of the right edition of music. Your gift of $50 will go toward the music library fund this year. At the end of the season you can send a follow-up stewardship and accountability letter to all donors of record indicating which pieces of music were rented this year (list), which were purchased (list), and a concrete story from the music librarian on the biggest challenge of the year (e.g., making music cuts in *Boris Godunov* to take the four-hour opera performance down to a 45-minute concert version— and by the way, all of the chorus parts are in Russian).

Good stewardship reporting delights the donors and helps cement an ongoing relationship and partnership between their money and the impact your organization is making in the community:

> With the heightened level of competition, donors are expecting more from their philanthropic experiences. . . . Institutions that are able to provide significant and meaningful donor experiences, more fully integrating the donor with the organization, may set themselves apart from the rest.[1]

Reports

In many ways, foundations have led the way with stewardship reports. To ensure an easy time in keeping their tax-exempt status, most staffed foundations ask for evaluation reports at the end of a grant project. They want to have written evidence the money was spent on what you proposed. What was the impact of the grant? If changes were made in delivering the grant from the proposal, what were they?

The habits you form in reporting back to foundations should be replicated with individuals who have supplied you with special-project funding. You won't have a form to fill out, but a stewardship letter that is created, hand delivered, and discussed will give the donor a great sense of comfort.

The Center on Philanthropy at Indiana University reported on a research survey of 945 households, which had an average income of at least $200,000 or liquid assets of at least $1 million:

> . . . seventy-five percent of the donors said charities that spend less on administrative costs could reap additional contributions. . . . Fifty-eight

percent said donations could also increase if charities showed donors the results of their gifts.[2]

Remember one of Cialdini's influence principles from Part II, Seek Winning Gifts for Your Organization—to gain influence show authority but admit weakness. Stewardship reports are an excellent place to use this principle. You want to show how expertly your organization carried out the project, of course. But don't stop there. Go the extra step and be honest in sharing a few of the weaknesses that you uncovered in working on the project.

For example: We created a new marketplace for our orchestra by developing a new *Pops* concert series (lighter concert offerings of musical tunes, movie themes, and popular guest performers compared with the more traditional heavy classical music of the regular season) in our neighboring town. The audiences loved this type of programming and we got some of our traditional classical concertgoers to drive to the next town for these concerts. We learned, however, that we did not budget enough for marketing and therefore sold only 75 percent of our tickets instead of the 90 percent we had budgeted. Thus we lost money that first year on the concerts. We now know that more marketing dollars for ads, flyers, and personnel will be needed next year and that additional sponsors will be required so we can break even at 75 percent (and net a solid profit for anything above that more conservative projection). We also began to realize that it might take several seasons to build a loyal following for this new *Pops* concert series. We shared these findings with our board, major donors, and concert sponsors to provide a stewardship report, an investor report in this aspect of our operations.

This honesty in sharing new discoveries, human errors, and simple mistakes in planning helps your donors to develop a partnership in your organization's development. Bring your donors closer to you by sharing what you have learned the hard way. Not everything is perfect in your donors' life experiences. Keep your organization real by admitting some weaknesses.

Organizational annual reports are an excellent way of providing collective stewardship reports to all of your donors. You can present a series of project vignettes that help tell the story of how contributed funds make a difference with your organization and the people you serve. If you don't have an annual report, look for samples in your community. What works well for other organizations? Realize that many groups are moving to electronic annual reports to help save mailing costs and to keep the information fresh (quarterly updates are recommended).

You can also use organizational newsletters to provide periodic stewardship updates to all donors and potential donors. Keep the stories short and to the point. Use a short, three- to five-minute DVD movie of a program from this year. Show the impact of giving to your organization.

Events

Stewardship events for current donors are different from cultivation events for prospective donors. For stewardship events your total focus is getting donors to feel the impact of their gifts rather than telling the story of why you need additional funding. Scholarship luncheons are a great example. Asking the students who received scholarships to meet with the donors at these luncheons is a wonderful activity. Each donor sits by a student and selected students are asked to give testimonial speeches to the entire group about the impact the scholarships have made on their lives. These stories can get highly emotional and have a profound impact on donors. Having the recipient of the scholarship gift report directly to the donors makes the gifts concrete, real, and meaningful. The donors know they have made a difference in a student's life. They can also begin to see the diversity of students in terms of background, geographical location, age, and ethnicity. Experiential learning (meeting scholarship students) is the most powerful tool you have to get your current donors to understand and appreciate the power of their giving on your organization.

If you are not in higher education, be creative with the type of stewardship event you have. Look at the products of your organization, the results you have created, and the impact your nonprofit has on society.

One private school, Tucker-Maxon School in Portland, Oregon, teaches deaf children how to speak. The school focuses on preschool through grade two. By third grade most of the students are successfully mainstreamed back to their neighborhood schools. Tucker-Maxon School develops a strong bond with parents of these students. It takes a strong team of teachers, audiologists, and parents to help the students succeed in their silent world. Tucker-Maxon keeps in touch with all parents as their children move on to other schools and has developed a tradition of bringing back new high school graduates. Even though these former students of Tucker-Maxon left after second grade, they are still alumni of the school. These 18-year-olds come to an all-school event for current students and their families. It is inspirational to parents of a first-grader who is profoundly deaf to see what grown-up alumni are like, to hear their college plans, to learn of their school activities, and to appreciate the impact the Tucker-Maxon School can have on its student and their families. It inspires hope in these parents. It is also a wonderful stewardship opportunity for selected donors to see the impact of their gifts of 8 and 10 years ago in these newly minted high school graduates.

Look at the impact your organization has made and capture that impact now, later, on video, in written stories, whatever it takes to prove you have had an impact. That's good stewardship.

Personal Stewardship

All of the written stewardship reports and group events are wonderful. You need them as tools and to reach the many donors that you cannot possibly see in person. However, for your best donors, a personal stewardship meeting is critically important. As professional, philanthropic fundraisers we know that the relationships we have built with donors as we have cultivated them for a gift, learned about their values, and presented a gift opportunity are the beginning of deep, professional friendships. The donor looks to this trusting relationship and assumes you will be his personal stewardship ambassador to the organization to ensure that his money is well spent.

This expectation on the part of donors that their fundraiser will ensure good stewardship can set up some interesting tensions within a nonprofit organization. The fundraiser naturally wants to play this stewardship role. The organization new to philanthropy may not be responsive to providing stewardship information to the donor or fundraiser. For some public universities, libraries, or public schools, the faceless, unknown taxpayers have provided operational revenues for a century or more. All of a sudden a donor gives a million dollars and wants special treatment. What is going on? Or the hospital with a $150 million operating budget and thousands of patients gets a special-project gift for $150,000, and the donor wants specifics on how the money was spent. This personal accountability to one person, who can ask tough questions, can be a new and disconcerting experience. The philanthropic fundraiser now becomes the negotiator and communicator between the organization and the donor.

Director of Stewardship Movement Individual major-gift officers can shepherd their donor clients through stewardship when they start their career at an organization. You may only have 25 to 30 donors to work with. As your track record builds over time, this group of past donors gets larger and larger and more difficult to stay in touch with.

As large organizations hire many major-gift officers, and as donors begin designating endowment gifts across time (the development officer 10 years ago secured the endowment, that person retired and two others have come and gone in the organization), the role of a professional, full-time director of stewardship has developed. Higher education took the lead with donor relations and stewardship by formally staffing these types of positions.

One hospital realized it needed this type of position when it hit the threshold of 65 named endowment funds. Its efforts in endowment building were slowing because of the need for consistent and persistent stewardship reports. The hospital found it more efficient to hire a full-time stewardship manager to handle the formal reports and specific endowment reports. The stewardship manager also worked with divisions of the hospital to make sure dedicated funds were spent as intended and to gather the stories of their impact so these could be compiled for the annual report and for individual stewardship meetings with donors. This person also handled all the logistics of stewardship events. This enabled the major-gifts officer, who held the relationship with each donor, to use his time for the one-on-one personal time that the donor also values.

Others Are Starting to Hold You Accountable

The Internet age has brought many interesting ideas to nonprofit organizations fundraising—e-philanthropy, prospect research databases, Webinars, online newsletters, and the ability to research your organization through charity clearinghouses. The most prominent is www.Guidestar.org. This organization has set up a database of all IRS 990 forms filed by nonprofit organizations. All nonprofits with budgets of $25,000 or more must file 990 forms (except for religious organizations). Realizing that donors may be doing their gift due diligence by using your organization's 990 form, you may want to assist your chief financial officer in completing the forms each year.

We hear that some of the stock brokerage firms that have set up family-advised funds for their customers are advising these donors to use electronic tools like Guidestar to determine which charities to make donations to.

Other watchdog organizations are starting to set up Internet charitable review databases. They include:

- www.charitynavigator.org—"Find a charity you can trust. Charity Navigator, America's premier independent charity evaluator, works to advance a more efficient and responsive philanthropic marketplace by evaluating the financial health of America's top charities."

- www.charitywatch.org—"American Institute of Philanthropy (AIP) offers ratings organizations in its Charity Rating Guide. AIP considers a group's willingness to provide basic documents to serious donors as an important factor in one's giving decision. These documents include an annual report, complete audited financial statements, and Internal Revenue Service form 990, with Schedule A where applicable. Groups which have complied with AIP's request and sent these documents are marked in the list by an open book symbol."

- www.give.org—"Better Business Bureau (BBB) Wise Giving Alliance. The goal of the Alliance seal program is to offer a highly visible accountability tool that will help inform donors, will assist charities in establishing their commitment to ethical practices, and will encourage greater confidence in giving."

Many, if not most, Americans have trouble finding the information they need to evaluate charities and make decisions about giving. A detailed donor expectations survey of 2,003 Americans commissioned by the Alliance in the spring of 2001 found that 70 percent of adult Americans said it was difficult to tell whether a charity soliciting their contribution is legitimate. Public attention on charity accountability has grown in recent years, particularly in the wake of September 11 and a series of high-profile charity scandals. In turn, charities themselves are seeking credible means to ensure donors that they operate ethically and in accordance with donor intentions.

Even community foundations are undergoing public scrutiny:

> The Council on Foundations (www.cof.org) has developed a new standards program for community foundations that engage in ethical and effective practices and highlight transparency and financial responsibility. . . . Community foundations are required to document their performance in donor services, investment management, grant making and administration.[3]

This trend of Internet nonprofit watchdogging will only increase over time. Just as it is important to check your credit rating on the Internet or to Google yourself to see what is there, nonprofits should monitor what is being said about them in cyberspace. Act like a donor and look up your organization on the web sites listed above. You may want to polish your web image based on what you find.

Keeping the organization anonymous, here is a front-page story from a major city newspaper:

> Mr. Y, the executive director of Z charity, found himself explaining how Charity Navigator, an independent watchdog agency, could rate the organization's finances as one of the worst in the nation. The rating stung because Mr. Y felt it reflected conditions before he took charge, when the organization was spending 31 cents of every dollar on overhead.

Even if donors aren't tracking these web sites, newspapers are.

Good Stewardship Is Good for Fundraising

In addition to being good manners, good stewardship helps promote the next gift from the donor. This seems obvious, yet it is not done as often as it should be in nonprofit fundraising.

In reviewing the literature for this book, numerous examples of post-sales contact are cited as a standard method of good sales. In Spencer Johnson's and Larry Wilson's *The One Minute Sales Person*, the authors recommend:

After the Sale: A Summary

1. I contact people after the sale to be sure that people are feeling good about what they bought and about themselves for buying.
2. If they are not happy, I take the opportunity to help make things right for the other person.

3. When they are pleased, I praise their buying decision and specifically point out something they did that helped that action come about.
4. I exceed their expectations by providing some form of added value.
5. When they are feeling good, I ask people for active referrals. I ask for the names of people they know whom I can contact, using the buyer's name as a recommendation.[4]

This type of post-sale contact and bonding is just as important, if not more so, for the intangible selling we do for nonprofit fundraising. Oechsli's research on influence found that the most powerful marketing technique to the affluent is word of mouth from friends and family.[5] Post-gift referrals and post-gift recruitment to IQ (Identification and Qualification) rating committees should be established as standard operating procedures in fundraising offices. It's a winning-gifts approach as your goal is first to delight donors with the gifts they made to your organization and then to keep strengthening those relationships through post-gift stewardship.

Another parallel view of this same concept comes from Peter Senge's book, *The Fifth Discipline: The Art and Practice of the Learning Organization.* In Chapter 5, A Shift of Mind, he talks about reinforcing loops.

> . . . "virtuous cycles"—processes that reinforce in desired directions. For instance, physical exercise can lead to a reinforcing spiral; you feel better, thus you exercise more, thus you're rewarded by feeling better and exercise still more. . . . *Reinforcing Sales Process Caused by Customers Talking to Each Other about Your Product* . . . a reinforcing feedback process wherein actions snowball. . . . If the product is a good product, more sales means more satisfied customers, which means more positive word of mouth. That will lead to still more sales, which means even more widespread word of mouth.[6]

As you think through his snowball effect, replace satisfied customers with happy donors. While not mentioned explicitly in *The Tipping Point,* one can see that this snowball effect helps to tip a trend in society. Your job as the philanthropic fundraiser is to aid the process through good stewardship, recognition, and thanking methods.[7] This bandwagon effect is the influence that Cialdini mentioned in his principle #6, Consensus—unleash people power by showing responses of many others, the testimonials of others (see Part II).

APPLY WHAT YOU'VE LEARNED

1. *Thank-yous.* Do you have a formal thank-you system documented in writing? What tiers do you have? How disciplined is your office when it comes time to thank donors? Don't worry if you're not at a model level. The first thing to do is to write down what your culture of thanking currently is. Don't be judgmental; just capture what is happening right now. What is written? What is informal? Who does it? How do you know if it is getting done? Now that you know what you're currently doing, determine what you should be doing. Set a plan for updating your system to take effect in the next 30 days. How can you refine this system further six months from now? What do you want to be doing a year from now? Be realistic. If you are the only person in your fundraising shop, your plan had better be simple and leveraged through volunteer help. If you're in a big office, ask everyone to advise you on improving your processes. Who is most interested? Would they like to own the process? Having an internal, donor-relations champion who is passionate about great thank-yous will make your newly improved system hum.

2. *Recognition.* Visit with five of your top donors that you are close to. Ask them to give honest feedback about the recognition systems you are using at your organization. Does the donor listing work for them? Is their name listed perfectly? Have they heard feedback from their friends about their listings? Do the recognition events make them feel good? Is there too much recognition or not enough? What advice would they give you to improve what you are doing? What have they liked from the other organizations that they give to? Write a report of your findings and a plan for improvement for next year.

3. *Stewardship.* What ideas did you pick up in this chapter? What could you start doing in the next three months to improve your program? Look at your "aging" list of donors from your database—your longest-term donor by number of years of giving regardless of gift amount. Interview five of the longest-term donors who have a history of small gifts; interview five with mid-level giving histories; and then five of your big gift donors of long duration. Ask them about stewardship issues in general with all of their philanthropic giving and then specifically with your organization. What are they suggesting

you could do better? What are you doing now that is working well? Institutionalize this through procedure guides so this activity does not stop even if you do.

NOTES

1. Tanise L. Chung-Hoon, Julie M. Hite, and Steven J. Hite, "Searching for Enduring Donor Relationships: Evidence for Factors and Strategies in a Donor/Organization Integration Model for Fund Raising," *International Journal of Educational Advancement,* vol. 6, no. 1, 36.
2. Nicole Lewis, "Half of Affluent Americans Say Tax Policy Doesn't Affect Their Giving," *The Chronicle of Philanthropy,* November 9, 2006, 14.
3. "New Standards for Community Foundations," *Advancing Philanthropy,* November/December 2006, 12.
4. Spencer Johnson and Larry Wilson, *The One Minute Sales Person* (New York: William Morrow, 1984), 59.
5. Matt Oechsli, *The Art of Selling to the Affluent* (New York: John Wiley & Sons, 2005).
6. Peter M. Senge, *The Fifth Discipline: The Art and Practice of the Learning Organization* (New York: Doubleday Currency, 1990), 80–82.
7. Malcolm Gladwell, *The Tipping Point: How Little Things Can Make a Big Difference* (New York: Little, Brown, 2000, 2002).

Coda—The Summary Review

The Winning Gifts concepts presented in this book are a philosophy of philanthropic fundraising whose goal is to delight the donor as you raise funds for your organization. Donors need to feel like they are making winning gifts as the organizations, the fundraising volunteers, and the fundraising professionals win those gifts. Using fundraising management techniques outlined in The Six I's of Philanthropic Fundraising, you can help guide and coach people into donating to your organization or increasing their philanthropic commitments.

In People Centered Fundraising (Chapter 1) we mentioned the importance of treating people as personalities first and bank accounts a distant second. Yes, you want them to be donors to your cause, but slow down and take the time to share your organization's impact on the community so the potential donor can begin to understand why a donation to your nonprofit is a win for society. Be sensitive to the different needs of corporate and foundation donors as they will vary from individuals. And, involve volunteers in your fundraising to keep a humanistic approach to your donations program.

To accomplish this lofty goal, study Chapter 2, Donor Values, to see survey research, and data gathered on giving and to hear from prominent donors on why they give. This will help sensitize you to pick up additional donor motivations in your local newspaper and as you interact with your donors.

Deep listening (Chapter 3) may be the most powerful tool in this book. Taking this marketing approach to philanthropic fundraising to understand the people who are or will be your donors is important. Both collective and individual listening and data gathering techniques were discussed. Use them to practice your listening skills so you can add to the database in your mind, in your notes, and in your organization's systems of donors and potential donors to your organization.

The insights reviewed in Part II from Gladwell's *The Tipping Point* and Cialdini's *Influence* help shift our thoughts from the donor perspective to the organizational one. Of course, you want to know answers to questions such as: How can we inspire giving? How soon can we get the gift? How can we raise the sights of donors so they make a larger investment? How do we get buzz in the community about our campaign? Our organization? Fundraising has used many of the *Tipping Point* elements intuitively—an inspiring leader and board champions (mavens), volunteers willing to help open doors and tell the basic message (connectors), and the always-important askers (sales-people) who know how to pitch and close the deal. Cialdini's *Influence* factors show us ethical ways of helping to promote our cause—using authority figures to provide public testimonials, admitting our weaknesses as we promote our vision and strengths, doing favors for people first (reciprocity), starting small and building through gifts and verbal displays of enthusiasm, being likable—all help to influence donors ethically to our cause.

Telling your campaign story, making your case, and presenting compelling reasons for people to support your organization were covered in Chapter 4. Techniques to develop your case, share it within your organization to build an internal marketing team, and share it through external leadership briefing focus group meetings and face-to-face interviews all help to build ownership in your organization, its vision, and its urgent need for funding. As you share the case with others and seek their constructive criticisms, you strengthen through the case through this continuous feedback.

With the basics covered in the first chapters of the book, it's time to pop the question and ask for the gift and close the deal. Chapter 5 covered concrete preparation steps such as recruiting members of the ideal ask team, preparation of strategy memos, determining the best setting for the ask, rehearsing the ask with your team, and envisioning the actual gift request meeting. Embracing the silence of the pregnant pause after the gift request and reviewing options for action at the end of the ask meeting round out this chapter.

Finally, Chapter 6 outlined a systematic way of thanking donors for their gift. Opportunities for gift recognition and stewardship complete our philanthropic fundraising journey.

Use all of these techniques and your fundraising program will be wildly successful. Use some of them and you will improve your program. Are there other ways of raising money? Of course. Use ideas from this book, the sources mentioned here, other books, friends, and your own intuition to craft a fundraising style that fits you, your organization, and your community.

Best of luck, and please delight donors through winning-gift propositions.

In closing—here is a wonderful story of a person whose life was transformed through the power of inspired community philanthropy.

From Dr. Chris King, Cardiac Surgeon, Harrison Medical Center in Bremerton, Washington after hearing a presentation on Andrew Carnegie's *Gospel of Wealth*:

> Because of a community-minded individual who believed in Carnegie's philanthropic principles, I was able to participate in a gifted program for promising elementary-school-aged children.
>
> During my first year in that program I completed a report on "hematology." I was able to interview several physicians regarding this subspecialty, and by the conclusion of this study, I had decided to become a physician.
>
> As I grew up, I was keenly aware of the opportunities that existed for me due to the extraordinary contributions of a few select families. The Carnegie Museums of Art and Natural History, Heinz Hall, The Phipps Conservatory, The Aviary, The University of Pittsburgh Transplant Programs, and Children's Hospital all stood out as remarkable products of the generous contributions by a group of people determined to improve the lives of everyone in their community. This philosophy over-flowed into every aspect of life in the Pittsburgh region.
>
> As a child I felt valuable, important, and worthy of the dreams my life experiences brought to me despite my family's rather modest means. The most important thing that came out of this experience in my childhood was my ability to believe in my dreams. Not only could I have dreams, I could then look around in my real-world physical environment and find the tools and motivation to make them come true.

Postlude

To end this book with a smile, review this advice to fundraisers from the late nineteenth century. Please excuse the sexist language of that era as well as the "victim" comment.

HOW TO RAISE FUNDS (CIRCA 1891)

1. Dress well with costly clothes, immaculate linen, and well brushed shoes. See also that your hands are kept clean.
2. Hunt in pairs: A call by two men would have a greater dignity than a call by one; but only one should talk.
3. Both men should have an elegant personal card to present at the office door.
4. At the outset, ask for only a few minutes of the prospective giver's time, and by plunging into the subject create the impression that the call will be short.
5. Enter the room in genial and radiant good nature; allow no provocation to disturb this good humor; keep your victim also good natured, and this throughout.
6. If you find him big with gift, do not rush too eagerly to the birth.
7. Let him feel that he is giving it, not that it is being taken from him with violence.

8. Appeal only to the nobler motives. His own mind will suggest to him the lower and selfish ones. But he will not wish you to suppose that he has thought of them.

9. Let the victim talk freely, especially in the earlier part of the interview, while you use the opportunity to study his peculiarities.

10. Never argue with him. Never contradict him. If he is talkative, let him talk, talk, talk. Give your fish the reel and listen with deep interest.

—Frederick T. Cates in *Study in Power* by Allen Nevins

Contact me with your reactions, your stories, and to get more examples and tools for your winning gifts program.
Tom Wilson
(503) 789–4366
Tom.Wilson@WinningGifts.INFO
www.WinningGifts.INFO

Appendixes

- A—Definition of Steps in The Six I's of Philanthropic Fundraising
- B—Written Survey Form
- C—Donor Bill of Rights
- D—AFP Code of Ethics for Professional Philanthropic Fundraisers
- E—Gentle Letter of Intent

Definition of Steps in the Six I's of Philanthropic Fundraising

#1 Identify, Qualify & Research	
Identify	Who are your top 100 cumulative donors? Longest term donors? Best community prospects?
Qualify	Who has the capacity to make a significant gift? $1 million or more, $100,000 to $999,999, $25,000 to $99,999.
Research	What can you find out about them from public records?

#2 Introduce, Interact & Connect	
Introduce	Begin sending newsletters, invitations to events.
Interact	Get acquainted at cultivation events to start building a relationship.
Connect	Ask your board members to bring your best prospects on site.

#3 Interests & Needs (Listen)	
Interests	Is the prospect intrigued with your cause? What other nonprofits do they invest in?
Needs	Why do they need to give money philanthropically? How visible do they want to be?
Listen	Be an active, empathetic listener. Take notes for future reference.

#4 Inform & Deepen Understanding	
Inform	How can we get prospective donors knowledgeable about our impact, our vision, and our needs?
Deepen Understanding	Cultivation events held. Site visits conducted. Presentation outline guide should be completed. DVD movie produced. Q&A document ready. Structural proposals copied for donor use. Campaign brochure printed.

#5 Involve, Acknowledge & Engage	
Involve	How can we involve the best prospects in the campaign committee? On our board?
Acknowledge	Treat potential donors as advisors rather than bank accounts.
Engage	How can we engage all donors in meaningful relationships with our organization over time?

#6 Invest, Recognize & Steward	
Invest	Ask for a thoughtful, win-win gift.
Recognize	Delight the donor through mutually agreed upon donor recognition.
Steward	Provide accountability reports to donors to show their gift has made a difference in your organization and the community.

Written Survey Form

The "5-Minute" Survey
for
ABC Symphony Orchestra

1) Relationship to the ABC Symphony Orchestra:
- ❏ Long-time subscriber
- ❏ New subscriber
- ❏ Long-time donor
- ❏ Periodic donor
- ❏ Other _____

2) Why is the ABC Symphony important to the community?

To you?

3) Please rate the following statements and comment on each of your ratings:

I enjoy the performances of the Orchestra and recommend them to others

Agree   1   2   3   4   5   6   Disagree

Please comment on your rating:

This organization is highly responsive to community needs

Agree   1   2   3   4   5   6   Disagree

Please comment on your rating:

I am highly satisfied with all aspects of service to me as a donor

Agree   1   2   3   4   5   6   Disagree

Please comment on your rating:

(OVER)

I definitely will make more gifts to this nonprofit in the future
        Agree   1   2   3   4   5   6   Disagree

Please comment on your rating:

Donations to ABC Symphony have an impact
        Agree   1   2   3   4   5   6   Disagree

Please comment on your rating:

Based upon your review of the Campaign Case Statement, please answer the following:

4) How supportive are you of the campaign?
- ☐ Very supportive
- ☐ Supportive
- ☐ Only somewhat supportive
- ☐ Not supportive

Why?

5) What are the three most important projects to you in the case statement?
Please rank 1, 2, 3 with 1 being your highest priority.
- ___ Artistic enhancements
- ___ Youth & education outreach
- ___ Capital improvements
- ___ Financial stability

Why?

6) Would you consider serving in a volunteer role for the campaign?

	Yes	Possibly	Not Sure
Leader	☐	☐	☐
Committee member	☐	☐	☐
Door opener	☐	☐	☐
Other _____			

7) Where does ABC Symphony rank among your philanthropic priorities?
- ☐ Top third
- ☐ Middle third
- ☐ Bottom third

Why?

8) If you were asked to make a 5-year commitment to the Symphony to help support the campaign, where would you find yourself on the gift chart today? This isn't a promise, just a sense of where you might be.

- ❏ $100,000 or more
- ❏ $50,000 to $99,999
- ❏ $25,000 to $49,999
- ❏ $10,000 to $24,999
- ❏ Other _____

9) Estate Gift Status (optional)
- ❏ ABC Symphony Orchestra is already included in my/our estate plan(s).
- ❏ I would consider including ABC Symphony in my/our estate plan(s).
- ❏ I need more information.
- ❏ Other _____

10) What advice would you give us to make this a successful campaign?

_____   _____
Name(s) (please print)   E-mail (if you are willing to be contacted this way)

A Donor Bill of Rights

PHILANTHROPY is based on voluntary action for the common good. It is a tradition of giving and sharing that is primary to the quality of life. To assure that philanthropy merits the respect and trust of the general public, and that donors and prospective donors can have full confidence in the not-for-profit organizations and causes they are asked to support, we declare that all donors have these rights:

I.

To be informed of the organization's mission, of the way the organization intends to use donated resources, and of its capacity to use donations effectively for their intended purposes.

II.

To be informed of the identity of those serving on the organization's governing board, and to expect the board to exercise prudent judgement in its stewardship responsibilities.

III.

To have access to the organization's most recent financial statements.

IV.

To be assured their gifts will be used for the purposes for which they were given.

V.

To receive appropriate acknowledgement and recognition.

VI.

To be assured that information about their donations is handled with respect and with confidentiality to the extent provided by law.

VII.

To expect that all relationships with individuals representing organizations of interest to the donor will be professional in nature.

VIII.

To be informed whether those seeking donations are volunteers, employees of the organization or hired solicitors.

IX.

To have the opportunity for their names to be deleted from mailing lists that an organization may intend to share.

X.

To feel free to ask questions when making a donation and to receive prompt, truthful and forthright answers.

DEVELOPED BY
Association for Healthcare Philanthropy (AHP)
Association of Fundraising Professionals (AFP)
Council for Advancement and Support of Education (CASE)
Giving Institute: Leading Consultants to Non-Profits

ENDORSED BY
(in formation)
Independent Sector
National Catholic Development Conference (NCDC)
National Committee on Planned Giving (NCPG)
Council for Resource Development (CRD)
United Way of America

AFP Code of Ethical Principles and Standards of Professional Practice

STATEMENT OF ETHICAL PRINCIPLES
Adopted 1964, Amended October 2004

The Association of Fundraising Professionals (AFP) exists to foster the development and growth of fundraising professionals and the profession, to promote high ethical standards in the fundraising profession and to preserve and enhance philanthropy and volunteerism. Members of AFP are motivated by an inner drive to improve the quality of life through the causes they serve. They serve the ideal of philanthropy; are committed to the preservation and enhancement of volunteerism; and hold stewardship of these concepts as the overriding principle of their professional life. They recognize their responsibility to ensure that needed resources are vigorously and ethically sought and that the intent of the donor is honestly fulfilled. To these ends, AFP members embrace certain values that they strive to uphold in performing their responsibilities for generating philanthropic support.

AFP members aspire to:
+ practice their profession with integrity, honesty, truthfulness and adherence to the absolute obligation to safeguard the public trust;
+ act according to the highest standards and visions of their organization, profession and conscience;
+ put philanthropic mission above personal gain;
+ inspire others through their own sense of dedication and high purpose;
+ improve their professional knowledge and skills so that their performance will better serve others;
+ demonstrate concern for the interests and well being of individuals affected by their actions;
+ value the privacy, freedom of choice and interests of all those affected by their actions;
+ foster cultural diversity and pluralistic values, and treat all people with dignity and respect;
+ affirm, through personal giving, a commitment to philanthropy and its role in society;
+ adhere to the spirit as well as the letter of all applicable laws and regulations;
+ advocate within their organizations, adherence to all applicable laws and regulations;
+ avoid even the appearance of any criminal offense or professional misconduct;
+ bring credit to the fundraising profession by their public demeanor;
+ encourage colleagues to embrace and practice these ethical principles and standards of professional practice; and
+ be aware of the codes of ethics promulgated by other professional organizations that serve philanthropy.

STANDARDS OF PROFESSIONAL PRACTICE
Furthermore, while striving to act according to the above values, AFP members agree to abide by the *AFP Standards of Professional Practice*, which are adopted and incorporated into the *AFP Code of Ethical Principles*. Violation of the *Standard* may subject the member to disciplinary sanctions, including expulsion, as provided in the AFP Ethics Enforcement Procedures.

Professional Obligations
1. Members shall not engage in activities that harm the member's organization, clients, or profession.
2. Members shall not engage in activities that conflict with their fiduciary, ethical and legal obligations to their organizations and their clients.
3. Members shall effectively disclose all potential and actual conflicts of interest; such disclosure does not preclude or imply ethical impropriety.
4. Members shall not exploit any relationship with a donor, prospect, volunteer or employee for the benefit of the member or the member's organization.

5. Members shall comply with all applicable local, state, provincial, federal, civil and criminal laws.
6. Members recognize their individual boundaries of competence and are forthcoming and truthful about their professional experience and qualifications.

Solicitation and Use of Philanthropic Funds
7. Members shall take care to ensure that all solicitation materials are accurate and correctly reflect the organization's mission and use of solicited funds.
8. Members shall take care to ensure that donors receive informed, accurate and ethical advice about the value and tax implications of contributions.
9. Members shall take care to ensure that contributions are used in accordance with donors' intentions.
10. Members shall take care to ensure proper stewardship of philanthropic contributions, including timely reports on the use and management of such funds.
11. Members shall obtain explicit consent by the donor before altering the conditions of contributions.

Presentation of Information
12. Members shall not disclose privileged or confidential information to unauthorized parties.
13. Members shall adhere to the principle that all donor and prospect information created by, or on behalf of, an organization is the property of that organization and shall not be transferred or utilized except on behalf of that organization.
14. Members shall give donors the opportunity to have their names removed from lists that are sold to, rented to, or exchanged with other organizations.
15. Members shall, when stating fundraising results, use accurate and consistent accounting methods that conform to the appropriate guidelines adopted by the American Institute of Certified Public Accountants (AICPA)* for the type of organization involved. (* In countries outside of the United States, comparable authority should be utilized.)

Compensation
16. Members shall not accept compensation that is based on a percentage of contributions; nor shall they accept finder's fees.
17. Members may accept performance-based compensation, such as bonuses, provided such bonuses are in accord with prevailing practices within the members' own organizations, and are not based on a percentage of contributions.
18. Members shall not pay finder's fees, or commissions or percentage compensation based on contributions, and shall take care to discourage their organizations from making such payments.

Amended October 2004

Gentle Letter of Intent

_____ **Art Museum**
Capital Campaign

<u>Gentle Letter of Intent</u>

Please include me/us among those who support _____ Art Museum and its
mission to exhibit and collect contemporary and historic art with a focus on _____
(region) and to generate an understanding for visual arts with the purpose of enriching our
community.

1) <u>Continue annual membership and sponsorship support</u>

I/We _____ (please print names) agree to continue our

operating support of the Museum by _____

Payment Option _____

2) <u>Donation of a Multi-Year Pledge, Appreciated Assets, or Cash</u>

I/We _____(please print) intend to give the sum of

$_____ over the next _____ years for the capital campaign.

Payment(s) will be made on the following schedule: _____

❑   Automatic payment option: I/We   authorize _____ Art Museum to

charge $_____ monthly on my/our credit card until my/our pledge is

fulfilled *(Visa, MasterCard, Discover, American Express)*.

Card # _____ Expiration date _____

❑   This gift is eligible for a matching gift by: _____

❑   Optional – it is my/our desire that my/our heir(s) honor(s) this intent to help

_____ Art Museum.

_____
Initials

(OVER)

3) <u>Legacy Society</u> for estate giving (bequests)

I/We intend to provide a planned estate gift to _____ Art Museum in the

following manner: ❑ Bequest (last will & testament) ❑ Life Income Plan

(charitable unitrust, gift annuity) ❑ Life Insurance (existing or new policy) ❑ IRA

(or other retirement plan)

❑ Other gift instrument _____

Special instructions:

_____

I/We conservatively estimate this gift to be $_____.

My/Our current age(s) by decade: ❑ 90-plus ❑ 80s ❑ 70s ❑ 60s ❑ Other

<u>Recognition</u>

I/We wish our gift to be:

    ❑   Visible as a role model to others.
    ❑   Visible only to the extent we are recognized as members in one of the
             Museum's gift clubs.
    ❑   Anonymous (but you can mention our gift to encourage others to give).
    ❑   Completely anonymous.

I/We understand a portion of our gift (20% for annual fund and 10% for the campaign) will go toward fundraising marketing costs to encourage others to support _____ Art Museum.

Name(s) – *please print*

Signature   Date

Signature   Date

_____ Art Museum Representative's Signature _____Date

Index